KEEPING EACH OTHER ALIVE

A Vietnam War Memoir

NORMAN HILE

KEEPING EACH OTHER ALIVE
A VIETNAM WAR MEMOIR

iUniverse books may be ordered through booksellers or by contacting:

iUniverse
1663 Liberty Drive
Bloomington, IN 47403
www.iuniverse.com
844-349-9409

ISBN: 978-1-6632-1689-2 (sc)
ISBN: 978-1-6632-1691-5 (hc)
ISBN: 978-1-6632-1690-8 (e)

Library of Congress Control Number: 2021914463

Print information available on the last page.

iUniverse rev. date: 07/20/2021

Contents

Preface

This memoir is based on letters I wrote home to my family, which are quoted throughout (full copies of most of them are in the appendix), photos I took during my tour, and most important my memory of my unforgettable wartime experience. It is a day by day, month by month account of my combat tour fifty years ago as an artillery forward and aerial observer in South Vietnam from August 1970 to June 1971.

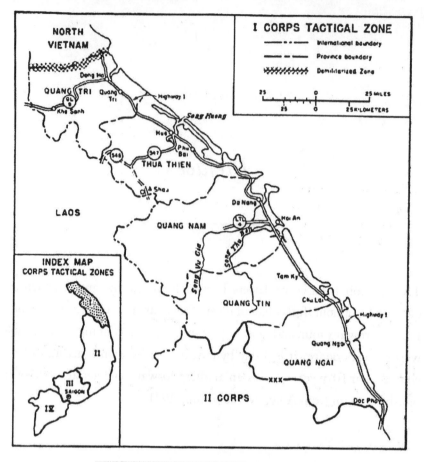

PART ONE

In The Field

AUGUST 1970

ON AUGUST 4, 1970, I BOARDED a chartered Boeing 707 taking me and other U.S. Army soldiers to fight the war in Vietnam. The airplane could be described as a cattle car of cannon fodder: every seat filled, six soldiers across. Feeling like prisoners, we faced our sentence: 365 days. Our newly assigned DEROS (Army acronym for "Date Expected Return from Overseas") was Aug 4, 1971. If we survived until then, we could come home. And for me, having served my time, if I lived I would be able to leave the Army and the job of soldier for good.

I was completely numb. I doubt any of us had slept much in several days, trying to get every minute of partying, or sex, or whatever it was that we hoped would last us for the next year, assuming we lived that long. We weren't going to this war as a unit or a team, just as individual soldiers who would be assigned to an outfit we had never seen before, to fight alongside soldiers we didn't know, to try to stay alive fighting an enemy we didn't hate, in a war that was clearly a mistake. Since that's the way we, as replacements, were being sent to the war, each of us would have to fight, and survive or die, as an individual.

How did I get into this? To a great extent, it began on January 28, 1968 when, at the height of the U.S. involvement in the war in Vietnam, the North Vietnamese Army and Viet Cong launched the "Tet Offensive," against South Vietnamese and U.S. forces throughout South Vietnam.

While the NVA and VC ultimately suffered a military defeat during those attacks, they nevertheless proved to the world, and for the first time to the American public, that South Vietnamese and U.S. forces were not anywhere near "winning" the war in South Vietnam. Instead, in the wake of the Tet Offensive, General William Westmoreland, the commander of U.S. forces, asked for 200,000 more U.S. troops to fight the war, and requested the mobilization of the Army Reserve.

At the time of the Tet Offensive, I was 22 years old and in my first year at Columbia Law School. I had become firmly disenchanted with U.S. involvement in the Vietnam War, and I had lost confidence in President Lyndon B. Johnson and his administration. When the Tet offensive revealed that the U.S. government had been misleading the country about how the war was going, I was appalled and dismayed.

My draft status at the time was 2S: a deferment classification given to college and graduate school students to complete their degrees. I had expected to remain 2S until I finished law school.

The Tet Offensive upended that. To draft the soldiers Westmoreland demanded, the Selective Service System decreed in February 1968 that in June, at the end of that current academic year, all graduating college seniors and first-year graduate school students would lose their draft deferments and be reclassified 1-A. Since local draft boards were under orders to draft the oldest eligible men first, in most cases first-year graduate school students were automatically the oldest available men. Those of us without other grounds for deferment were drafted into the U.S. Army.

My family was neither wealthy nor well connected. My brother had recently served in the Navy and my father had served in the Army during World War II. They were neither able, nor inclined, to help me avoid being drafted. Seeing no way out, and not wanting to flee to Canada and perhaps end up a convicted felon, I decided to take the chance that Richard M. Nixon, then the odds-on favorite to win the presidency that fall of 1968, would thereafter succeed in his vague "secret plan" to end the war. So, as I was about to enter the Army in the summer of 1968 as a draftee, I volunteered for Officer Candidate School. Going to OCS meant that I would have to spend three years rather than two years that drafted enlisted men were required to serve. Here was my calculation: if I underwent the six months of basic and individual training as an enlisted man, then completed an additional six months of training that OCS required, Nixon would have time to end the war, or at least to begin enough of a withdrawal that Westmoreland would no longer need me to fight in Vietnam.

As we now know, Nixon's "secret plan" was a hoax. U.S. involvement in the Vietnam war was nowhere near being over. Indeed, it had almost seven more years to run.

And so, in August 1970, as a 25-year-old soldier on an airplane on my way to fight a useless war, I had to deal with the uncertainty of whether in the coming year I would live or die. How would I deal with combat, with possible death? What would happen to me in this war?

One small comfort was being able to sit next to Ralph Oser. Ralph was an OCS classmate with whom I had suffered and laughed throughout training to be an artillery officer. Like me, Ralph had been drafted in 1968 to meet the Army's apparent need for soldiers to fight in South Vietnam. Ralph was tall, thin, bookish and bespectacled. He had an impish, clever but very dry sense of humor. He'd graduated from college and was planning to attend law school when he finished his service. Ralph shared my disdain for the military and the Mickey Mouse games we had been forced to play during training to prepare us to fight in a war we didn't agree with. Now he was sitting next to me as we flew toward that war and whatever our fates would be.

We made small talk, told weak jokes and tried to catch up on our sleep to the extent our strangulated legs would permit it. The numbness that we felt in our minds transferred down to our legs enough that we caught up a little bit on the sleep we hadn't had in our last few days in "the world," as we soldiers then called the U.S.

Ralph and I had met at the curbside at Travis Air Force Base in Fairfield, California, around 9:00 o'clock that morning. The night before had been a long one—lots of food, drink, and partying. As I drove back to my hotel, a California Highway Patrol cruiser pulled me over for speeding, obviously intrigued by the New York license plate on the borrowed car I was driving. When the trooper started to write me a ticket, I told him I wasn't going to be able to appear to contest it because the next day I was being shipped off to Vietnam. He snorted but showed no sympathy at all. He told me that I could just pay my fine by mail from overseas, a tipoff of what those of us who fought in Vietnam would face for years after we returned home.

The flight to Bien Hoa Air Base near near Saigon, South Vietnam took over 20 hours. We made two stops, in Anchorage, Alaska, and somewhere in Japan. Typical of the Army, there was no food or drink service on the plane other than every three hours a meal of typical airline fare was dropped in our laps. In between, there was no beverage service and certainly no alcohol. I asked once for a Coke and was told by the flight attendant that I could go back to a water cooler for a cup of water.

When we reached the air base in Japan for refueling, we were ushered into a small shopping mall where we could buy watches, jewelry and stereo equipment at Army PX prices. A number of us spent our last dollars on gadgets we weren't going to be able to use for the next 365 days, if at all.

Our first steps onto the tarmac in South Vietnam were filled with dread. We had heard stories of planes filled with "newbies" being greeted by mortar shells exploding on the runway, forcing an evacuation of the plane in flak jackets and helmets. Fortunately, it was quiet when we arrived. We were bused to Long Binh military base to wait in the first of many interminable lines for processing so the Army could officially count us as what was termed "in country."

One recollection of those first few days was the contrast between us newbies and the other soldiers in the barracks. Showing the Army's macabre sense of humor, we were housed with our opposite numbers— soldiers who had lived through their 365-day imprisonment in Vietnam and were about to return on what we called a Freedom Bird to the U.S. Two bunks down was a totally inebriated soldier screaming at 30-second intervals: "Short!" "Short" was the term we soon learned to use for being within weeks or days of going home. These short-timers looked at us with, as I saw it, sneering condescension and blatant pity. They had lived through what we could only imagine.

How did we remain sane, staring at a one-year sentence to go into combat and fight, and perhaps die, in a war we didn't believe in, and which experience now showed we couldn't win? It's hard now to comprehend. There was some consolation in being surrounded by fellow soldiers feeling the same way and going through the same thing. Also, we had been subjected to a long period of Army brainwashing. At this point I had been in the Army for just shy of two years. That included 10 weeks of basic training, 8 weeks of advanced individual training, 23 weeks of Officer Candidate School and a year as an instructor at the artillery school in Fort Sill, Oklahoma. By the time I reached Vietnam, I was a 1st Lieutenant. First as an enlisted man, and later as an officer, I had been subjected to so much haranguing that I had become pretty numb myself. But that did not change the uneasy feeling that I had because I really didn't know where I would be assigned, what job I would have, and what I would face in the war over the next 365 days.

I knew that many soldiers would have jobs in the "rear," out of harm's way. Later, I came to know them as REMFS for "rear echelon motherfuckers." REMFS were the ones who went through their year in Vietnam with a job at a rear base or in a staging area, with a hooch maid who "put out," R and R trips to Australia and Thailand, and the smug self-satisfaction of being able to say that they'd fought in a war, but without ever having seen any actual combat. Like just about everything in the Army, whatever happened to any of us was by lot and with the Army's perverse, contrary spin thrown in. At that moment we had no idea whether we were going to be in actual combat or whether we were just going to spend a year bored to tears but nevertheless almost as safe as at home.

I had hoped for an assignment in a part of South Vietnam that was not "hot" in terms of the war, such as near Saigon or in the south of the country. Or perhaps, even if it was in the north, where the war at that moment was "hotter," I hoped for a job in a rear area, or, at worst, on a firebase in a fire direction control bunker for an artillery battery, where I would not be on the front lines.

That was not to be. Having been in the wrong place at the wrong time several times already, my bad luck didn't quit. After processing at Long Binh, my orders sent me north to I Corps (see map, p. viii) and within it to the American Division, whose area of operations included the scene of the My Lai massacre. It was also the birthplace of the Viet Cong. It was one of the hottest areas of operation for the North Vietnamese Army in South Vietnam. In mid-1970, at least from the reports on U.S. radio and TV, the southern part of South Vietnam, such as the Delta, Saigon, and the mid-country highlands, had pretty much been quiet for a year or two. But the fighting was still going on in the north, from I Corps to the so-called DMZ. And that's where I was being sent.

In a bizarre twist of fate, in the few hours I was in Long Binh I was able to meet up with Peter Beeson, my college roommate. Peter was now an infantry officer who, because of a medical condition discovered in Vietnam, was completing his tour in the rear. Ralph Oser, Peter and I had a few scotches in Peter's air-conditioned trailer for an hour or so. Then I got ready to ship out to the war to the north. Ralph's assignment was to the Central Highlands. We had no idea what that area would be like or what he would encounter.

I wrote my first letter home on August 7 as I waited for a flight to Chu Lai, the headquarters for the American Division. In that letter (included in the Appendix) I reported:

"So far the heat and humidity have been bearable but somewhat oppressive in mid-afternoon. Conditions are horribly primitive, especially for the enlisted men. Everyone [in our group] acts somewhat jumpy but tries to make light of the whole situation."

I FLEW NORTH ON A C-130 military transport plane to headquarters of the American Division Artillery, at Chu Lai, a major U.S. post in the north and located on the picturesque South China Sea. The American Division Artillery staff gave two other artillery lieutenants and me a week of in-country training. It was then that I learned that, in the American Division, all newly arriving artillery lieutenants were assigned to the field to be artillery forward observers for infantry companies. In other words, I had struck out on getting anything near a safe assignment. I was going to be on the front lines fighting, along with other soldiers I didn't know, struggling to stay alive.

In-country training was a sweltering, boring, uncomfortable process. The oppressive heat and humidity–especially the humidity—was unbelievably debilitating. As a youngster, I had lived for six years near the equator in Venezuela, and I had also spent a summer in Hong Kong, so I thought I would be able to withstand a tropical climate. But this daytime heat and humidity was something else again. It sapped all my strength, and at times I wondered if I would even be able to keep breathing.

One afternoon we flew by helicopter to a small mountaintop outpost overlooking Chu Lai for a practice mission to adjust artillery fire as foreword observers. The outpost was located overlooking the so-called rocket pocket, where NVA and VC units launched rockets into the base at

Chu Lai. Our camp consisted of two tents and a building made of C-ration boxes. Three of us were alone on a small outpost without infantry support to adjust artillery rounds onto made-up targets in the rocket pocket. I didn't sleep much that night, both because we were totally outside the post compound in a hostile area, and because we were trying to sleep on the ground on the edge of a cliff.

Upon returning to Chu Lai, I got my first taste of being under actual fire, perverse as it was. After lunch one day, I returned to the barracks for a 20-minute nap before the next training session. Our hooch was made out of screen and wallboard—hardly something to withstand any type of gunfire. The bunks were Army-issue iron pallets with dirty, beaten-down straw mattresses. As I lay there in the noontime heat trying to breathe the sweltering air, I suddenly heard two screams, then sounds of a scuffle outside. Then three M-16 rounds crashed through the wall of my hooch. I rolled onto the floor and pushed myself underneath the cot, trying to find solid cover, wondering why someone was shooting at me and how the war had suddenly come so close. I heard more shots, though no more came through my hooch. I heard someone running down the dirt road outside the building. More shouts, a few more shots, and loud crying.

I never actually saw the U.S. soldier who fired the shots. I never learned what made him start shooting. I have no idea what the Army authorities ultimately did to him. But as I lay on the floor under the cot, I shuddered at how close I'd come to being killed. It was the first time I had heard the different, and awful sound of bullets coming at me instead of heading away. Afterward, all I learned was that some soldier had simply "lost it" and grabbed at the ever-present means of venting frustration—a handy M-16 automatic rifle. He was subdued, and who knows what happened to him afterward. But thereafter, I braced myself for danger coming anytime, day or night, and from any direction.

IN THOSE FIRST FEW DAYS I learned where the U.S. and the South Vietnamese really stood in this war I had been sent to fight. By 1970 the U.S. government propaganda machine had managed to submerge the debacle of the 1968 Tet Offensive. From news reports in the United States, it seemed that the war was going better. After Tet, the U.S. television audience was dazzled with maps showing areas that were now claimed to be "pacified" and purportedly under either U.S. Army or South Vietnamese government control. Each week TV news reports showed a new portion of the map, claiming "pacification" on the way to another victory for control of South Vietnam. Yet in August 1970, after finishing my mini-training in Chu Lai, as I flew in a helicopter to Duc Pho to join an infantry company as an artillery forward observer, I pointed to the ground and asked the helicopter pilot, "what part of this area do we control?"

He looked at me, smirked and replied: "None of it."

None of it? Not even Highway 1, which was just west of the South China Sea, where we were told convoys could move without harm? Not even the beach near Chu Lai with surfboards rear echelon soldiers could rent? Not even the flatlands filled with rice paddies stretching west from Highway 1 to the cities and towns, like Quang Ngai, we had been told were now filled with Vietnamese "friendlies?"

"None of it."

I confirmed that assessment, at least in the Americal Division, when I reached Firebase 411. It was on a knob of a hill in the western portion of the flatlands between the South China Sea to the east and the Truong Son Mountains to the west. Firebase 411 was headquarters for the infantry battalion and, within it, the infantry company for which I was to serve as an artillery forward observer. Firebase 411's core was D Battery of the 6 Battalion, 11 Artillery, with its six 105 mm Howitzers and its bunkered fire direction control center, which were on the southern section of the hill. The northern part of the hill contained headquarters for the 3rd Battalion 1st Infantry Regiment, consisting of four infantry companies who worked off Firebase 411 in an area of operations in all directions. Firebase 411 housed six perimeter bunkers and six supplementary bunkers, the latter built to give the infantry on the hill supplementary fighting positions. Ringing the hill on all sides were barbed wire and Claymore mines plus Quad 50 mounted machine guns. Within the firebase's perimeter were two helicopter landing pads and an aircraft control tower. The firebase housed an infantry Battalion Operations Center and a mess hall. Just outside the perimeter of the firebase, on the northwest corner of the hill, were a rifle range, and an M-79 and machine gun range.

Firebase 411 maintained constant surveillance from its bunkers. The territory outside its perimeter was a desolate, flat plain, unoccupied and pockmarked with artillery and bomb craters. There was no farming being done or other outward signs of human habitation. About a kilometer and a half to the east was a South Vietnamese resettlement camp, essentially an armed fortress, where Montagnards, the indigenous people of the central highlands, and lowland Vietnamese civilians had been relocated for protection from Viet Cong and NVA attacks. It was a living sewer, a man-made ghetto from which the inhabitants dared not venture at night.

About five miles to the southeast, along the Song Tra Khuc, a major river, was the town of Quang Ngai—capital of Quang Ngai Province. The dirt road between Firebase 411 and Quang Ngai was unsafe to travel unless mine sweepers had just inspected it because Viet Cong mined it almost nightly. Shortly before I arrived, the mine sweepers had not done their job well enough, and several trucks of a convoy from Firebase 411 were blown up by land mines. Several miles to the south were some small villages with no apparent inhabitants in them. To the north was a flat plain with nothing to speak of leading to another river emptying into the sea from the mountains in the west. The mountains were jungled-covered and steep, and extended all the way to the Laotian border.

My assignment as an artillery forward observer was to join one of the infantry companies who worked the area surrounding Firebase 411. Charlie Company, 3rd Battalion, 1st Infantry Brigade at that moment was in the field operating to the north of Firebase 411. The artillery battery executive officer gave me my radio call number and frequency, and minimal advice before putting me aboard a resupply helicopter to take me out to join Charlie Company. After a five-minute helicopter ride, I found myself on the ground, in the field and on the absolute front line of a very hot war.

Luckily, during my first few days in the field, Charlie Company was not under attack. On the other hand, I knew none of the other soldiers, and I was an unknown quantity to them and to the infantry company commander, to whom I was supposed to be always within a few yards. Charlie Company had had no artillery forward observer for some months. I was told that the last one was a sergeant who had almost blown up some of the company's men. These infantrymen didn't have any reason to trust a green, newbie artillery officer who had no experience in the field.

Above: Firebase 411, in a picture I later took from the air, showing guns firing.

Essentially, I was now a combat infantry grunt with an additional job of lending support by shooting artillery when the company commander thought we needed it. Meanwhile I would be carrying my own M-16, trying to avoid booby traps, sleeping on the ground, eating C-rations, drinking canteen water, and carrying on my back everything I needed to survive.

Charlie Company had set up camp for several days on level ground to the east of a small hill and just south of an abandoned village. There were trees in clumps and lines surrounding us, but no obvious cultivation. About two or three kilometers to the west and south were hills that formed the beginning of the mountains. Charlie Company's command post, consisting of the infantry company commander, his three radio operators and a medic, stayed in that spot for several days, while each of the company's three rifle platoons patrolled to search for Viet Cong or NVA. The company commander, whose last name was Moran, was a stout, baby-faced captain in his second tour in Vietnam. He was about my age and was a curious mix of gung-ho career officer and pragmatic ass-saver. During his two-year tour in Germany, which had been sandwiched between Vietnam tours, Moran had become somewhat overweight. He had made the decision that his second tour in Vietnam was at least going to be the means by which he trimmed down. Despite the sweltering heat and humidity, he always wore a fatigue shirt tightly buttoned at the neck and totally soaked with perspiration. Cpt. Moran was somewhat aloof in his dealings with me, but at least he was a seasoned combat commander.

I also had an artillery radio telephone operator (RTO) already in the field to assist me. His name was Terry Brennan. Terry was one of the many misfits I came to recognize in the field—a young (at the most 18 years old) outcast who saw this war as a chance for an unparalleled adventure while advancing his status with his friends back home. Having failed miserably at impressing the dullards on the artillery guns at 411 who were NCOs, Terry had volunteered to go out into the field. That was where the real fighting was, and Terry was hoping for some peak experience that might lift his life above the muddle that it was. He was about as scruffy-looking as they come. His attempt at growing a mustache and beard had been

14

unsuccessful. His steel-pot helmet, much too big for him, was always down around his eyes, making it almost impossible to see the thick eye glasses peeking out from underneath. Terry must have weighed all of 130 pounds. He revelled in being a combat veteran (after a few months in the field), and had made good friends with all the infantry riflemen. They must have found it amusing that someone had actually chosen to be with them instead of back on the firebase. Terry had no love at all for the artillery—in his own heart he was now an infantryman.

Each night before dark we plotted defensive targets—delta tangos in artillery lingo—for points of reference from which to adjust during the night when we would have no light to see reference points. That first night in the field I shot artillery for the first time in a combat situation. We received incoming mortar rounds shortly before we tried to go to sleep. When the rounds came in, all hell broke loose. Soldiers were scrambling into their foxholes, firing their M-16s and M-60 machine guns, and shooting blindly into the night to discourage anyone who was out there from coming closer. Meanwhile, Captain Moran yelled at me to put some artillery out there in the direction of what somebody reported had been the flash of an enemy mortar to the south of us. I radioed Fire Direction Control on Firebase 411 for my first combat fire mission.

"Riverside 81 [the call sign for Fire Direction Control], this is Stoney Brook 45 [my artillery call sign]. Fire mission, over.

"Stoney Brook 45, this is Riverside 81, send your mission, over."

"Grid 5-3-2-4-7-5-9-2, direction 0, mortars firing, over."

The FDC at the guns on Firebase 411 repeated the data for the fire mission, and we waited—interminably it seemed—for something to happen. When the first rounds finally landed, Moran said they weren't anywhere near where he was talking about. "No, no!" he yelled, "over there," pointing into another pitch black area. Although I had no idea what he wanted me to shoot at, but wanting to show that I knew what I was doing, I called in adjustments to the guns.

"Riverside 81 this is Stoney Brook 45. Right 500, add 300, over." FDC repeated the command and we waited.

"Stoney Brook 45, this is Riverside 81. We can't fire there, over," came the reply.

"Riverside 81 this is Stoney Brook 45. Why not, over."

"Stoney Brook 45 this is Riverside 81. It's a no-fire area, over." I relayed the information to Moran. "Damn artillery motherfuckers," he said. "Move it as close as you can."

I called in another adjustment, and the shells landed about 200 yards away from the original rounds, a waste of time and ordnance. With nothing more we could do, we would have to wait until dawn to see where the mortar rounds might have come from.

Charlie Company spent over a week at that spot. We did have some contact with what we thought to be VC one afternoon when Sgt. Robbins, an E-6 who was the highest ranking NCO in the field, gave chase with his platoon through the sweltering heat. They returned having bagged no one, but with one wounded infantryman. When I saw the platoon members, they were almost unconscious from the heat.

When I say Sgt. Robbins was the highest ranking NCO in the field, what I really should say is he was virtually the only one. In the field, Charlie Company consisted of approximately 80 men, down 40 from its full strength. This was because of casualties, illness and R&R. It was not anything like an infantry company that my OCS infantry tactics class had posited. An infantry company was supposed to have a captain company commander, four lieutenant (officer) platoon leaders, four E-7 platoon sergeants, four E-6 squad leaders and numerous E-5 sergeants within each squad making up various teams. Charlie Company bore no resemblance to this. Besides Captain Moran, in the field we had only one lieutenant platoon leader, one E-6 platoon leader (Robbins), and a bunch of "shake and bake" Spec 4's as additional platoon leaders and squad leaders. "Shake and bake" was a term that referred to the instant NCO program the Army had developed to make up for the lack of NCOs available for the field in Vietnam. A draftee could sign up for this special school, do an extra 13 weeks of training and, with the maximum of six months in the Army, be sent out to the field as an E-4 noncommissioned officer. Meanwhile, all of the lifer NCOs—those who had earned their stripes through a few years of service and were making the Army a career—had reenlisted for special duties involving noncombat specialties, which meant that they were exempt from being in the field with the infantry company.

But it wasn't just that Charlie Company had only one officer platoon leader and only one true NCO in the field. The infantry riflemen in Charlie Company, be they shake and bakes or private E-1s, were virtually all draftees and 60 percent or more were soldiers of color, like Robbins, who was Black. Even our medics were special cases—a Peruvian who had gained U.S. citizenship by enlisting, and two former left-wingers who had claimed conscientious objector status and been assigned to the medical corps. So virtually the entire force of Charlie Company were draftees attempting to survive day to day on their wits, building up bitterness that would most likely manifest itself back home if they survived.

Charlie Company had not trained together as a unit before being sent into battle. Nor did it have any leadership other than its company commander. These soldiers had been given the task of fighting in a war just as I had: plopped into the field without knowing anyone in the unit, without leaders to look up to, and without any mission other than trying to stay alive. It was no small wonder that they didn't have any respect for me, an inexperienced artillery officer who had been in country for less than two weeks.

During that first week, mercifully given the heat, Charlie Company's CP (or "Command Post") stayed in that one spot. My job was to stick with the CP, which consisted of Moran, three infantry RTOs and a medic. For some reason, Moran's three RTOs were white. So even within Charlie Company, the safer spots went to white soldiers, while the platoons were mostly soldiers of color.

From the CP Moran monitored the rifle platoons on their patrols. Fortunately, for that week I didn't have to march anywhere. But about three days after I arrived, I was forced to find out where I could empty my bowels. With that in mind, I had to make a rather embarrassing inquiry, which showed how little I knew about life in the field. Summoning all my courage, I went right up to leadership: Moran.

"Where do you go to take a shit around here?"

His answer confirmed my worst fears. "You take your entrenching tool and you walk out there." Moran pointed outside the perimeter to no-man's land, about 50 yards from the CP and a good 25 yards outside the machine gun bunker perimeter we had built around the ground we were holding. "And don't forget to tell the perimeter guards that you're going. Otherwise they might mistake you for a VC and shoot you."

That was it. There were no trees among which to hide. I was going to have to walk out into no-man's land by myself, hoping no sniper was waiting, avoiding stepping on booby traps, then assume the most defenseless position one could be in, for all the world to see, including any VC who might be watching for a chance to pick off a G.I. It took me several hours to get up the courage.

One thing we had been taught in Vietnam training was that booby traps were perhaps the greatest danger we faced. We heard all sorts of stories about soldiers putting a foot down and being blown up. We were taught that you could try to avoid booby traps by walking in the exact footsteps of the person in front of you. This way the only person who was likely to step on a land mine or plunge down into a bungee pit was the first man through, or "point man." My problem for this mission was that I was the point man. After giving notice to the perimeter guards, I walked to the edge of our perimeter with my entrenching tool and my M-16, finger on the safety, ready at any moment to alternatively dive for cover or start quick firing. I planned each step I would take while eyeing where I was going to put the rifle down to dig my hole. I surveyed the flat plain in front of me, reassured myself that the people who were on the perimeter knew it was me going out, and took the first few tentative steps into no-man's land.

In the middle of such a mundane and yet life-threatening situation, I confronted what soon became the game I was to play for that entire year. Each step I took, each decision I made, had to include considering the risk of some greater unknown danger. The dilemma was that, risky as some steps were, I simply could not always choose not to move. Moreover, I didn't know for sure whether action or inaction was safer. Every moment of every day was like playing Russian Roulette. Almost every minute I had to make a decision of where I was going to move next, whether it was riskier than staying where I was already standing, and whether the risk of moving was worth it to alleviate the uncertainty, or sheer boredom, of standing still. And the boredom, which was severe in the field, became one of my worst enemies. It grew so bad that it made me take chances; it made me willing to take risks simply to make the time pass. The boredom was sometimes as hard to endure as the terror. At least when I took a step, I had an awareness of being alive, and at least it made the minutes go by. When I stopped moving, time stood still.

I'm not going to say that going out to take that first shit was some life-affirming act. I was so frightened, I almost couldn't see. Yet, on arriving safely back inside the perimeter, I felt an adrenaline rush, and for a few moments, anyway, I felt incredibly alive.

WHILE WE WERE STILL IN THAT same spot, almost a week after I'd gone out to the field, the artillery battery on Firebase 411 sent out to the field another artillery RTO, PFC Ed Williams, to join me and Terry.

I'd been told by the artillery battalion executive officer that we would soon have another RTO to help with carrying the radio that connected us to the artillery battery on Firebase 411. Since I hadn't yet had to carry the radio or my pack anywhere, I didn't yet have a full appreciation for how heavy that radio felt in the heat and humidity. I did intend, however, as they told us, to train both Terry and the new RTO to shoot artillery in case anything happened to me, and also so that we could split up our spotting capability among the three of us.

Ed arrived aboard the resupply helicopter we saw every couple of days that brought fresh water, mail and, once in a while, cans of unrefrigerated soda.

Ed was fairly large: about 6'1" and probably 200 pounds. He was 19 years old, a recent high school graduate from a small town in Texas near Fort Worth. His head was fairly shaven. He looked a lot like pictures I'd seen of the prizefighter Jack Johnson. And yet, by his eyes, I could see a wounded, scared draftee drawing into himself for protection.

At the outset, Ed basically wouldn't talk to me. All I could get from him were fairly intelligible grunts indicating "yes" or "no" in response to my questions. The communication gap between us was impenetrable during those first days. I asked him the first night he was there if he wanted to call into the artillery battery our defensive targets over the radio. He grunted no. Later I asked Terry what he thought about an RTO who wouldn't talk on the radio. Terry told me Ed had never used a combat radio before and had never been trained to do so. Ed also had no training in reading a map or to calling in artillery.

When it came to sleeping, Ed and I were to share a tent, because Terry already had someone else he was bunking with. Actually, calling it a tent is an exaggeration. What we slept in was a two-man shelter made by snapping together two rain ponchos and stringing them over a horizontal stake and held up by two-and-a-half foot long stakes planted vertically. The ponchos weren't big enough for the stakes to be any higher than two and a half feet. One couldn't sit up inside this tent. That tiny space was sleeping quarters for two soldiers.

The Charlie Co. command post. Sitting in the left foreground is Ed Williams, my RTO.
In the background with his hand on a tent pole is Captain Moran. That's Ed's and my
tent, with the radio and antenna sticking up. In the right foreground eating C-rations is
our medic, a native of Peru, who hoped to get U.S. citizenship by serving in the Army.

Getting Ed and me into that tiny space was quite a task, since I too was just over 6 feet tall. It didn't help that I used an inflatable mattress I blew up each night. Initially, Ed wanted to save the weight of the mattress in his pack and thought he would sleep on the ground. He tried that for one or two nights and then called back to the rear for his own air mattress. I did bring another item to our tent that few other soldiers bothered with: a mosquito net. We tied the unfurled mosquito net to the roof pole of the tent and, just as we were climbing in to go to sleep, we slipped underneath it and spread it out. It didn't keep the millions of mosquitos from buzzing in our ears throughout the night, but it was comforting to know that, unless there was a hole in the net, none could bite us while we slept.

Tied to one pole of the tent was the radio that linked Ed and me to the artillery on Firebase 411. The radio was mounted on a backpack, and we lashed it upright to the front tent pole with the antenna sticking up three or four feet above the top of the tent. We didn't take clothes off before going to bed—actually that was the time to put on any clothes we had because it was the coolest part of any day. We did, however, take off our jungle boots to try to air out our feet, and we lovingly placed our M-16s right next to us on the ground inside the tent in case the enemy hit us at night. In front of the entrance to the tent we dug a foxhole deep and wide enough so that we both could get in and crouch down if we received incoming fire.

Throughout those first days Ed continued to say almost nothing to me. Only once in a while would he answer my questions, and then usually with only a grunt.

After about 10 days, infantry battalion headquarters on Firebase 411 radioed to Moran that Charlie Company was to rotate onto Firebase 411 for a few days. The next morning a fleet of helicopters—Bell UH1 Iroquois choppers known as "Hueys" or "Slicks" —appeared on the horizon. We dropped smoke bombs to show them where they should land (right about where I had dug my hole a few days before). We boarded the helicopters for a flight back to Firebase 411. I had survived my first days and nights in the field.

WHENEVER SOMEBODY TELLS ME NOW THAT you shouldn't eat something that has fallen on the floor, or suggests that we've got to change sheets that someone else might have slept on for a few nights, I think about the bunker that the Charlie Company CP occupied on Firebase 411. It was our home when we pulled our rotational stint on the Firebase. That bunker proved that human beings can live in the most filthy, inhuman conditions. It's just a matter of ignoring the filth.

Photo of me taken just outside our bunker on Firebase 411.

At least eight of us in the CP occupied that bunker, which had about four "beds" in the main room. It was approximately 12 feet by 12 feet with a table in the middle. To one side was a smaller room with just enough space for a double-deck bunk with little else and no light. The bunks were the iron type with straw mattresses so old they were brown. We took turns sleeping in those bunks.

Charlie Company's job for the five or six days of our rotation on the firebase was to defend the perimeter. Accordingly, the individual infantry squads spread out around the perimeter in bunkers that faced the surrounding landscape. Communication among the bunkers and the CP was by radio. At the highest point of the hill on which the firebase stood, of course, was the artillery battery consisting of six 105 mm howitzers. Also at the firebase was the battalion infantry headquarters where the infantry battalion commander, a lieutenant colonel, and his staff decided where individual infantry companies would operate around the firebase. No piece of land in the approximate five-mile radius of the firebase, which was the battalion's area of operations, was controlled by the U.S. forces or the Army of the Republic of Vietnam (ARVN). The job of U.S. infantry around the base was simply to find and engage any Viet Cong or North Vietnamese regular soldiers within that radius.

Creature comforts at the firebase were slim, but at least it was better than in the field. We had plenty of water and a makeshift shower made out of an oil drum with nail holes in the bottom. The problem was that you had to haul your own shower water up from the water truck and pour it into the overhead drum. The water was cold, but that was no problem given how badly we needed showers and how hot and humid it was.

When we arrived at Firebase 411, Charlie Company's First Sergeant was there. He had quite a reputation among the infantrymen as an organizer. He had brought us a couple of cases of beer, which he managed to chill by stealing some ice from the mess hall. We all drank a beer and then took off the jungle fatigues we'd been wearing for the past weeks in the field. We then put on a new pair that would be our only clothes for the next several weeks until we came back to 411 for another rotation.

The fatigues we took off were so soiled, torn and disgusting that the first sergeant had them burned.

On August 26, while on Firebase 411 for the first time, I wrote home reporting:

"The artillery in our area has a bad reputation because of problems caused by the My Lai incident. We can't fire anywhere near villages or huts, and must get political clearance from the Vietnamese before any firing. Most of the time, we can't fire at all, or if we can, not where we need it. As a forward observer with the infantry, this can be both frustrating and hair raising since I'm only trying to support myself and the people around me. The F.O. our company had before me was a sergeant and was prone to fire on his own people as much as the enemy. So my biggest job has been to convince the infantry I'm safe and can do them some good and then try to talk the artillery into firing."

I also had this to report about Cpt. Moran and the infantry:

"Our company commander is very good and has a prior tour here. I have much more confidence in him than I usually would in the infantry, and we're beginning to work together to get some tactics on call. ... I'm taking the platoon leaders out tomorrow to teach them to adjust mortars and artillery. Since I stay in the command post with the CO while the platoons maneuver, they will have to adjust what I can't see."

DURING OUR STAY ON 411, CAPTAIN Moran decided to go into Quang Ngai, the only "city" within a day's drive, to look for souvenirs and ice. He asked if I wanted to go. I had heard that the road from Firebase 411 to Quang Ngai was frequently mined by the VC, and that recently some Army vehicles had been blown up and soldiers killed on the road. But combat engineer minesweepers were now combing the road every morning for mines. So I debated what I'd rather do: take a chance on seeing something new, or swelter through another hot, boring day on Firebase 411. As I did so many times during my tour, I wanted to take my mind off the boredom. So I decided to go.

The dirt road reminded me of the roads I had traveled as a boy when my family lived in the interior of Venezuela. Here's what I wrote about that excursion in my Aug. 26 letter home:

"I just got back from a trip to Quang Ngai for ice for our beer. Population is 60,000, but it looks like another San Felix [a city near our home in Venezuela in the 1950's]. All the roads are dirt, and the outskirts are all huts and cardboard shacks. The ARVN have big headquarters there so I didn't feel too unsafe. We still had to carry M-16s locked and loaded with steel pots. The really discouraging part is that our areas are so primitive."

When we reached Quang Ngai, the unpaved streets were narrow and clogged with ARVN troops and people shopping at food stalls. Almost all the men were in military uniforms, and a few places were serving beer. Lots of kids and many malnourished dogs roamed the streets. I decided not to eat or drink anything that was offered. Moran bought some clothing and ice for Charlie Company's beer.

Quang Ngai was not far from My Lai, where Lt. William Calley and his troops had massacred over 300 Vietnamese villagers. So I was wary about being a white U.S. Army lieutenant without much of an entourage. I was glad I had my steel pot and was carrying my M-16. But we ran into no problems and soon drove back to 411. Luckily, again the road was not mined.

ED HAD BEEN TRAINED ONLY TO load and shoot a howitzer and keep it functioning. That was irrelevant to what he was doing now. I wanted him to be able to talk on the radio and adjust artillery if needed. So it was up to me to train him.

Fortunately, Ed was bright. When he had been in high school, he had been a good football player. I later learned he had been contacted by a few recruiters about playing college ball. I really don't recall why he turned that down and ended up in the Army.

My first job, besides getting Ed to speak to me, was to get him proficient at talking on the radio. The easiest way to get started was to give him a script. Defensive targets were perfect for this. When we called in the grid locations of the "Delta Tangos" each evening, they had to be encoded using a "kak" wheel. The wheel had numbers and letters. The grid locations had to be encoded in advance using the wheel. Then they were read over the radio to Fire Direction Control just before dark. Ed quickly became adept with the kak wheel, no small chore. He wrote the entire message he was going to give each night and then read his "script" over the radio. He soon became comfortable with radio lingo and talking "artillery talk" with FDC.

As we worked together, Ed opened up a little and became more friendly. He began to address me as "LT" (no trooper in the field ever called me "sir," and that was fine with me), and we began to share ideas for making C-ration meals palatable.

Soon we began going over the various commands for calling in an artillery fire mission. We talked about when to call for the different type of fuses, including variable time and illumination. Most important, I worked with him on reading our maps, including determining our exact position through triangulation. We worked on locating a target's position on a map in terms of grid coordinates. We also discussed when to use high-angle and low-angle shell trajectories. One day, when we were about to move from one camp to another, Ed put together an entire fire mission, and put rounds where we were going to walk to blow up any booby traps. Meanwhile, I critiqued his target locations and his adjustments. Within a week, I declared him a full-fledged forward observer.

THE TANK WAS PROBABLY THE LEAST effective piece of military hardware I saw being used in Vietnam. Trying to fight a guerrilla war with armored vehicles is like trying to kill a fly with an elephant gun. And, perversely, tanks and other armored vehicles were a perfect target for the Viet Cong's and NVA's most lethal weapon: the rocket-propelled grenade, or "RPG" as we called it. Some of the enemy's RPG's were even armor piercing.

The Viet Cong's and NVA's only ordnance that we ran up against beyond automatic weapons and mortars was the RPG. It was ineffective against individual soldiers in the field since it consisted of a single rocket. Against a target as large as an armored vehicle, however, an RPG was extremely deadly.

U.S. armored units were operating in our area. I'm sure that the brass hats from the armored units weren't about to let a war go by without a chance to get some combat experience. Unfortunately for Charlie Company, when our five day stint on Firebase 411 ended, our next maneuver was with an armored unit: E Troop, 1st Battalion, 1st Cavalry.

Initially, I wasn't fully aware of the target that tanks provided the enemy, and I was thankful that, when working with the armor, we as infantrymen in Charlie Company didn't have to walk. We boarded armored personnel carriers that traveled with the tanks and headed south out of Firebase 411 for a two-week operation.

We struck camp in the flatlands about 10 kilometers south of Firebase 411 around 4 p.m. in the afternoon that first day, putting up our poncho liner tents and digging foxholes within a perimeter made up partly of armored vehicles. After calling in our defensive artillery targets, Ed and I bedded down for the night feeling safe because we were close to the armored vehicles.

At dawn, an explosion ripped me awake. I rolled out of the tent into our foxhole, trying to grab my rifle, steel pot and ammunition all at the same time. My first sight was Doc, our medic, running at incredible speed toward one of the tanks but crouched so low that his rear end was almost hitting the ground. I heard screams from one of the tanks, but they were soon drowned out by the roar of retaliatory fire from the armored vehicles and our own weapons. A few explosions from within our perimeter were drowned out by our return fire. The tank where Doc had dragged his medical bag was on fire, looking like a rumbled heap of torn metal. Doc started attending to a clump on the ground. I found out later that one soldier died and three were wounded in the RPG explosion, which struck the side of the tank. One victim Doc was attending to had his leg blown off and later died. The survivors were taken out on medevac helicopters.

I measured the distance from our foxhole to the larger foxhole dug by the CP for Captain Moran and his RTOs. I saw nothing blowing up anywhere within the perimeter for about 30 seconds and decided to get to Moran to see if he wanted me to shoot any artillery. As I jumped into the hole I couldn't help thinking how ridiculous Moran looked. He had also been woken by the blast and was crouching in his foxhole in his T-shirt, no boots and his steel pot.

"You want any artillery?"

"Sure."

"Where?"

"I don't know. RPG must have come from over there." He pointed. "Try putting some rounds over there."

I dashed back to Ed, and we called in a fire mission. Then, as always, we waited.

After a good 20 minutes, Fire Direction Control radioed back that it couldn't get clearance to fire artillery where I had asked.

As I made my way back to Captain Moran's foxhole, something kicked my leg out from under me. I spun to the ground as if tackled. My knee was burning and twitching. I crawled into Moran's foxhole, unable to keep my leg from jerking up and down. To me it looked like the bodies of lizards after being shot by a BB gun. I still couldn't figure out exactly what had happened. But when I rolled my jungle fatigue past my knee, there in the side of my kneecap was a hole about a quarter inch in diameter with a piece of metal sticking out. There was surprisingly little blood. The metal was still hot. I pulled it out. It was about half the size of my thumb nail.

Captain Moran summoned Doc, who plunged a morphine shot into my thigh, dressed the wound and bound my knee. Moran laughed—more a snicker—and said to me "Purple Heart."

When we stopped firing at whoever had fired the RPG, we made sure no one from Charlie Company had been hit. Later, however, when Moran reported to the infantry battalion, he mentioned that his "Redleg" had been wounded by a piece of shrapnel in his knee.

The wound didn't require me being air lifted out. I was just an inch or two from a million-dollar wound, that is a wound that would have taken me off the battlefield and perhaps back to the States to recuperate, but didn't cause a lasting disability.

What was I feeling in those moments? I do recall thinking how surprised I was that I was not petrified. I can only attribute that to over two years of Army brainwashing. In fact, I felt almost a sense of exhilaration when, during such intense action, I was still alive, functioning and capable of acting. Jumping into Moran's foxhole was a result of two things–lack of any constant fire coming near me for a moment, and the hope that perhaps I could do something to help out.

That feeling grew into a philosophy for acting during any firefight, as well as for my day-by-day actions. I wasn't particularly hungry to kill the enemy; rather I was doing whatever it took to keep me and as many of us as I could alive. Whether we knew each other or not, we were all stuck in the same situation. We couldn't refuse to fight. We couldn't desert because there was nowhere to go. Basically, our mission was to do what we were ordered to do while trying to survive. And that meant doing everything we could to keep each other alive, since we had to rely on each other if we were going to survive for a whole tour. If I failed to do my job, not only was I more likely to die, but also so might many others.

I also realized that, whenever we got hit, often there were no more than one or two of the enemy firing at us. The Viet Cong and NVA were much like the Americans in the Revolutionary War. Chances were, whatever damage they were going to do, they did during the first one or two seconds of any firefight. After that, the enemy would be doubling back and away from us. All our fire could do was let them know that we weren't going to let them pick off any more of us.

The next day we were hit again—another RPG into the side of a tank and at least five more casualties. Once again the battle was over before we knew what had happened. I distinctly heard a "whoosh" go just past my head before an explosion behind me told me that an RPG had barely missed me.

The medevac choppers arrived within minutes to take out the wounded and the dead. It was here that I saw my first body bag, which was quickly filled with a soldier's body and flown back to the rear.

The area we were working was against the foothills of the mountains to the west that ran the length of the Americal Division. We were in a plain interrupted by tree lines, irrigation ditches, berms, and an occasional rice paddy. Within a kilometer or two the hills rose up and quickly became the foothills of the interior mountain range. We would often return to this area, and the foothills, in the future.

Like the rest of us, Captain Moran had had enough of working alongside armored vehicles. He convinced the battalion staff that our company would be better used sweeping the area to the south on our own. We left the armored vehicles carrying our packs, and baking in the hot sun of the late Vietnamese summer.

HUMPING WAS THE TERM WE USED to describe marching with our packs and equipment. I soon learned how difficult, if not at times impossible, it was to march in the heat and humidity with what we were humping. Put aside for a moment the 20-pound radio that Ed's job required him to carry so we could communicate with the artillery guns. Let's just concentrate on what else there was that each of us individually was humping.

I estimate our full pack weighed about 30 pounds. It was stuffed full with C-rations—mostly cans not unlike wet cat food filled with franks and beans, fruit cocktail, and packages of coffee, hot chocolate, cookies, toilet paper, etc. Add to that any personal belongings we needed such as a poncho, towel, poncho liner to use as a blanket at night, canteen cup for cooking, fork and spoon. For recreation, a deck of cards, maybe a paperback book, and a pen and writing paper and envelopes for letters home. Also an M-16 cleaning kit. On our belts we carried ammunition for our M-16s—each metal clip filled with multiple rounds of ammunition. A bandolier of clips probably weighed close to four or five pounds.

"Humping" with my pack in the field. Note my folded maps
tucked into my pants leg pocket and my steel pot.

Next, and probably the heaviest, were the canteens of water. We never knew how long it would be before being we were resupplied, and given the heat and humidity, we had to hydrate constantly. So we each carried at least three canteens of water. (We also humped iodine pills to purify water if we ran out of canteen water, and pills that supposedly prevented malaria.)

After that came mortar rounds. Charlie Company had a mortar squad with a mortar tube and set-up. But virtually all of us carried one or more mortar rounds attached to our packs. These rounds weighed close to five pounds each.

Then came a few hand grenades and smoke bombs. In general, these were worn around the periphery of our packs or along our belts. Each weighed about a pound and we would average roughly five or six per soldier. In addition, of course, each of us had our M-16 and steel pot, the latter an absolute necessity but surprisingly heavy. With close to 50 pounds on our backs, heads and belts, we would bend forward. To carry that much weight in the sweltering heat and humidity of Vietnam meant that we couldn't march more than about 15 minutes before taking a break.

If there was any uphill grade at all, it would take practically a whole day to go more than a kilometer.

A word or two about the M-16. It was a wonder weapon: extremely light, capable of single or semi-automatic fire, easy to use and deadly as hell. M-16s had been designed so that their bullets would tear apart the internal organs of any person they hit. Compared to what the enemy was using, the Soviet made AK-47, the M-16 was much lighter and more maneuverable. The one problem with the M-16 was that it tended to jam when not cleaned. This raised an ironic question: how were we supposed to keep a weapon clean when we were living in dirt, mud, rain, sweat, and all sorts of filth? Where could we even find a place to spread out and dismantle, clean and re-assemble a weapon given the conditions in which we were living? And what would happen if, while our weapon was dismantled for cleaning, we got hit?

SEPTEMBER 1970

WHEN WE LEFT THE ARMOR, WE swung south along a small river that ran through flatland dotted with tree lines. We spent the night in sand dunes stretching along the riverbank. Because we didn't get to set up camp until late in the day, we had no chance to erect our tents, so we were at the mercy of the mosquitos all night. We faced a choice of suffocating underneath our poncho liners or being eaten alive by mosquitos. I barely slept that night and remember saying to myself that if I was going to be in this horrible assignment for six months, I would either die of malaria or lack of sleep. I had no idea, however, how much worse it was going to get.

The next day began as did all of the others. We awoke shortly before the sun rose, around 6 a.m., when it became too hot to remain asleep under the mosquito net or poncho liner. We ate a C-ration breakfast—mainly canned fruit because that felt cool compared to anything heated, along with cheese spread on crackers. By 7 a.m. we were underway with hopes that we would be far enough by 10 a.m. to rest during the midday heat before continuing in the late afternoon.

We moved out in our usual formation: one platoon leading to the left, another leading to the right, the command post and the mortar platoon in the center and a last platoon split to the rear to cover us in case of attack from behind. Within the CP, the radio operators walked first, Morgan behind, and then Ed and me behind them. Terry was with the platoon to the left, having told me that he felt confident he could help best by being there to spot artillery if they needed it.

We had been moving about an hour when the enemy hit us. We were approaching a tree line about 25 meters ahead of us in a flat field. Irrigation ditches crisscrossed the field several times between us and the tree line.

We knew immediately that this was a different situation than a strike by one or two VC. When the shooting started we could hear not only enemy automatic weapons fire, but also the noise and impact of larger explosives all around us. I dropped to the ground and tried to find out where the firing was coming from. I turned around and saw that Ed and I were alone in the field. The rest of the CP had jumped into an irrigation ditch about 10 meters in front of us. Behind I could see no one. We had crossed a ditch about ten yards behind. Our packs, including the radio Ed was carrying, lay on the ground next to us. I yelled to Ed that we better try to go forward rather than be cut off from the CP. His eyes widened, but he muttered, "Okay." We grabbed the straps on his pack with the radio, one on either side, and ran forward as low as we could toward the irrigation ditch ahead. As we ran, I heard no sound but simply scrunched my face as if trying to avoid being pummeled in a rainstorm.

We landed in a heap in the ditch next to Captain Moran and the rest of the CP. That was when I recognized the racket the enemy's fire made when they saw us running. And the explosions behind us and a constant whistle of rifle fire had been aimed at Ed and me.

The tree lines and creek area where we fought the NVA in early September.
I took this picture from the air after I became an aerial observer.

Captain Moran told me that the left platoon had been hit first and suffered several casualties. He had called for medevac helicopters. Meanwhile, he was trying to figure out what enemy force we had run into, and what we should do to fight back. He ordered the right forward platoon to move around the flank, but they were immediately pinned down by automatic weapons fire. I asked Moran if he wanted artillery. He said "Yes" and pointed to a spot about 30 yards in front of us.

"Can you walk it in?" he asked. I told him we were on the gun target line to Firebase 411 and would have a difficult time using its four guns for such a delicate mission. But two of the battery guns were now at an outpost to our east. With those, I felt I could walk in artillery rounds right on top of us. I called in my fire mission, requesting the two guns to our east.

When word came back that we had clearance, FDC told me they would be firing the four guns from Firebase 411. I told them no, explaining that we were on gun target line to those guns. I told them this was a "dangerous close" mission. I wanted to walk artillery rounds into an area about 20 meters from us. I asked them again to use the artillery guns to our east.

FDC came back in a few minutes insisting that they needed to use the four guns on the hill and saying that they were going to start firing. I told them to add another 200 yards to get the original rounds farther from us just in case.

When they radioed that the first rounds had been shot, I told Moran to tell everyone to get down. He radioed to all the platoon leaders. We all crouched low in the ditch. The first round was long past the target and over our heads. The round almost killed people in the platoon to our left. I called off the fire mission.

By this time the infantry battalion had been able to scramble Cobra helicopter gunships out of Chu Lai. I gave Moran our exact grid position on the ground and the best estimate of where the firing was coming from so he could guide the gunship commanders and direct their fire. The gunships started a series of passes that lasted for several hours. First they used rockets on their rocket pods. When they ran out of rockets, they used their Gatling guns to fire into the tree line directly in front of us. The noise was deafening.

As the the gunships pounded the enemy positions, some of the wounded were able to make their way back to the CP, where they could be airlifted out. They began to tell us of the dead and dying where they had been attacked. Meanwhile their own blood began to turn the water in the our ditch red. We ordered body bags brought out on the medevac · helicopters.

After an hour, with the gunships running out of fuel and ammunition, I convinced Captain Moran to let me try the artillery again. This time, I told him that, if I couldn't get the guns to the east, I would start the first rounds at least 500 meters to the north of us and "walk them in" as carefully as I could. We needed additional cover because as soon as the gunships left for a few minutes, the enemy fire in front of us increased dramatically. We knew the gunships couldn't fire forever.

I called in another fire mission, again requesting the guns to the east. Again I was denied. Therefore I gave target coordinates well out of range of us and began slowly walking it in. We were never able to get it closer than 200 meters from us, but the fact that it was there seemed to inhibit the enemy's fire.

When the first rounds came in, we all ducked, and felt the ground shake from the explosions. Then it was my job to look up and see where the shells had landed. Right after I stuck my head up above the lip of the ditch, there was an explosion behind me. At first I thought it was a stray round. But when I saw the smoke from the two rounds in front of me, I realized that somebody was shooting an RPG at me. From then on, when I looked up, I kept my head a lot lower.

During the next hour I was the only one to peer out from our ditch. On our right, what was left of the forward platoons continued to fight skirmishes with the enemy in the tree line. As the day wore on, several more Charlie Company soldiers died and more were wounded. An armored group tried to close on our position, resulting in two more tanks being hit with RPGs. In addition, the enemy shot down one Cobra gunship and one medevac helicopter.

By nightfall our forward platoons had to withdraw because they were out of ammunition. To get them through the night, the CP gathered what M-16 rounds we had left and sent them by runners out to the platoons. We hoped at least to give them enough ammunition to be able to return fire. The infantry battalion commander back at Firebase 411 ordered us to make an assault before dark. Moran radioed back that we couldn't do it because we were virtually out of ammunition.

During that day, when I had time to think, I realized how scared I was. I also began to understand that, while up to then it had been sort of unreal, now I had to confront that I was likely going to die. If I managed to live through the end of this day, there was no prospect of living through the next day, much less getting through a week, a month, or, most improbably, a year at this rate. I tried to think about whether there were ways out. I knew I couldn't simply walk away because there was nowhere to go. I began wishing for a million-dollar wound. We had kidded some of the less wounded soldiers about their good luck before they were airlifted back to the rear. It no longer seemed like a joke. Now I even started thinking about whether I could shoot myself in the leg.

I also began to wonder, if I weren't killed by enemy fire, would I survive the conditions. We were in an open field with no shade. We were running low on water. I recall that I did eat something during the day, but was never able to eat more than a snack. I also knew that it would be virtually impossible to sleep that night in the water-logged ditch, where we couldn't really lie down and where mosquitos would eat us up.

The night passed uncomfortably but at least without further enemy engagement. The next morning a Huey supplied us with more ammunition. Orders came over the radio to assault the position that had been firing at us. If we were going to move forward on the enemy's position, I wondered again how long I was going to live.

As our first platoons moved out, the tree line in front of us was strangely quiet. The platoons radioed back to the CP that they were encountering no opposition. Those of us in the CP left our packs at the ditch and moved forward toward the tree line.

No one fired at us. When we made it to the other side of the trees, very little ground was not pockmarked with craters from the gunship rockets. Any enemy soldiers who were alive must have gone underground. Within a few yards of the trees, we began to find enemy bodies.

The sight of a dead enemy was no less gruesome than the sight of our own dead. I don't recall how many corpses I saw that day, but I do remember one in particular—he was the biggest Vietnamese I'd ever seen. He must have been close to six feet tall and weighed about 175 pounds. He was clearly a North Vietnamese regular. We even speculated that he might have been Chinese.

We searched the enemy's bunkers and found that they had been abandoned during the night, leaving a number of weapons and some papers. When we were certain that no hostile soldiers were still alive, we called in the intelligence people from Firebase 411 to begin their analysis.

We touched nothing, afraid that anything left behind might be booby-trapped. One of our tunnel rats found an extensive network of underground caves. After the tunnel rat emerged from the last cave, we set off explosives inside the tunnels to make sure no one remained alive. By mid-afternoon we had marched to the other side of the plain to set up camp.

The following day the infantry battalion commander, a lieutenant colonel, whom we had never seen during the fighting, arrived on the resupply helicopter to visit with Moran. He looked sheepish, especially considering he was in washed and starched jungle fatigues in contrast to our two-week old filthy and torn jungle attire. I remember at one point he told Morgan: "You guys saved my career. If you hadn't moved forward, I don't know what I would have done."

Besides that, he could offer little help. Charlie Company was now down to approximately 55 men from an original strength of over 100. We had no remaining infantry lieutenant platoon leaders, no remaining NCOs, and the squads were disorganized. Those of us who remained wished that we had been shot in a limb so we could have been taken back to the rear.

I asked the battalion commander why we hadn't been able to use the two artillery guns to the east. He said he didn't know that I had asked for them, and told me I'd have to speak to the artillery battery commander when we got back to the hill.

We had only one more casualty on that maneuver. One morning, just after breakfast, a CP radio operator grabbed a pack of toilet paper from his ration pack and headed a few yards away. I was reaching down to pick up my canteen when he set off the booby trap. I remember freezing as I heard the explosion, waiting for something to hit me. It couldn't have been more than five feet away.

Somehow, I wasn't hit. His body must have shielded me and others near him from the shrapnel. The booby trap had torn open the front of his body. He was choking on his blood. It sounded like someone drowning. He died a few minutes later before a medevac helicopter arrived.

THE NEXT MORNING WE WERE ORDERED to join a battle another infantry company was fighting. This company had been pinned down for a day or two by an unknown enemy force close to where we had found the NVA battalion. We arrived just before dark and established a perimeter to act as reinforcements. The next morning we were joined by a group of South Vietnamese RF's and PF's (Regional Force and Popular Force) soldiers. These were not regular South Vietnamese soldiers but the equivalent of U.S. Army Reserves and National Guard. Whenever fighting erupted in their region, they were supposed to be brought in. The rest of the time their job was to patrol their home area and set up refugee camps. Nevertheless, they were well outfitted in green camouflage uniforms and sported American-made M-16s.

We spent the morning moving with these "Rough Puffs" into position. None of them seemed interested enough to dig a foxhole. Their main concern seemed to be procuring some of our C-rations and cigarettes. The rest of the time they spent standing around, talking to each other and smoking cigarettes. We couldn't communicate with them in anything but pidgin English. Our South Vietnamese "Kit Carson Scout" translated for their commander as he and Morgan discussed the plan of attack.

Around noon, with the sound of the firefight increasing, we got the order to move forward on what was suspected to be the enemy's right flank. As our first platoon moved in that direction, it came under fire immediately. Meanwhile, the rest of us moved out around the left flank.

The RF's and PF's jumped into our foxholes as the firing started. Their commanding officer sent the word that they were to move forward with us in a line moving west. Our CP dispatched the signal it would give when everyone was to come out of their foxholes and move forward.

As we waited for the signal, I thought we were finally going to be doing what we should be doing—fighting alongside the Vietnamese, showing them, if they needed it, what we knew. I was sadly mistaken. When the signal came, I started out of the foxhole along with everyone along the line. None of the RF's or PF's moved. Their officer came running up behind yelling and screaming at them, trying to stick his rifle butt into several behinds, jabbering obvious obscenities at all of them. None moved.

Nor did they even try to cover us with fire. When I looked back, they weren't sticking their heads above the foxholes to see what was happening.

We reconnoitered 100 yards forward, ducking behind the tree line for cover. Without the RF's/PF's, we were too spread out to move on the enemy effectively. Moran radioed to the platoon leaders to pull in ranks. Three squads dashed to the right to give protection to the initial platoon that had come under fire while we established a perimeter so helicopters could evacuate a couple of wounded soldiers.

Moran then radioed to battalion headquarters, telling them what had happened with the RF's/PF's. He told battalion that we weren't going to have anything more to do with them lest they got us all killed. Battalion agreed. We spent the night in the tree line.

The next morning, the enemy seemed to have disappeared again. No resistance, no fighting. We found a few old AK-47's. We sent our demolition specialists to blow up the tunnels we found. Later in the day we got orders from battalion to ride east with the armor. They could get us there a lot quicker, and we could start operations based on new intelligence. Reluctant on the one hand to join the armor, but happy on the other to be riding instead of humping our packs, we climbed aboard the armored personnel carriers for the trip east.

We were about 100 yards from our loading zone when we heard a "whoosh," and then an explosion a few yards behind us. It was an RPG, fired toward the armored personnel carrier I was riding in. The tanks and personnel carriers immediately scrambled into a circle and we bailed out. I was firing my M-16 into the bushes in front of us when I heard Moran yell to stop firing. I realized I had expended half of my M-16 rounds without hitting anything. But it did relieve some of my frustration knowing that, once again, I and the other soldiers in the armored personnel carrier had managed to miss being killed by about a foot.

OF COURSE, I WAS NOT GOING to tell my family what had just happened: about the men we lost, and about my conclusion that staying alive for a whole year seemed impossible. That would have been cruel. But in the aftermath, on September 2, when the battalion commander had come out to congratulate us, I wrote a letter home from the field:

"It's about time, I guess, for a comment on this stupid war. We had two platoons of Popular Force Vietnamese go with the infantry today, and as soon as the shooting started they hid and refused to fight. Here are the South Vietnamese with two companies of [U.S.] infantry, a troop of tanks, all the air support in the world, and they won't fight the NVA who have been bombed for two days and have only small arms and a few anti-tank rockets. But the NVA put up with all we have and hold their ground. You almost have to conclude they deserve this place, not the South Vietnamese. The Americans fight well, but Nixon's stupid Vietnamization is a hoax, at least up here. From where I'm looking, I'm just hoping we don't lose any more men in this ridiculous place. We fight well and hard, but for no good reason. I only hope I'll be out of this area soon."

I'm somewhat disbelieving that this letter got by whatever censorship the Army applied.

The next day, I wrote to my uncle and aunt in New York:

"The war from this angle is even more ridiculous than from the States. The South Vietnamese are afraid to fight, even with our units going in with them.

49

The NVA, whom we have been up against lately, fight about as fiercely and as dedicatedly as the Japanese in WWII. It seems to me they deserve the country if they're willing to fight for it. I doubt Vietnamization is doing any good at all. When we pull out, the North will take over."

On September 5, as we continued to clean up the area, I reported:

"The fighting has stopped now and I'm combatting a heat rash. This morning we got food [C-rations] and water for the first time in three days—a banquet was had by all. We had been drinking stream water with purifying tablets which makes it taste like iodine. I even managed to shave and wash a little. Mail came for the first time in four days... and I got a Sports Illustrated from Dad. It has been well passed around by now.

"We routed the 60ᵗʰ NVA Battalion and got credit for 40 kills. However, they were bigger than Vietnamese, and they are investigating the possibility of Chinese help. I sure hope not. If things go as planned we'll go in for a rest in four days. We can really use it, especially some cold beer and soda and maybe a few hot meals. I have learned to cook C-rations to an edible mess, but the last two days it has rained regular monsoon type deluges, and we've spent the morning drying out and trying to make some fires. We also get LRRP's out here — long range reconnaissance patrol meals which are instant type—which enables us to add water to achieve beef stew, chicken & rice etc. They are somewhat like a lump in your stomach but make a good change from C-rations."

Before we headed back to Firebase 411 we had to weather the first monsoon rain of the season. We spent two days trying to stay relatively dry, but found it impossible. As I wrote:

"So far (knock on wood) my stomach hasn't rebelled too badly. Only my skin from the dirt. I'm also drying my socks and boots for the first time in a while. Such breaks should come more often."

The next day I described in a letter home a fire mission, commenting again on how artillery support might keep me and others alive:

"Yesterday was a good, quiet day and I even got a chance to wash, shave, trim my mustache and wash my hair. For dinner I had a hot LRRP spaghetti and meat sauce and wrote many letters. Then at night I had a hairy experience. Each night when we reach our defensive position I plot defensive targets ... of

likely enemy attack positions. Then later at night they fire them in to make sure they are where we want them. We shoot white phosphorous up in the air first to make sure they're safe and then fire the same location 'on the deck' for pin-point. Since there are other companies around us now, it's hard to make sure they aren't close to a [defensive target]. I only know where our company is.

"Anyway when they fired our second target last night up in the air, it came close to where I thought another company was situated. They told the guns it was safe for us but not, I thought, for another friendly element. They argued with me that it was either safe or not safe, but I refused to let them fire on the deck. Five minutes later the other company got through to the guns to say the WP round was right over their heads, please don't put it on the ground. They had failed to tell the guns they had moved an element out during the night. Sweet vindication and much relief for this FO and plenty of static to both the guns and the other company's FO. It may give me a small amount of satisfaction to know that in one instance it was worthwhile for me to be an officer who can save some lives and limbs."

In the same letter I offered my assessment of the structural problems facing those of us in the field:

"Another comment on this war, prompted by a column by Stewart Alsop (who I don't usually listen to) in Newsweek. He talks of the fighting situation here being messed up because only draftees are fighting. All enlisted men who signed up were given the chance to choose their job and of course chose non-combat specialties. The NCO's who re-up do the same thing. This is very true, and the result is a non-professional combat force of 18 and 19 year olds who get the worst jobs and have no experience. 90% of our company is PFC, Spec. 4 personnel, all drafted with no higher NCO leadership. Each platoon should have an E7 platoon sergeant and 3 E6 squad leaders. Now our highest [ranking] squad leader is E5 (he made rank over here). We have three E6 platoon sergeants and 2 E6 platoon leaders (a lieutenant's job). So you have a civilian, drafted fighting force with no experienced leadership, and a professional rear in the soft jobs.

Of course this is bound to happen when the army tries to keep people by job incentives. But it shows how horrible the draft system is: if you're drafted, you'll be the one being shot at, and you better learn by yourself because there are no experienced people with you. Since a high percentage of draftees are black, you create a bitter bunch of trained killers. This war will have continuing repercussions for many years to come. And the draftees are the ones losing their lives. It's no wonder the career people love this war and volunteer to come back."

Despite being scheduled to return to Firebase 411 after several weeks in the field, our brief chance to kick back was postponed. On September 9 I wrote home:

"This is our 12th day on this field trip, and according to the original schedule, we should go in today for 4 days of guarding the firebase. However, because of the major size of this operation we'll probably be out another eight days. Long time between showers and change of clothes.

...

"Things have been quiet now for several days, and my heat rash seems to be disappearing. So I'm trying to get as much of a tan as possible to guard against the inevitable ringworm and jungle rot. It's a real scorcher already, even before 9 a.m.

The Chaplain spent the night with us and is now trying to catch fish in a bomb crater with our radio antenna and a few worms. He's a real character whose favorite pastime is liar's dice..."

Two days later, on September 11, I wrote home:

"We all took a bath in a nearby river today—with the villagers and their cows. We figured it was safe if they were willing to risk their animals. Besides, the NVA have apparently left for the time being and the VC haven't reappeared."

The next day, I wrote and asked my folks to send me a Kodak Instamatic camera. I figured that I could carry it with me to take photos of our operations. The photos in this memoir were taken with that camera, which I received a few weeks later. In the same letter I wrote:

"We had our second mechanical ambush claymore mine go off on our perimeter last night — and bagged our second rabbit. But you should have seen the people scurry when the explosion went off. At least it keeps the troops alert."

I also reported:

"Last might I fired a defensive target and one of our ambushes called up to say it was right over them — they were 1000 meters away from where they thought they were. I'll have some gray hair when I get home."

WHEN WE FINALLY GOT BACK TO Firebase 411 for our rotation, I learned that military intelligence had determined that the heavy fighting a few weeks earlier had been against the 60th North Vietnamese Army Regiment. Their report confirmed 40 enemy bodies. I never saw anything close to that amount of carnage. I sincerely doubt that they found that many dead enemy. But body count was what mattered to the higher ups, and body count was therefore often exaggerated, as I later found out.

Military intelligence had translated the captured documents, which defined the NVA battalion's mission as shooting down two helicopters, putting four tanks out of commission and killing 55 U.S. soldiers. Eerie, but that was close to what they had done before the NVA survivors disappeared. I couldn't imagine what it must have been like for them. The most they could throw at us was machine gun fire and rocket-propelled grenades. We threw at them infantry, artillery, cobra gunships and napalm. Having met their quota, the survivors had, not surprisingly, stolen off into the night.

I also caught up with the battalion chaplain. He told me he was a Southern Baptist. He thought it was amusing to go around with no weapon except a large slingshot tucked in his belt. He wasn't a bad guy, making what seemed a sincere effort to seek out anyone who wanted a chaplain's guidance. From what I saw, however, everyone humored him but no one took him up on it.

The chaplain visited us in the field as well as at Firebase 411. Note the slingshot in his belt; he bragged about its being his only weapon.

I also sought and confronted the Firebase 411 artillery battery commander. I wanted to ask why he hadn't let us use the two guns to the east of us when we needed them. I found him at the gun emplacement, introduced myself and told him I wanted to talk.

He was a typical young lifer captain—trying to deal with all situations in as tough a way as possible. The men on the guns hated him. This was his first tour in Vietnam. He had managed to get through his years as an artillery lieutenant without being a forward observer, so he had no experience in the field and no way of understanding what it was like to be on that end of the guns.

I told him I was the forward observer for Charlie Company. He appeared eager to swap war stories with someone so recently in action. He asked how I liked the shooting his battery had done for us. I told him it was responsive when I called for it but it had almost killed me and a number of other people. He asked what I meant. I told him that, during the recent battle with the NVA, the guns at 411 were directly north of us, which put us on the gun target line for a danger-close mission. I told him that because I had wanted to "walk" artillery in, I specifically requested the two guns to the east, which would take us off the gun target line. I told him that twice I had been denied the use of those guns. I asked why.

He had no answer. He just said it was a decision he made. He could offer no other explanation. I could only assume he had no comprehension of what I was talking about or about the danger we had faced from our own guns. And I had the sense he wasn't going to lose any sleep over it.

In a letter written on September 15, I summarized the encounter this way in a letter home:

"I really had it out with the Battery Cmdr when we got back, and I may have made a few enemies here. It is rare that I have really told someone off, but the artillery support was so bad, I felt something had to be done. He was belligerent and defensive since he'd been getting it from all sides anyway; it may have been the wrong thing to do, but I'm very concerned for the safety of our company, and my disposition suffers when I get such a response from someone not getting shot at and merely protecting himself. It also helps that I'm not worried about my Army career."

I recall later talking to Ed about that battle with the NVA. He and I kidded about the way we got up the courage to drag the radio, ourselves and our packs forward to the ditch with the rest of the CP. I asked him what he would have done if he had been stuck out there in the middle of the field alone. He grinned and said he had no idea. I also asked him if he had ever had any training as an infantryman. He said, "No."

I asked Ed how he got stuck going to the field instead of being back on the guns, as he had been trained. At that point I could see his anger rise.

As Ed told me, when he first arrived at Firebase 411 on a chopper, he was one of a group of three newbie artillery gunners. They all had the same Military Occupational Specialty (gunner), the same training, the same rank. They all got off the helicopter together. They reported together to the battery commander. He looked at the three of them, and then told Ed to get a pack. He then sent Ed out to the field to be an RTO. He assigned the other two to be gunners on the firebase in the relative safety of the firebase. Both of them were white.

That was why, Ed said, during those first few days he had refused to talk to me, a white artillery officer.

WHAT ED LEARNED DURING OUR SHORT course was how to be an artillery forward observer in Vietnam. In a conventional war, artillery is used from behind the front lines to bombard an enemy before infantry and armor moves forward to meet the enemy. The artillery forward observer usually looks out from a position on a hill or high terrain, choosing targets that are visible. Once the observer determines where that target is on his map, he calls in the location of the target, using his map's grid coordinates corresponding to that exact spot. When the first rounds land, which can be off by some distance because of weather factors or poor map reading, the forward observer then "adjusts" fire from where the first rounds landed to hit the target.

In the Vietnam War, there were no front lines. Forward observers were on the ground with roving infantry companies. So as a forward observer I had to send in artillery fire missions from the vantage point of the center of the infantry company's position. This made knowing the infantry company's exact position incredibly important. We didn't want to have artillery rounds land on us and our fellow soldiers.

As I soon learned, the Charlie Company and infantry in general were terrible at reading a map. They rarely knew exactly where they were on for purposes of safely using artillery or air support. As someone who could read a map, and most important as someone who could figure out exactly where we were on it, I brought an important skill to the table.

Artillery maps are divided into grid squares. Each square is 1000 square meters. Each grid square can be identified by a north/south number and an east/west number. Any particular spot within a grid square can be identified first by its grid square and more specifically by tenths of a grid square. So any position on a map is describable in grid coordinates down to as little as approximately 100 meters.

Sometimes our location on a map was easily determined, such as when we reached the point where a road crosses a river. Map grid coordinates of that position are simple to determine. But what if you do not have a specific landmark to establish your grid location on the map? Another bit of assistance was that the maps had contour lines. These lines enabled the forward observer to see the terrain's went elevation. A contour map allows for a three-dimensional view of the landscape even though the map is two dimensional. If you were on top of a hill, you could locate that spot with accuracy by determining the grid coordinates that correspond to the highest contour point of that hill on your map.

But what if you were on flat land with no easily recognizable landmarks? You could determine your grid coordinates through what is called "triangulation:" using distant landmarks, particularly peaks of hills or mountains, as reference points. Placing a compass on the ground on your map, you orient your map in a north/south direction. Then, again using your compass, you determine how many degrees off 0 degrees the top of a far off hill is. You then draw a line at that angle on your map from that spot. You then do the same thing using another landmark that you see in a different direction and again draw a line on your map corresponding to the degree reading on your compass. Where the two lines drawn on your map intersect is your grid location on the map.

Knowing your exact grid location, you can safely fire artillery onto a target on your map that has different grid coordinates than your own position.

Artillery rounds are amazingly accurate given the distance they travel. This is because of many calculations done back at the guns that factor in not only the target location, but also the outside temperature and humidity, the current wind speed and direction, the temperature of the powder used at the guns to propel the rounds and the grid location given by the forward observer. The 105 mm howitzers, like those we had at Firebase 411, could shoot accurately a distance of over 5 miles.

The maps the artillery provided us were made of thick stock. They were in color and, when unfolded, were about 2 feet X 2 feet. These color maps with contour lines, I was told, derived from the French Indochina War. Despite their age, I found them mostly quite accurate.

The fundamental problem was keeping a paper map from disintegrating from sweat, rain, dirt and simple rough daily use. I solved the disintegration problem as best I could by encasing my map in the plastic wrapping used to preserve cartons of cigarettes. That wrapping, with a judicious use of tape, not only protected the maps from the elements, but also allowed me, using a grease pencil, to write on an unused section of the map any grid coordinates and radio call signs. Most important, I could draw lines on the map when I was doing triangulation to establish our position. I spread the map out on the ground, oriented it north/south with my compass, and drew lines with a straight edge to calculate our grid position. Whenever I was done with the information I had written on the map in grease pencil, I would wipe the map clean with a damp cloth.

I found a great place to carry my maps: in the cargo pocket on the right leg of my jungle fatigues. This made my map quickly available at any moment. Even when I was humping my pack, I could easily grab my map to see what lay ahead.

I BEGAN TO WONDER IF MY skin would fall off from the dirt and sweat. I stopped wearing the green cotton undershorts the Army provided—they rode up uncomfortably during a march. More fundamentally, after about a week, they rotted off anyway.

The green T-shirts were a little better. While they were absolutely grotesque looking, they didn't seem to be affected by whatever it was that ate our undershorts.

The pants and shirts of our jungle fatigues were made of the thinnest fabric; given the heat and humidity, I appreciated that. Like cargo pants, they had large pockets along the thighs.

Our jungle boots were made of breathable material on the sides, which helped in the heat. The soles had metal plates in them, reputably designed to withstand booby traps. I doubted they would help protect against a booby trap explosion, but they might have withstood a step onto a bungee stake planted in a hole and hidden by foliage.

Most days, I would have killed for a shower. About every three days, when we were resupplied with water, I would fill my steel pot with fresh water and try to wash my hands, face and neck the best I could. Most of the infantry never bothered with such niceties. I shaved about once a week. The feeling of cleanliness from that one shave would last about a day. Meanwhile, for the first time in my life, I grew a mustache.

Still, what I felt I needed most was a complete bath. I finally got what I asked for—at least I thought—when we had a rain shower. Everyone ducked for cover. I took off my shirt and undershirt, and stood in the rain looking up into a cloud to catch every drop, rinsing off the best I could. My pants and boots were soaked, but at least I felt refreshed.

I didn't know what a mistake I had made until I went to lie down that night. I noticed a tingling over the upper half of my body, which soon developed into a maddening itch over every inch of my torso, neck and face. Then my scalp began to itch. I couldn't use a light to see, but I could feel the bumps all over my skin. I couldn't bear having my skin touch anything and had to try to sit up to sleep. The next morning, I could see I had what I assumed was the worst case of prickly heat in medical history. Whatever was in the rain, or the combination of rainwater, dirt and sweat, had apparently created the perfect conditions for a rash. I suffered for the next day and a half. I did manage to find someone who had a can of Army-issue talcum powder, but it only made the rash worse. I decided from there on out I was better off dirty.

What had started with a short shower soon turned into the first monsoon rain of the season. We had been in the field almost three weeks. At last, Morgan got a call from battalion that we were to march several kilometers east to the location of the two howitzers in a small village. There we would be picked up by helicopters for rotation back to Firebase 411.

Marching in the rain to be picked up for a chopper ride to Firebase 411.

It started raining so hard it was almost impossible to see in front of us. We walked on a dirt path in several inches of water. We were also humping several kilometers with our packs. But I was elated. I had made it through a horrible engagement, and I was alive. I knew I would really enjoy a few days on Firebase 411. And I knew that no matter how exhausted I was from this march, we were going to ride the rest of the way in by chopper. This time I marched behind Ed, singing with joy to myself, but placing my boots exactly in his footprints, as he did in those of the trooper in front of him.

FOR OUR NEXT MANEUVER, WE BOARDED helicopters just outside Firebase 411 for what the Army called a combat assault. On a combat assault, we jumped off helicopters on a landing zone ("LZ") that intelligence sources thought was a likely location for the enemy. Artillery would first bombard the LZ, then a wave of Hueys would carry Charlie Company to clean out any remaining opposition.

My RTO Terry Brennan sitting on the left in the door of a Huey as we prepared to take off on a combat assault. Sitting in the chopper's door throughout the flight enabled us to jump out the moment we landed. Our packs were heavy enough to keep us from falling out.

Photo I took from the doorway of one Huey showing another Huey while on our way to a combat assault.

As we came in for the landing, the burning question was whether any enemy would shoot at us as we approached the ground. Seated in the doors of the choppers, we were particularly easy targets.

If the enemy was there, in the parlance of the Army it was a "hot" LZ. We were about as vulnerable during the landing as soldiers in the landing barges in WWII. Our only covering fire was M-60 machine guns manned by door gunners on each side of the helicopter. The door gunners had no clue what they were shooting at, and they were just as exposed as we were. The feeling I had as we landed on each combat assault was of bracing my face against a hard rain. I kept hoping that the rain would not be bullets from the other side.

Jumping off a Huey during a "combat assault." I took this photo as a second wave of Charlie Company arrived on the LZ, which was on a hill from which we could see the mountains to the west and the plains to the east.

Fortunately, this LZ was cold. We were now half-way up a mountain, on a peak that gave us a wide view of the valley below and the mountains to the west. We set up temporary camp and created a perimeter for the night. On September 18, I wrote:

"We're sitting on top of a mountain the choppers took us to yesterday afternoon. Last night was cool and clear, with few mosquitos. But today we have to climb another mountain, and I'm not looking forward to such a hike. My pack is heavy enough on flat ground."

On September 20, I reported on a successful artillery mission:

"Early this morning Cpt. Moran and I were making a binoculars reconnaissance of the valley to our rear. He spotted a small waterfall and pool and I spotted about 4 NVA taking a bath in it. They were about 3 miles away, so I called back for some artillery and we hit the waterfall after one adjustment, killing two of the enemy. When I called back to battalion that we had gotten two, the place went mad. The colonel came out to look over the area (from our location) and wanted my full story... He suggested all sorts of [Artillery] tactics for tonite in case they come back. Anyone who comes back for a bath after 2 batteries hit the

area is crazy. But the Arty has been so bad of late this is the biggest thing they've had and everyone wants to get all the facts for their rear war story...

"Of course maybe I should feel some short of emotion about killing people but this war has pretty much drained me of moral qualms. ... I was much happier later in the day to fire support for one of our platoons in trouble — they got hit on a hill and I got enough heavy stuff on the enemy for our people to pull back to their trenches. No one made much notice of it."

We continued to move up the mountains away from the sea and flatlands and closer to the Ho Chi Minh Trail. On the way we suffered from the lack of experience and leadership in the form of officers and NCOs, which I recounted again in a September 22 letter home:

"We've been trying to get the two platoons up a hill with resistance from some scattered NVA. The terrain more than anything is against us since the mountains are so steep and the woods so thick. I'm somewhat frustrated with Arty because I'm on another hill about 1000 meters away with our CP and two platoons and can't observe most of the stuff we call in.

"I have my SP/4 [Terry] with the two platoons and he's getting a lot of practice firing and adjusting, but it just shows the old story. They have someone just out of [Advanced Individual Training] with no training doing an E7's job because it's in the field and the NCO's stay in the rear. Since one of our platoon leaders was wounded and one platoon had no NCO's we had an E5 with two years experience leading two platoons. The men were scared and didn't want to move up the hill. We had to send a LT from another platoon and an E6 over to them to up the hill. What a war.

"Our company has had a drastic change of personnel in the last month and most of the people are scared and inexperienced. Unless we get some leadership in the platoons we might as well just sit in one place. ... Cpt. Moran is realistic in figuring we'll just have to move slowly and do little until people get some time to get oriented. Otherwise the company will fall apart.

"Of course we also have the problem that no one wants to be a target in a war that means nothing. We have no use for taking land, just finding the enemy and that means getting shot at. So morale in the platoons is rather low."

WE CONTINUED PATROLLING THE MOUNTAINS FOR the next week. On September 24, as I reported in a letter home, we had some action.

"I killed three VC yesterday on a mountain top with artillery. Whoopee. Of course everyone was once again exhilarated, but I found the bloodthirsty hoopla somewhat incongruous. As a confirmed killer now I'm not sure any woman will like the look in my eye and the wild appearance I take on when spotting a potential victim…

"However it does afford me a certain amount of status among the people here. All the grunts want me to fire at anything that moves and they give me twice as many rounds as I ask for back at the firebase. All this is fine as long as they don't decide to keep me in the field longer to have a higher body count."

WE WERE LUCKY DURING THE NEXT several weeks that whatever action we got into was brief and caused no casualties. We were severely short-handed, not only in leadership but in bodies as well. This made it difficult to affect the appearance Charlie Company wanted the enemy to see—a fully staffed infantry company of 100 plus men that no one should want to mess with.

I did, however, adopt a strategy that helped reduce the booby trap danger. Before we moved, I fired artillery onto what was to be our line of march. When the lead platoon point man put his foot in a recent artillery round crater, he knew he wasn't going to step on an unexploded booby trap. These craters also tended to clear a path where the undergrowth was thickest. We accepted that the enemy might notice that we were going where the artillery rounds had just fallen and set up an ambush. But we were more afraid of the booby traps.

Still, being so short-handed, we would be in trouble if we ran into any significant enemy force. Captain Moran reported this to the battalion and asked for replacements. For several weeks, nothing happened. Then, finally, we got our answer. A resupply chopper left Firebase 411 to bring us water and mail, and we were told that three infantry grunt replacements would be aboard.

As the helicopter landed within our perimeter, 1 could see three scared faces. They couldn't have been more than 18 years old. We knew then that we weren't getting the leadership backup we had been hoping for. All were private E-1s. They also had a strange demeanor about them as they got off.

The next morning I found out why. Captain Moran had called battalion and told them to retrieve the three replacements. When the resupply helicopter arrived, he and the platoon leaders stuffed the three of them and their equipment onto the helicopter in disgust.

Our platoon leaders had found out by the end of the first day that all three were on heroin. Sending them to the field was the rear commander's way of cleaning out some battalion problem children. It was easier to send them to the field than to deal with what the Army required for a soldier with a drug problem. The fact that these soldiers might cause the death of some of us in the field, for instance should one of them fall asleep on perimeter guard, was apparently not something that was deemed important to those who had sent them.

AT NIGHTFALL THE TEMPERATURE FELL ENOUGH to let us breathe a bit. It was dark from 6 p.m. to 6 a.m., and we didn't want any light or sound coming from within our perimeter lest we create a target for the enemy. We secured the perimeter with soldiers from each platoon, who lay in foxholes peering into the darkness, M-16's and M-60 machine guns at the ready. Each platoon also set out Claymore mines about 25 meters in front of their section of the perimeter. One soldier had to be awake on guard at all times during the night at each perimeter position.

The CP was at the center of the perimeter, surrounded by the platoons as they looked out into the darkness. The CP's radio was in contact with the battalion HQ at Firebase 411, and was turned down to its lowest volume. Meanwhile, during the night, Ed and I placed the artillery radio that was in contact with the guns on 411 next to the company radio so one person could monitor both.

Just like the platoons on the perimeter, the CP had one of us awake and alert all night to monitor the radios. So each of us in the CP pulled at least an hour of "radio watch" during the night. We rotated shifts so that each person, on at least one night in six, got the first watch and the last. Those were cherished the most because they allowed uninterrupted sleep if nothing happened during the night.

The biggest challenge of radio watch on most nights was staying awake. In the darkness, with no sound but an occasional soft squeal from a radio, there was nothing to see or do. We couldn't talk or read or even play solitaire. The only permitted "activity" to pass the time was smoking, as long as the cigarette was lighted under a poncho and the glowing cigarette was concealed by a curled hand.

For me, each hour of radio watch seemed to last an eternity. Checking the time periodically only made it last longer. When my hour was finally up, and I woke the next person to take over, it felt wonderful to get back into the poncho liner tent, pull the mosquito net over me, and fall asleep.

WE RAN OUT OF JUST ABOUT everything at some point in the field. During certain times we ran out of ammunition, and particularly during monsoon rains we ran out of food. We ran out of purified water frequently, but we then took water from a river or stream and purified it with iodine pills.

But we never ran out of cigarettes. The Army, I'm sure through the federal government, had made a deal with the tobacco companies to provide troops in Vietnam with free cigarettes, as many as we could smoke. Whenever we got back to the firebase, or went to the rear for a day or two, or even when the resupply helicopter brought us more C-rations, we were submerged in cartons of cigarettes. Bear in mind: cigarettes were very light, so they didn't add much weight to our packs. As a result, at every rest stop on a march, and after every meal, or during the night when we were on radio guard, cigarettes became the way we would "treat" ourselves when we had nothing else we considered a treat.

I'm sure the tobacco companies considered their contribution a well-paying investment. Here were thousands of young men who would come back from a year's tour in Vietnam hooked on nicotine, thus becoming profitable customers, many for the rest of their lives.

As always, a racial angle developed. Black soldiers seemed to prefer menthol-flavored cigarettes, such as Kools (the top choice) or Newports (a second choice, at best). When we split up the cartoons of cigarettes before heading to the field, given the number of Black troopers and the relatively low percentage of Kools and Newports among the cigarettes, the white guys would trade their Kools and Newports to the Black guys for double the number of non-menthol cigarettes.

In the field, other drugs were a constant problem, particularly troublesome because we needed our guards alert at night while on perimeter guard. All of us were relying on one another; we could not tolerate any of us falling asleep on perimeter guard by getting stoned during the early evening. As time went along, and I became more trusted by the riflemen, I saw that virtually everyone was smoking marijuana, laced, at times, with opium. However, in Charlie Company the men were watching out to make sure that no one was impaired when they pulled perimeter guard or when we set out on an operation. If someone was under the influence, one of his buddies took over for him on guard or as point man. No one was permitted to be stoned when it counted, or to use any real hardcore narcotics. That was supposed to wait until we were back in the rear.

I was invited several times to join in smoking marijuana with one of the platoons, particularly when we were back on Firebase 411. The first time, I struggled with myself as to whether, as an officer, I should report it. I knew that I couldn't for a couple of reasons. I had heard enough stories of officers being shot in the back of the head by their troops, whether because they had given an order the soldiers knew was dangerous, or because the officers were about to turn them in for drug use. I also felt that, by monitoring drug use and having the confidence of the troops who were doing it, I was more likely to be able to keep it under control. I was not in the infantry riflemen's direct chain of command, so I was in less danger in turning a blind eye than Captain Moran, as company commander, or the platoon leaders.

WHETHER IT WAS BECAUSE OF OUR battle with the NVA, or because we were so short-handed, at the end of September the infantry battalion scheduled Charlie Company to be sent to the battalion headquarters in Duc Pho for a three-day in-country R&R. Here's how a letter home on September 29 describes what happened:

"I suppose I've been in the Army long enough to know that there is no justice and if you can get screwed, you will, but this last crusher takes the cake.

Every 90 days each company gets a 3 day "stand down" in the rear where the troops can relax, they don't pull guard, and they can party and get some USO type entertainment. This is looked forward to almost as much as regular R&R because for the field troops it's the only chance to let off steam and get out of danger.

Today we were supposed to be in stand-down. Instead the higher ups cancelled it and sent us back to the field because a company found 5 NVA. Last week our company found a platoon [of NVA], had 10 people wounded and got no help. Now another company sees some people and we have to go help them. The morale is now non-existent in the company but the highers won't listen. Anything to help their careers. The really stupid thing is that one of the other companies that just completed stand down was not sent out. They are returning for a second tour of guarding the hill. Talk about SNAFU. It's all so stupid and meaningless, with the draftees paying the price once again."

As we returned to the field, Captain Moran told me that he had put a number of people, including himself, up for medals relating to the recent battle with the NVA. A couple of the medals were posthumous. He had also recommended a medal for my RTO Terry for bravery. Moran had nominated himself for the Army's second highest award for bravery—the Silver Star. I knew that the people out in the platoons, including Terry, had gone through 10 times more hell than any of us, including Captain Moran, in the CP. I was beginning to learn what medals actually meant.

CHARLIE COMPANY WAS ASSIGNED ONE TO three Vietnamese "Kit Carson" scouts. These local soldiers were part of the unit in every way, eating, sleeping, humping and fighting with us. Here's how I described them in a letter home on September 5, 1970:

"We have with the company three Kit Carson Scouts: former VC who have come over to our side and work as scouts for strategy and uncovering booby traps. They are funny to talk to in their pidgin English, but prove invaluable in their jobs. I have been using them to plan harassing fire at night where they can point out suspected enemy escape routes and camps."

In the top margin of the letter, I had one of them, whose name was Thin, write his name to say hello to people in the U.S. Thin was a member of the CP and gave us great local knowledge of where we might expect trouble, whether by ambush or booby traps, from the Viet Cong.

Another way we interacted with the locals was spending time with the Vietnamese kids. Whenever we were in the lowlands and things were quiet, during the day Vietnamese kids would show up. Most of them were probably 8 to 12 years old. They would wander into our perimeter or join us as we were humping from one place to another. They hoped to get us to give them C-rations or cigarettes, and they often offered to carry such things as mortar rounds or tent poles. What I most liked about having them around was that I figured they knew when the VC were likely to hit us. I also figured they knew where the booby traps were. So I mostly worried when they weren't around or, even worse, when they would suddenly disappear.

A Vietnamese kid who befriended me for a day while we were in the lowlands. He helped Ed and me carry our tent poles and wore my steel pot.

You would have thought that the best thing we had to trade with these kids was tropical Hershey bars that were included in some C-ration packages. But these kids had no interest at all in these purported sweets, and I saw one kid throw a bar back at the soldier who offered it. I guess that proved what we already knew: these supposed chocolate bars were completely inedible. Yes, because they were so-called "tropical," they didn't melt in the heat. But they tasted like dirty wax.

The kids usually had stuff to sell: mostly cans of warm Coca-Cola or Pepsi-Cola and most useful: packs of stir fry noodles (like Top Ramen in the States). The going price for a Coke was $.50 in MPC. That was worth about $5 dollars today. While it was a fortune to us, it was hard to turn down. Where else were we going to spend our money, anyway? Even warm, a Coke tasted pretty good after days with only water or canteen cup instant coffee to drink.

Photo above is of my RTO Terry Brennan (center), our medic (right) and a CP RTO drinking Pepsi Cola we bought from the Vietnamese kids.

The noodle packages were even more highly prized. We would boil water in a canteen cup, pour in the noodles, and when they were cooked, add whatever C-ration entree we had. Then we shook in lots of Tabasco sauce to kill the taste of the C-ration, and somehow we had something that resembled an edible stew. Ed and I discussed many recipes, but this was our favorite.

OCTOBER 1970

AS A GROUP, THE SOLDIERS OF Charlie Company liked being in the mountains a lot more than being in the flatlands and rice paddies. Sure it was tough to hump our packs in the mountains if we had to move. But there weren't as many booby traps, and we were much less likely to be ambushed. And we weren't as likely to be attacked at night. Captain Moran liked having the CP sit in one place in the mountain foothills for several days with a view of the terrain below while sending out platoons on patrols that lasted only a few hours.

A new first lieutenant infantry platoon leader joined us in the field. His name was Sam Gracio. Sam looked and acted the part of a tough, hard-bitten warrior. He always cut off his fatigue sleeves so that his biceps showed. He also always wore a vest that had magazines of ammunition, far more than anyone else in Charlie Company. He was always ready to talk about anything, particularly infantry tactics. He cared about the men in his platoon, and they responded by following him no matter what he demanded of them. I took a photo of Sam just before we moved out one day to hump into the hills.

Sam Gracio in the field ready to hump.

Sam was wounded within a week or two of joining Charlie Company, but it was not a serious wound, and he rejoined us less than a month later. It was great to see him lead his platoon the way all our platoons should have been led: with conviction and a bit of sass. Sam was always the first to be ready to move out, and he was constantly checking the gear of his grunts to make sure they were ready for a firefight.

The weather, however, was changing and we were caught in an extended monsoon storm. I wrote home on October 7:

"Sorry for the delay in writing. We got caught in a storm in the mountains for five days — everything wet and cold, and no re-supply of food and water or mail, and we just tried to stay warm & dry for the duration. There was major flooding in the lowlands, bridges out and towns under water, and we had to wait until it was over to get out.

Photo of RTO calling in Hueys to pick us up.

When I said cold, I really meant it. We were soaking wet with only our thin jungle fatigues between our bodies and the wind and rain. I guess the temperature dipped as low as the 50s, but I had no way of really knowing. Ironically, I think the hottest I've ever been was in Vietnam and, thanks to the monsoon rains in the mountains, also the coldest.

When the storm finally petered out and helicopters could retrieve us, we were taken back to Firebase 411.

Choppers arriving to take us back to Firebase 411.

INSTEAD OF PULLING A NORMAL ROTATION at Firebase 411 we were finally in for the break we were due. Because of our significant casualties and fairly constant action, but mostly because it was our turn, the battalion finally gave us our three-day, "in country R&R" back at Duc Pho.

It seemed strange to be back in a compound in a rear area. It was gated and designed for us to use for a three-day drunk. The compound had a series of barracks, a theater-like auditorium, a dirt courtyard and a mess hall. The first sergeant had been hard at work getting together enough beer, ice cream and soda to last us for three straight days of partying. Helicopters plunked us down into this compound straight from the field. We peeled off our filthy fatigues, showered in outdoor stalls, and donned fresh fatigues.

We weren't really confined to the compound—it's just that no one was allowed out unless he could prove that he wasn't so drunk as to cause a problem. Most of the infantry enlisted men just stayed there. Captain Moran approached me, however, about a trip to the base PX and the steam bath. He said it was an Army-run steam bath and massage parlor where, for a dollar, you could be bathed, steamed and massaged by a Vietnamese masseuse. By the tone of his voice, I suspected more might be involved.

When we got to the steam bath we each paid a dollar and sat down with a ticket. About five minutes later a Vietnamese woman in white tennis shorts and a white blouse took Moran's ticket and led him by the hand down the hall and into a small room. A minute later, another woman came for me.

The room she took me to was probably 12 feet by 16 feet. It had a standard steam locker with a hole for your head, an open shower and a massage table. In pidgin English the woman told me to take off my clothes. She led me to the shower and washed me down. Then she stuck me in the steam locker. I'd never been in one before, and I found it uncomfortably hot. I felt ridiculous with my head sticking out the top. After 10 minutes, she wrapped a towel around me and took me to the massage table. As I lay on my stomach, she pounded and kneaded my back, and then hopped up onto the table and walked up and down my back.

Finally she stopped and bent over, whispering into my ear: "You want a hand job?" "How much?" I said. "Five dollars," she said. "Okay," I said. She reached for the Jergens Lotion.

On our way back to the compound, Moran and I stopped at a small PX. I bought some junk food to keep in the barracks, and gazed at some of the cheap radios and watches for sale. I stocked up on an essential for our next trip to the field—two bottles of Tabasco sauce that Ed and I would use to kill the taste of C-rations.

We also passed what was clearly a prisoner of war enclosure. It had barbed wire atop about eight feet of thick chicken wire. Inside I saw two or three prisoners sitting on their haunches in the dirt, sweltering in the heat. They looked to be suffering horribly. I decided not to pass that way again.

When I returned to the compound I tried to take an afternoon nap in the barracks where the CP was bunking. Outside, small groups of soldiers, mostly drunk, were milling around. I went inside and lay on the top bunk against the back wall in the barracks.

After about 10 minutes I heard a squeaking sound coming through the wall next to me. I saw a crack between two boards in the wall and looked through.

On the other side of the wall was another barracks. On two lower bunks, two Vietnamese women, naked from the waist down, were gazing up at the ceiling while G.I.'s pumped away. The women looked strangely detached. I looked toward the door and saw a rear area sergeant collecting money and directing traffic for a long line of soldiers snaking outside the door. As each soldier finished and left the room, the sergeant collected a $5.00 MPC note from the next soldier and handed him a condom. I assumed the sergeant was taking a big cut and making a killing.

The squeaking continued the rest of the day, through the night and into the next day. Periodically I looked to see whether or not there were different women. It didn't appear so. Morgan later told me they were getting about half of what the sergeant was collecting.

The next morning the chaplain conducted a service for the men of Charlie Company who had died. Out of respect for them, I attended. However, I left when the chaplain started saying how lucky those men were to now be in heaven, having done their duty for their country. I couldn't believe that someone in this century could seriously spout such tripe, much less think anyone else would believe it. If any god were going to choose a side in this war, he certainly would have chosen the Viet Cong. After all, it was their country, not ours. And they were winning, despite our superior firepower. To classify the American role as a holy crusade was, at least to me, obscene.

I headed for the artillery battalion headquarters, where I had undergone a few days of early training before heading for Firebase 411. When I entered the battalion FDC, the same people were sitting at the same machines doing the same job. It seemed unbelievable to me that, after all I had experienced for the past three months, they were going on with life as usual. They seemed unimpressed that I was one of the forward observers who had been calling in fire missions from the field for the last two months.

I left FDC and went to the Officers Club. I was the only one there. Feeling sorry for myself and nostalgic for home, I found two hand-held cassette recorders. I poured a large glass of scotch and began to sing into the first recorder. I had been in a a cappella singing groups in high school and college, and singing four-part harmony had always been an activity that raised my spirits. I knew all four parts to at least one song, "Aura Lee." After I recorded myself singing the melody, I played it back while singing the bass part into the second recorder. I then played back the two parts together while adding the baritone part into the first recorder. The three parts sounded in tune. Last, I played the three parts again while singing the 1st tenor part in warbling falsetto into the second recorder. Then I played them all back. There were some not-so-nice chords, but in general it sounded like a half decent barbershop quartet. Afterward, I turned on a cassette of Glenn Campbell and got quietly drunk.

When I returned to our compound, even though it was late, Charlie Company was celebrating something new. I learned that the U.S. Army Vietnam Command had declared a currency changeover. The piaster, the Vietnamese local currency, had been suffering from skyrocketing inflation for the past several years. MPC, the "military payment currency," G.I.'s used for their transactions in Vietnam, was pegged to the American dollar. This created a very active black market for the South Vietnamese, who hoarded MPC as a hedge against the piaster's inflation. Periodically, to discourage the black market and without any advance warning, the U.S. Command would do an MPC changeover. American soldiers had 24 hours to exchange old MPC notes for new MPC notes. Then old MPC notes became worthless. Any Vietnamese holding old MPC notes as a hedge against the piaster's inflation suddenly found that old MPC notes were worthless.

This changeover, which was countrywide for all U.S. forces in South Vietnam, held up all operations for 24 hours. As a result, Charlie Company got an extra day at the R & R compound. The celebrating was intense. I found the sergeant who had been collecting money from the line of soldiers for the previous twenty-four hours. I asked him what had happened to the women in the barracks next to mine. He said they had left after he had paid them off a few hours earlier in old MPC. He giggled at the prospect that their two days of work had only earned them worthless pieces of paper.

WHEN WE GOT BACK TO FIREBASE 411 from our stand-down, we got another infantry platoon leader replacement, a young second lieutenant. The new officer showed up just before we were told we should prepare for another combat assault.

As we made plans at the CP for where we would go after being dropped off at the LZ, I introduced myself to the new lieutenant. He was younger than I, tall but thin, and he had a healthy, almost boyish look. He was from a rural community in Northern California. He was totally green, an ROTC first lieutenant whose last name was Redding. He had been in country about two weeks. This was his first combat assignment. Nevertheless, I was relieved that at least we had another officer who, with a couple of months' experience, could give one of our platoons some semblance of leadership.

That night, however, we learned that Lieutenant Redding, and the rest of us, were going to get a little bit more than we had bargained for on his first day in the field. Word came through from brigade headquarters in Duc Pho that they were holding a medal ceremony for, among others, our infantry battalion commander. The brass was awarding him a medal for his role in our operation against the NVA a few weeks earlier. All company commanders were ordered back to the rear to be present when the battalion commander received his medal. Moran was also receiving a medal.

I asked Captain Moran: "If you're going to the rear, are they at least going to call off the combat assault tomorrow?"

"No," he said, "Charlie Company is going ahead. Lieutenant Redding is in charge. You're going to have to watch him closely."

That was it. They were sending us on a combat assault without our company commander, the only experienced infantry officer we had in the field. Charlie Company was going into a potential battle led by a single infantry officer, a lieutenant who had never been in the field, much less in combat.

I took Redding aside. He looked scared. I asked him if he knew that he was going to be in command of the company for the combat assault. He said he had just found out, and he was putting together some ideas of what we should do once we hit the LZ.

I said to him: "Look, you don't know your ass from a hole in the ground out there. Even if you did, no one in this infantry company would believe it. They've seen a lot of their own people killed when they were following orders of infantry officers who knew what they were doing. They aren't going to listen to you. I don't know what's going to happen if this turns out to be a hot LZ. But if it isn't, let's just to sit there and dig in. We're going to land on the top of a hill, and from there we will be able to see all around us. When we land, if the LZ is cold, let's just sit there and not move an inch until Moran gets back."

Redding looked stunned, but he agreed. Who knows? That decision might possibly save him from a bullet in the back of his head.

Fortunately, the next morning, the LZ was cold, although we faced a problem of another kind during the landing. Whereas virtually all helicopter pilots in Vietnam were unflappable and brave beyond measure, we had one on this assault who must have become gun-shy. I can only guess he was new, or had about a week left before he went home. As his helicopter came in to the LZ, he saw an area with thick grass. He wouldn't put down to the ground. When our grunts wouldn't jump off the helicopter, which was still six or seven feet off the ground, he told the door gunners to start pushing them off. Several of our grunts ended up with sprained ankles from hitting the ground in full pack. But at least no one was shooting at us.

We immediately set up a perimeter we could defend. We were on the top of a hill in the second tier of mountains west of Firebase 411. From this vantage point we could see below a valley to our west and flatlands to the east. I suggested to Redding that he radio into the battalion headquarters that we had a good view of two important areas, and that we were going to stay there for the time being while sending out patrols during the daytime. Fortunately, we got battalion's permission.

The next three days, while we waited for Captain Moran to return to the field, we kept ourselves occupied playing cards in the CP. During the daylight hours, the rifle platoons sent out small squads on patrol, with the goal of spending the shortest time possible away from our hilltop perimeter.

During the second day, two of the patrols spotted what they thought were a couple of VC in a ravine below us to the west. Luckily, as I saw it, we were blocked by a steep cliff from being able to pursue them. The patrols asked if I would put some artillery rounds on the spot where they had last seen them. I said sure.

Because we sat atop a steep hill, and because we were directly on the gun target line between Firebase 411 and where we were shooting, I ordered high-angle fire from the guns. This would not only give us greater accuracy in the ravine, but it also would reduce the danger that the rounds would land on the brow of the hill where we were camped.

FDC was excited to have the fire mission, but said its calculation showed no chance of low angle rounds brushing the side of the hill. They requested using low-angle fire to avoid hitting aircraft.

I didn't see any aircraft, but if FDC was sure we would not catch any rounds on the brow of the hill, I said they should go ahead. After hearing that the rounds were in the air, I turned to watch the ravine.

Suddenly, the blast of two artillery rounds went off about 100 meters from us, striking the side of the hill we were on and wiping out the north part of our perimeter. Miraculously, no one was hurt. I called off the fire mission.

On October 11, I wrote home from that hill:

"Well, ..., there isn't too much more to report. If I see any of the filthy commies, I'll be sure to pour lead on them, or steel, as they say in the Arty.

I closed with Army parlance for how many days before I could come home:

"297 and a wake up."

But who was counting?

When Moran finally returned from the award ceremony, Charlie Company carefully made its way out of the hills to the valley to the west. Once in the flat land, we slowly headed to Firebase 411. We suffered only one casualty—an 18-year-old rifleman died when he stepped on a booby trap as we set up camp just before dark. I felt partially responsible as it was our only casualty from a booby trap after I had begun firing pre-emptive artillery for the rest of my time in the field. Worse, this rifleman was only weeks from the end of his tour.

Charlie Company walking out of the hills into a valley near Firebase 411. A few minutes after we stopped for rest, we took sniper fire from the hill to the left.

Artillery round going off where we took fire from an enemy sniper. The gray dust is the explosion of the round just after landing. The sniper was in the green trees to the left, and I adjusted the next rounds onto the grove of trees.

CHARLIE COMPANY'S NEXT SWEEP WAS SOUTH of Firebase 411, in the flatlands where we had run into the NVA battalion a little over a month earlier. We were supposed to meet an armored unit. Moran told me that, although we would have to fight with the armor, we would set up our own camp each night as far away from them as we could.

Our first order of business, however, was a so-called "search-and-destroy" mission into a small village. Because the My Lai massacre and its repercussions still stung with I Corps command, a major from division headquarters tagged along as an observer.

Search-and-destroy was a different experience from what we had done in the past. Now we were actually going to sweep through a small village with Vietnamese inhabitants as we searched for Viet Cong. We walked off the firebase about 2 a.m. to surround the village before daylight. The major went with us as a member of the CP.

We discussed in advance what we would do if we got into a firefight. We had become used to having Vietnamese civilians, mostly kids, around our operations. I also knew that we would not be permitted to fire artillery if we got into a firefight because the village was in a restricted-fire zone. The inclination for most of us was to shoot anyone we met first and ask questions later. There was still a lot of resentment over the casualties sustained against the NVA battalion only a few short kilometers from this village. It had been enough time since that battle that I was hopeful our troops would not be trigger-happy. But I also worried that when the cordon was sprung on the unsuspecting village, we might shoot ourselves in the crossfire.

Fortunately, the trap was one big anticlimax. Apparently the villagers had been warned of our coming, and had deserted the place. We found no enemy and nothing that seemed suspect. By nightfall, I was relieved that we had finished our sweep and were marching south to join the armor.

BEFORE WE COULD JOIN THE ARMOR, infantry battalion headquarters ordered us to head west instead, to the foothills that rose out of the rice paddies. We camped at the base of a steep slope that rose up into the mountains. That night, headquarters sent us an encoded message telling us to proceed at 5 a.m. the next day from our current grid coordinates to a spot approximately one kilometer away. Captain Moran asked me to decode the grid destination and report to him. As I plotted our destination, I realized that it wasn't very far on the map. However, it was virtually straight up a mountain.

I showed my map plotting to Captain Moran. He looked up the mountain that lay in front of us. It was so steep that it hardly had any vegetation; just red clay. That meant we would have no shade, and just as bad, no cover. We calculated that, with packs, ammunition and our mortar team's rounds, it would probably take us about three days to scale the mountain to the assigned grid location. We also knew we would be sitting ducks for the enemy while we were climbing.

We discussed trying to make as much of the climb as possible at dawn and twilight to minimize the risk of being seen and suffering from heat prostration. We also considered asking battalion to send a helicopter to carry our heavier gear to the top of the mountain. We couldn't ask battalion in so many words whether they understood our task because of the danger of compromising our plans over the radio.

"I don't think they understand what we're facing," I said.

"Well let's let tell them it's gonna take three days," Moran said. I put together a coded message that read, "Will take three days."

Within an hour we got our answer. It read, "You're only going about 900 meters. You've got one day."

"See, I told you," I said. "Goddamn infantry can't read a map. They don't realize that the 900 meters we're supposed to go is straight uphill."

Captain Moran snickered. "You're probably right. Still, once we get up there, we'll be able to see the whole valley. We can probably set up camp there and send patrols out for a week or two."

Once again, fortunately for all of us, Captain Moran was no more interested in having us walk into trouble than the rest of us. He wasn't going to disobey any direct orders, but if he could interpret them in a way that would keep us from having to get into trouble, he sure was going to try to do it. But first we still had to climb a mountain.

"What we need to do," he said, "is distribute the weight among us as best as possible. I'll get the mortar platoon to spread out their ammunition among a lot of us. In the meantime, we've got to pack as little food as possible. If we can find a good place for a landing zone at the top, we can probably get resupplied. But the climb will be so hot that everybody better pack as much water as they can."

Before dawn the next morning, we started off. We looked a little bit like what I imagined Sherpas do heading their way up a mountain in the Himalayas. We weren't going anywhere near that high—probably at the most 250 meters—but the line of soldiers alternately picking their way up the side of the mountain and resting along the way looked like one long chain of climbers roped together.

It wasn't long before the heat and humidity made it impossible cover more than about 20 meters without taking a break. There were no trees or even shrubs on the side of the mountain, just clay and an occasional rock or clump or grass. The mortar platoon organized a human chain to carry the mortar tube, our heaviest piece of equipment, up the hill. When a group was resting, they would hand the tube up, one by one, along the chain of climbers. Our medics treated at least one soldier for heat prostration.

By noon, to our surprise, we had traveled about a third of the way up the side of the mountain. At least the most forward elements of the company had gotten that far. While the forward platoon spread out to do a short patrol around the side of the cliff, the rest of us began eating what would be our C-ration lunch.

The enemy firing started only a minute or two after we had sat down. Those of us in the CP inched our way around the side of the cliff to find out what was going on. We saw bullets kicking up clouds of dust around the forward platoon, which was pinned down on in the open. They were taking fire from a knobby precipice to the north and about the same elevation as our destination.

The radio report from the platoon was not good. A staff sergeant who had joined us about two weeks earlier, and was our lone NCO in the field, was dead. Several others were also wounded.

We called for a medevac helicopter, although we had no idea where it could land. We told the forward platoon to pull back. I radioed in an artillery fire mission. With binoculars, I thought I could actually see who was firing at us. The fire seemed to be coming from someone in a tree. Morgan called for our own sniper, who had joined us for the operation, to see if he could reach the tree with his high-powered sniper rifle.

Our sniper was armed with a converted M-14. It had a special scope that enabled the sniper to judge windage for long-distance firing and used special bullets that went much farther than a normal M-14 round.

Our sniper said he thought he was about at the limit of his range but that he would try to keep whomever it was pinned down. Meanwhile, I received clearance for the fire mission. Artillery clearance had come through quickly because we were in the mountains. Within ten minutes, the first rounds were out. Because the target was easily pinpointed on my map, the first rounds almost hit the tree.

As soon as the smoke from the first rounds cleared, our sniper started firing more rounds toward the tree. I called in a small adjustment, and the next rounds were on their way within less than a minute.

One of the next rounds landed on the tree. Something flew out. It looked to me like a body, but from that distance, it could as well have been a large limb. Nevertheless, everybody jumped up and down, screaming "We got him! We got him!" I yelled at Captain Moran "Did you see it? Did you see it?" He was grinning from ear to ear.

"Okay let's call it in," he said. "We've got one KBA." That was the abbreviation for killed by artillery.

"Do you think they'll accept it?" I asked. "We haven't anyone to verify it."

"Well, we all saw it. Anyway, when the medevac chopper comes out, if we haven't received any more shots at us, we'll ask him to do a little looking himself as he leaves."

I radioed that the fire mission was over and reported one KBA. Over the radio I could hear cheers in the background at FDC.

I wondered whether the medevac pilot would be willing to take a chance just to confirm a dead body. But I knew that medevac pilots, like most helicopter pilots, were basically crazy. Anyway, we would see.

The chopper had a difficult time landing on the side of the hill, but we cleared an area large enough for an LZ. The chopper set down and unloaded a body bag and a couple of medical corpsmen to help the wounded on the trip back. We loaded the helicopter, ribbing the ones who were conscious about their million-dollar wounds. The one I talked to didn't seem badly wounded—his left arm was bleeding and he had a bandage around his head, but he seemed to be pretty clear-headed. I avoided looking as they loaded the body bag onto the helicopter.

Ed tuned our artillery radio to the helicopter's frequency as it took off. The pilot appeared eager to try to confirm our kill. He went straight up from our LZ and headed toward the tree.

Within a few seconds he reported: "Go ahead and report your KBA."

"Did you see him?"

"Oh, fuck," he said. "I don't know, but it's good enough for me. You can tell them I saw it."

For purposes of this bit of action, the body count was confirmed.

We spent the night on the side of the mountain; the slope was too steep to lie flat. Early the next morning, Moran sent a platoon the rest of the way up the mountain without packs to make sure we weren't walking into something we couldn't handle while tied down by equipment. The rest of us divided that platoon's equipment and tried to make our way up as far as we could before they returned for their gear. Before dawn, the rest of us started up the slope again.

By noon the second day, the forward platoon without packs had made it to our destination. They radioed back that it was a fine place to camp, with a great view of the surrounding terrain. They also reported that the spot had recently been someone's camp—apparently NVA. They said that they were careful not to touch anything so they didn't set off any booby traps. In the meantime someone got the bright idea to ask for battalion headquarters to send us some ropes.

News of our casualties had reached infantry battalion headquarters. They were willing to send us whatever we needed to complete the ascent. By midday we had long coils of rope, which the most forward soldiers took to the top. Those on top started hauling the packs and mortar gear up the hill. Less burdened, we were able to make the summit shortly after dark.

A Huey resupplying us in the mountains. The most important item, the bag containing mail from the States, is barely visible in the back door.

THE SUMMIT WOULD HAVE MADE A beautiful base of operations, given the view of the surrounding terrain. But after two days, it began to rain so hard we could hardly see. All of our equipment, and especially our ordinance, got so soaked it probably wouldn't work. However, we comforted ourselves with the thought that the VC and NVA, who were in this war for the long haul, probably weren't enjoying being out in this weather any more than we were.

Accordingly, we felt fairly safe just lying in our tents. The only real danger we faced, as we figured it, was from a possible enemy mortar round or two around nightfall. We filled the time playing cards, writing letters to be mailed the next time we got resupplied, and rereading the ones received over the last couple of weeks. Ed and I also made a major project out of smoking different brands of cigarettes from our C-ration packs. We invented a contest to see who could get a cigarette going the quickest before the wind or rain blew it out the flame from the lighter.

The most uncomfortable duty was nighttime perimeter or radio guard. There was no way to keep dry with our foxholes filled with water. But somebody had to be awake to return fire in case the enemy sent anything our way. We couldn't see anything in the dark, particularly in the rain, but it was important to return any incoming fire to let the enemy know they were dealing with a significant force.

During the third night of this storm, we almost lost a soldier. A young rifleman, who had arrived in the field only a week before, suddenly and inexplicably leapt out of his perimeter guard foxhole and, screaming, tumbled off a cliff. He fell down the side of the mountain into the black mist below. It was so unexpected that no one had a chance to tackle him.

His platoon quickly organized a search party to head down the mountain after him. We figured that he had had some sort of seizure. We had no way of knowing whether he had survived the fall. But the thought that he was lying alone and in pain, without shelter from the rain and possibly suffering from a broken leg or neck, meant we had try to keep him alive.

I told Captain Moran that I could shoot artillery illumination rounds that might provide enough light so the rescue party could pick their way down the cliff. He agreed that should help, and I called in the fire mission.

It took almost twenty minutes to get the artillery battery ready, obtain clearances and begin to fire the first illumination round. The gun battery had never fired illumination for a rescue mission. But FDC at Firebase 411 agreed to try it.

The first round illuminated the sky but was not close enough to be useful. In the thick mist, however, I saw that it gave off more light than if it had been a clear night. We didn't worry about giving away our position because we figured that the Viet Cong and the NVA knew where we were anyway, and they probably didn't want any movement on their part to be exposed by an illumination round.

With the sky lit by consecutive illumination rounds, the rescue team scaled down the cliff far enough to find the trooper. I timed my request to fire each illumination round so, just as one began to burn out, another would burst above the scene. As each round floated down on its mini-parachute, I counted down the seconds before it would burn out, and then called for another round to light up the sky.

Finally, the search party found the wounded soldier. He was unconscious, but alive. It was clear that he had a broken leg at least, and the bleeding from his mouth suggested internal injuries.

The next step was to call for a medevac helicopter to pick him up. A Huey flew out into the night with word to home in on our illumination rounds. It didn't take long for the pilot and his crew to spot us and locate the small rescue party on the side of the mountain with the wounded grunt.

The helicopter pilot, however, faced problems with the wind, the rain and the lack of a flat area to land. He tried three or four times to fly in close enough to land near the wounded soldier. Each time, however, the wind began to blow the chopper into the side of the mountain. I continued firing illumination rounds, but the pilot finally radioed us that he simply couldn't land.

Although reluctant to move the wounded soldier, we were more afraid that he might die if we didn't get him up the hill where a helicopter could land. The search party constructed a stretcher out of a poncho and two stakes, and prepared to carry him up the hill. Before they could start, however, I got a call from FDC at Firebase 411.

"We've been giving you round after round of illumination for almost an hour. We can't afford to give you any more. If we do, we won't have any left over for any other missions."

"Look," I pleaded, "we've got six men and a wounded soldier on the side of a cliff in the dark and the rain. They can't get him back up here unless we have illumination so they can see where they are going. How often do you have a chance to keep one of us alive with your artillery rounds?"

They said they'd get back to us. Captain Moran said we should plan to have the search party stay put until morning unless the artillery agreed to give us more illumination. We waited about 20 minutes. It had become eerily dark after the last illumination round had burnt out.

Finally, FDC came back on the horn. "Okay, you've got your illumination. We had to go to battalion artillery to get permission. We'll keep firing illumination until we don't have any left."

I went back to counting the seconds after each round exploded and burned its way down toward the ground, then telling the guns to fire another round that would light up the sky just as the previous one went out.

It took close to another hour of struggling with the wounded soldier on the makeshift stretcher, but the group scaled up the side of the mountain to our perimeter. It was almost dawn when they made it back. Within an hour, as light made it possible for a medevac Huey to land near us on the top of the hill, the soldier was picked up and flown back to the hospital in Chu Lai.

We never learned what had caused him to fall off the mountain, but we later learned he survived.

ED AND I HAD BECOME GOOD friends, at least as much as we could given that I was an officer who gave him orders, and he was an enlisted man required to follow them. I called him Ed, not PFC, and he called me LT instead of lieutenant or sir. We shared some of what our families and homes were like, and our hopes for life after our tours were over. We constantly worked on devising better ways to make C-rations palatable, and we watched out for each other in many small ways. We kidded each other often and tried to raise each other's spirits on particularly bad days. We shared fresh water when one of us ran low, and we worked hard to make our poncho liner tent a home that repelled mosquitos and the elements. I chided him when he refused to take his malaria pills, and he said he'd rather have malaria than constipation, which was one side effect of the pills.

When Charlie Company did its stints on Firebase 411, Ed tended to pal around with the Black infantry grunts. I wasn't offended because I figured Ed didn't want anyone to think he was sucking up to me. But in the field, we were inseparable, tied together by our assignment, the radio he carried and our reliance on each other. I needed that heavy radio close to me at all times, and Ed made sure of that. I began carrying some of his food and other stuff so we could even out the weight of our packs. I kidded him about walking just a few steps behind me wherever we went, and he countered saying that he was just walking in my footprints so I'd be the one to be blown up by a booby trap instead of him.

Charlie Company stayed on the brow of the mountain about a week. While there, Ed's birthday arrived. He and I must have looked pretty awful after a week in close quarters without a chance to dry out. I decided, however, that we needed to liven things up, and a birthday celebration was just the thing. I figured all we needed was a cake.

Coming up with the base of the cake turned out to be relatively easy. Some C-ration packs included a pound cake. The cake was round and small, about two and a half inches in diameter and about an inch and a half high. But pound cake was a prized item—it was the only dessert in the C-rations menu that was sweet and somewhat moist.

Next, however, our cake needed icing. I tried a number of concoctions. First I melted a tropical Hershey bar in my canteen cup with some C-4 explosive. All that did was put a black burned gum on the bottom of my canteen cup. My next idea was to mix dried C-ration cocoa and coffee. But this concoction was runny. So I added some coffee whitening powder, a few shavings from the Hershey bar, a bunch of sugar cubes and some ground up dry noodles. The concoction was a bit firm, but at least it was dark brown in color and had a slightly chocolatey taste. And it was sticky enough to spread on the pound cake.

Next, I collected a few small sticks to mimic candles. Unfortunately the sticks were too wet to burn. I finally settled on sticking some of our camouflage matches into the "icing."

Proud of such baking prowess, I summoned the birthday boy. As we lit the matches, Captain Moran, others in the CP and I sang happy birthday to Ed. He seemed embarrassed, but I could tell he was touched by the gesture. He ate about a half of it in one big gulp, and then Moran and I split the rest. It tasted just like C-ration pound cake with gooey, somewhat chocolatey tasting glop on top. But to me it tasted almost like home.

WHEN WE FINALLY LEFT THAT SPOT, we worked our way down the other side of the mountain through the jungle to the flatland. The foliage on the west side included what I assumed were banyan trees and some bamboo. The tree canopy kept us relatively cool. It was much easier going downhill in a forest than uphill in the sun. In packing we had considered that fact as well as that we might run into another monsoon rain. That meant we might not be resupplied for an extended time. It also meant we could be wet for days, if not weeks.

Taking a break as we descended the mountain into the jungle below.

The jungle was thick, and the steep hillside made it difficult to move quickly. Our packs kept getting caught on the underbrush, At 5 p.m. the first day we still weren't anywhere near our destination, so Moran told everyone to set up for the night right there. I tried to carve out a little spot for my air mattress, but the slope was too steep to lie down without it and me slipping down the hill. Even when I tried pointing my feet straight down the mountain, I tended to slide off. Meanwhile, some of the men were rigging up ways to tie themselves around tree trunks so they wouldn't have to hold themselves on the side of the hill as they slept.

Fed up with the prospect of a sleepless night, and especially one without a tent and mosquito net, I studied my map and saw that we were not that far from what had to be a clear knob on the lower side of the mountain. I told Captain Moran there might be a clearing with a good vantage point.

"We're staying here," he said. "If you want to check it out yourself, go ahead."

I weighed my choices. I considered the danger of walking through the jungle alone against the prospect of lying awake all night on the side of the hill. As to going off alone, I could summon all sorts of visions of booby traps, or running into some NVA. But I couldn't imagine any of the enemy trying to set up camp here. As I often did in such situations, against my better judgment, I opted for doing something instead of nothing. I decided I would walk about 100 yards through the foliage to where, at least according to my map, there might be a clearing. As I took the first couple of steps outside our perimeter, with my M-16 on safety but my finger on the trigger, I began to think I must be crazy. To calm myself, I mentally planned what I would do if I suddenly encountered the enemy. In my mind I ran through the quick fire lessons we'd been given in training before I left Fort Sill, Oklahoma. I also studied each tree branch to make sure there wasn't a tripwire for a booby trap.

About 50 yards out, I began to see light through the foliage. A few yards farther I emerged onto a grassy slope with a view of the valley to the south. I studied the low grass to see whether it had been trampled recently.

There were no signs of life. I surveyed the size of the knoll and decided we could easily get most of the company comfortably set up for the night there.

I retraced my footsteps as best I could back to Charlie Company's position. When I described what I'd found, Captain Morgan agreed we should move to the grassy slope. By 6 p.m. we were encamped with tents set up and hopes of a good night's sleep. I kidded Captain Moran about how the infantry never could read maps, but the artillery could.

We stayed at that spot longer than any of us anticipated. It was a natural base from which to send out patrols. The morning of the first day we spotted what we thought to be a VC near a stream and waterfall about two kilometers away. I called in artillery on the spot. Even though we were all fairly certain that the first rounds scared whoever it was away, I did see something fly through the air after one of the second rounds. Moran said to go ahead and report it as a KBA. I asked him whether we would need confirmation. He said don't bother. As usual, body count was king back in the rear, and no one had time to confirm it.

Toward the end of the next day, it began to rain. Before we could get everyone back to their tents, we were all soaked. By early evening we not only had heavy rain, we had winds that at about fifty miles an hour. The temperature dropped into what I estimate was the high 50s, though it may just have seemed that cold. With wet fatigues and the wind blowing, we had no way to heat food.

Soon Ed and I began to suffer from the cold. By midnight I thought I was going to come down with pneumonia. I couldn't stop my teeth from chattering, and Ed and I had nothing to wrap around us as a blanket. We managed to dig a small ditch around our tent so that the water would not run through it. But without any means to dry our clothes, we were facing hypothermia.

Ed and I eyed Captain Moran's flab. He had to have a lot of heat in that body. We told him to join us in our tent. I suggested we try to make the mosquito net into a form of thermal underwear. The three of us wrapped the mosquito net over us, then threw two poncho liners on top of that.

Huddling together in this small tent we managed to fall asleep, warmed by each other's bodies under the poncho liners and mosquito net.

When we awoke the next morning, the rain and wind were still pounding our tent. However, my jungle fatigue pants had dried. My shirt was also dry from the warmth the three of us had generated. But I had to pee. I knew that if I did so, I would be soaked to the skin within a few seconds of emerging from the tent.

I tried to pee underneath one of the tent flaps. I rolled onto one side, lifted the flap up a little and saw the stream of water running by in our makeshift trench around the outlines of the tent. No matter how I contorted my body, I just couldn't manage it. So I had to get out and get drenched.

We stayed in our tent that whole day. By nightfall we had played innumerable games of cards, and managed to cook a little food to assuage our hunger. My muscles were beginning to ache from being cramped inside the small tent. We took turns emerging from the tent periodically wearing Captain Moran's rubber poncho pants to make sure that everything was all right around the perimeter.

The next day was more of the same. We were like hibernating bears. The time seemed to drift by without very much going on or happening. Our main concern was that we couldn't stay there long without being resupplied with food. After three days, we were forced to inventory what food we had left and to ration it.

At the end of the fifth day, we were down to one meal for the three of us to get us through the next day. We split that meal as best we could. Before we went to sleep that night the three of us divided up our last pound cake and tried to imagine how many days we could go without food while the storm lasted.

It was a curious feeling. I wasn't so much worried about hunger, but I needed something to keep me warm. By the same token, I would have been happy to go several more days without food, if we weren't likely to be attacked. The relentless storm created a strange sense of calm and safety. We slept most of the time except for our stints of radio guard, listening for any word from Firebase 411. We had plenty of rainwater to drink. And, characteristically, we didn't run out of cigarettes.

During the storm I wrote home. The letter was dated October 16:

"This may take awhile to get to you since we're on top of a mountain in a typhoon. It's really rather unpleasant. Poncho hooches are not made for 90 mph winds and driving rain. And of course we're out of food. Rain water is plentiful however, and we're making the most of what shelter we have...

However, we continue to march. We just laid the transom for an ark, and have 38 more days to find a mountain top. Were they pigeons or doves?"

On October 17, I wrote home again:

"Would you believe — I had to stop writing to move out. Into the storm we went, looking for Charlie. We finally made it to our present location at dark last night, somewhat wet and tired. But the storm ended at midnight and we got resupplied this morning. ...

Commenting on how the war was going in our area, and somehow again dodging Army censors, I wrote:

I'll try to answer some of your questions in the last few letters. First of all the VC/NVA are much fewer than a year ago, and they are mainly in the mountains. The movement of communities into the lowlands with all mountains free fire areas has cut off most of the enemy's food supply, and the rice denial program in the lowlands has them very hungry for this monsoon season. However, in the mountains the terrain gives the enemy the advantage and very good cover. So searching the mountains is still dangerous and rather unproductive. Since there's so little food in the mountains there isn't too much reason to fight there except to keep them from stockpiling for after we leave. The VC are very low on manpower and NVA are helping them now. This is the line we get but it seems to be true from what I've seen."

I also commented on our cuisine:

"I've been making some delicacies with my Tabasco, Vietnamese noodles and C-rations. However, if you ever see the "C-ration Cookbook" in any stores, we could use it out here."

Although the rain began again almost as soon as we were resupplied, we were ordered to move down the side of the mountain toward the area of the NVA battalion headquarters we had unearthed several months earlier. The route of least resistance followed a stream bed through the thicket of trees. This was the classic wrong trail to take from an infantry tactics standpoint, but we were convinced that no self-respecting VC or NVA would be out in such weather, and we moved along without any concern. Actually, the creek bed reminded me a great deal of some of the hiking trips I had taken in New England. The foliage, leaves under our feet, and smooth rocks of the stream bed created an almost peaceful aura.

We set up camp at the bottom of the hill on the border of a few rice paddies. We thirstily awaited what we knew would be soon coming—a visit from the Vietnamese kids selling warm cokes and, we hoped, noodles. We knew that the little Vietnamese entrepreneurs, however, wouldn't miss a chance to earn a bunch of MPC.

After a few more days of patrolling, encountering no opposition, we headed back to Firebase 411 for several days.

A RELOCATION CAMP FOR VIETNAMESE CIVILIANS from the area was located two kilometers directly east of Firebase 411. The barbed-wire perimeter and corrugated tin roof shacks were thrown together to create an instant ghetto where farmers and their families were forced to live. I had no idea how long these people had been there, away from their rice paddies and farms, but I suspected they weren't too happy with either the RFs who manned their perimeter or the GIs who were now patrolling and blowing up their homes and farms.

Defense of the camp included machine gun nests manned by the RFs throughout each night. Curfew was at nightfall.

Captain Moran told Lieutenant Redding and me that the two of us would lead a party off the firebase that night to the refugee camp, pick up a squad of RFs, and then head south a few kilometers to set up a nighttime ambush. He explained that we would leave after dark so the enemy would not see us setting up during daylight.

I couldn't quite figure out what good I was to this mission. The entire area from Firebase 411 east to the refugee camp and south to Quang Ngai was an artillery no-fire zone. If we managed to ambush anyone, or if we stumbled into an ambush ourselves, I wouldn't be able to support us with artillery. But it was someone's idea, either Captain Moran's or the infantry battalion's, and the artillery approved their request that I should go.

When Redding and I explained our mission to his platoon, the men were incredulous. They saw immediately the likely result. As we walked in the dark toward the perimeter of the refugee camp, some uniformed or trigger happy RF was going to open fire on us with a machine gun.

Throughout the day we heard the riflemen grunts were deciding whether to refuse to go on this potentially disastrous mission. Meanwhile Redding and I did everything we could to convince Moran that it was a stupid and dangerous. He asked battalion headquarters to give him assurances that the RFs knew we were coming.

About an hour after dark, Ed and I met Redding and his platoon at the gate on the perimeter of Firebase 411. The men milled around waiting to learn whether we could satisfy them that we weren't going to be gunned down by the RFs. We did our best to display an air of confidence that we didn't feel. Finally one of the squad leaders told us that he had discussed it with all the men and, without further assurances, they refused to go.

Here was the essential Vietnam combat dilemma involving a potentially dangerous mission in a pointless war. Redding and I knew this was the sort of situation that caused officers to be shot in the back, and mutinous enlisted men to be imprisoned at Long Binh jail in Saigon. As I saw it, the decision to put us in harm's way had been made somewhere up the line, probably with minimal concern for our lives, and certainly without any real consideration for the ways it could go wrong. Meanwhile, as pawns, we on the front lines were forced to weigh the risks of obeying the orders and potentially losing our lives, or disobeying them and ending up either dead or in jail. Moreover, this conflict might ultimately cause the death of two officers at the hands of their men.

I weighed the alternatives Redding and I faced. We could simply report back to Captain Moran that the men wouldn't go. That seemed the easiest alternative in the short run. It clearly wasn't an attractive alternative, however, in the long run.

It would be nice to say that we were thinking of the men, that we didn't want some of them court-martialed. But frankly, reporting a mutiny would not be in our best interest either. Those who were court-martialed might be gone, but the remaining soldiers might at any moment drop a hand grenade in our tent, or put an M-16 bullet in the back of our heads. We were a fragile group, but we were nonetheless a team that was trying to keep each other alive. We relied on one another every minute of every day and night. Even if we didn't go on this mission, the next day, and the day after that, and the day after that we would be relying on each other and the rest of our company to keep us alive. The only positive thing to come out of the battles we had fought was a sense that we had survived together and, if we kept together, we might have a chance to survive for the future. To tear that apart created a much greater risk.

By the same token, how could Redding and I end the stalemate? Our order for the men to follow us had clearly failed. We didn't want to create any more of a wedge among us by repeating that order and having it refused again.

Redding and I pulled away from the group. I asked him if any men were willing to follow him and me if we went. He said that his RTO and another man had told him that they would go. I told him that Ed said he would go with me if we went. We decided to attempt to shame the rest into joining us.

We walked back to the spokesman. He was obviously as uncomfortable with the mutiny as we were. I told him: "Look, we're not any more excited about this than you are. We know that we've got to rely on a bunch of RFs getting word from our battalion to hold their fire. But we have all the assurances we can get from battalion that the refugee camp has been alerted we are coming. We've got the radios, so if they do open fire we'll be able to let them know back at the hill. They'll be able to hear the firing on the hill. And the RFs probably couldn't hit the side of a barn anyway. We'll go very slowly and, as we move along, ask for further confirmation that they know we're coming."

"We're not going, LT," was the answer.

"Okay," Redding said, "but we are. Four of us are going to go because we've got no choice."

I signaled to Ed. Redding nodded to his RTO, and the four of us started down the road into the blackness. I wondered whether we would continue to go if they didn't follow. I also wondered how many steps we'd have to take before we knew.

We got about 50 yards down the road when we heard a voice behind us. "LT, wait up. We're going with you."

In silence, the rest of the platoon caught up with us, and we began to march.

To reduce our risk of casualties, we spread out rather than marching in one line. The terrain was flat with low vegetation. Periodically we encountered small ditches, but mainly we had no place to take shelter. As we moved forward, we began to see the distant outline of what we knew to be the walled fortifications of the refugee camp.

As we marched, I felt vulnerable in the way I had so many times before when danger was the greatest. I felt as if I were sticking my face out of a moving car, just waiting to be hit in the eye with a dead bug. My reflex was to clench my jaw and grimace, waiting for the inevitable. I figured we would see the light from the guns firing before we heard the sound of the shots, so I kept my eyes glued on what had to be the fortifications. Mentally I rehearsed how I would hit the ground and cover up if the firing started. I also tried to keep in mind the closest place to take shelter. I cursed our luck that a partial moon revealed our silhouettes as we moved forward.

Every few hundred yards or so we called back to 411 saying we were closer, seeking confirmation that the RFs knew we were coming. We kept getting the same answer: "Yes."

I tried to guess when we would be so close that the RFs couldn't possible fail to see us, and that we were safe because they hadn't started firing. We thought of shouting out to them, but no one wanted to take the chance that that would set off firing. Suddenly, about 20 yards from the wall, we stumbled onto a platoon of RFs, who were sitting in the dark, waiting for us.

So we were safe. The RFs had sent troops out to meet us so we could move to the ambush site. I felt, once again, that I had rolled the chamber, put the gun to my head, and pulled the trigger. Miraculously, all I heard was click.

The subsequent ambush was uneventful. After we marched another two kilometers to the south along the road to Quang Ngai, we set up on either side, hoping we would later catch the enemy mining the road. I'm sure that whoever was doing it had been warned in advance of the ambush. Even if they hadn't, they couldn't have missed all of us moving through the night. We, of course, had a vested interest in that—we didn't want to have to confront anyone either. We'd had enough excitement for one night. Ed and I radioed in some defensive targets, and then slept fitfully on the ground for the rest of the night, keeping our equipment and belongings close to us so that none of the RFs could steal it.

NOVEMBER 1970

WHILE WE WERE ON FIREBASE 411 we learned that Captain Moran was immediately rotating out of the field, and that he would start a staff job back at brigade infantry headquarters. With only two days' notice, the company commander who had somehow kept us together and alive was gone. Suddenly we were without Captain Moran's knowledge of the strengths and weaknesses of our company, and all his experience from two tours in the field in Vietnam.

None of us knew our new company commander, who joined us before we left Firebase 411. Captain Stancyk turned out to be a soft spoken infantry captain who also had a previous tour in Vietnam but virtually no combat experience.

*Photo of Cpt. Stancyk and one of the CP RTO's rigging up a radio
antenna on a long tree limb to improve radio reception.*

On November 4, I wrote home:

*"Well today is my anniversary — 3 months in country. The job [in the rear]
I was going to get fell through... and to top it off I learned that they are going to
rotate one of the other FO's before me because he came in country before I did. I
have twice as much time in the field as he does — me bitter?*

*That's the way things seem to go. We have a new company commander. Cpt.
Moran has a rear job at Brigade and tomorrow he'll go in. Our new CO came
out today. At least he's been here before and seems to know what's going on. Cpt.
Moran and I were getting along very well so I hope things won't be much different.*

Fortunately, Captain Stancyk turned out to be a truly nice guy, malleable
in some ways and always ready to consider suggestions. The platoon leaders
and I quickly acclimated him to our preferred program of moving the whole
company only when we had to, of making a lot of noise when we did, and
doing whatever we could to avoid any major contact with the enemy. Stancyk
quickly let us know that his favorite pastime was playing cards. His passion
was a game called "Spades," which is like Hearts but less demanding, and
his joy in playing with those in the CP permitted us to spend several days
at each place we set down, sending platoons out on non-risky patrols while
the bulk of the company laid around where we had pitched our tents.

*Captain Stancyk (left) and some of the CP playing Spades
on a card table made of C-ration boxes.*

But we couldn't lie low forever. Within a week we were ordered to take part in our first combat assault with Stancyk, which took us directly west of Firebase 411 into a valley cut into the mountain foothills and widened into the Song Tra Khuc, which coursed from the western mountains, past My Lai to the South China Sea.

Thank goodness that once again the combat assault LZ was cold. We set up camp at the foot of a mountain among a series of rice paddies for the first few days of the operation. Charlie Company's first sergeant sent a pinochle deck on a resupply chopper, and those of us who didn't like Spades were set for a week.

A member of the CP repairing a hole in a mosquito net. C-ration boxes are behind him.

On November, 6 I mailed my first roll of slides taken with the Kodak Instamatic camera home for my family to see.

We didn't run into any of the enemy face to face on that maneuver, but there are some events that stuck in my mind.

First, in a letter home on Nov. 11, I discussed my participation in the U.S. mid-term election on Monday, Nov. 3:

"I got my absentee ballot on the 1ˢᵗ. of November and it had to be received by Scott Township [PA] on the 30ᵗʰ of Oct., so I doubt my vote was decisive. Thanks anyway for sending it so that I could vote for most of the Democrats…

I also wrote:

I got another kill yesterday with Arty, sending the company into paroxysms of joy. I still don't know how to take it. But we lost two wounded to a booby trap the day before, so it does help morale to even things out."

Second, after several days of C-rations, one of the riflemen spotted a much more tempting dinner in the form of a chicken wandering across a rice paddy. With visions of chicken stew cooked in a steel pot, he told everyone to be quiet and took off low crawling across the rice paddy, M-16 pointed menacingly at the chicken. I figured he was trying to get close enough to shoot the bird. From what I knew of ballistics, however, if he hit the chicken with an M-16 round the chicken would disintegrate entirely. It quickly became apparent that he had made the same calculation. His rifle was along only for protection since he was outside our perimeter. He stealthily crawled across the rice paddy embankment into the water and began to move on the chicken.

Back within the perimeter all of us watching started making book on whether or not he'd be able to catch the chicken. We also started plotting how to get a piece of it. In my own mind I felt the best tactic was to offer that I knew how to pluck the feathers out of the chicken, something I had once seen as a 7-year-old in Vermont.

The grunt's stalking continued across the rice paddy but the chicken, apparently alerted that something was about to happen, would only sit still for about five seconds before taking a few running steps to a new location. Finally, after about twenty minutes of drama, the chicken had widened the distance between himself and his pursuer by so much that the pursuer called off the hunt. We were all back to C-rations for the evening.

ON NOVEMBER 13, I WROTE HOME about the infantry battalion commander being relieved of duty. For us in the field, it suggested that things were falling apart up the chain of command. Here's what I wrote:

"Our Battalion Commander was relieved this week; the circumstances are rather vague & we really don't know what he did wrong. There have been several mining incidents on the road leading to the firebase from Quang Ngai. There doesn't seem to be anything that can be done since the mine sweep team that goes out every day doesn't pick up the charges and the road isn't paved so there's easy access to digging a hole. Really all they can do is pave the road, but even after about ten incidents with about 12 killed there's no help from the rear to pave the road. That's the way it goes here — the troops that are left are support personnel, so we're fighting the war with about half the support we should."

I also wrote for the first time about what was called a drop, which was having your tour shortened. I wrote:

"Now they are giving drops for Christmas to anyone going home before Feb. 15. This will leave everyone very short. Just hope the 'ceasefires' are effective."

All of this lowered the morale of those of us in the field with months to go before we could leave. Sure, we were happy for anyone who got to go home early. But what did that mean for us? It probably meant less support, fewer replacements and a lower chance of staying alive until our own return.

On November 19 I received from my family the book version of Erich Segal's novel *Love Story*, which had become a best seller in the United States. I had taken a course on tragedy from Segal at Yale, and I had heard that the book related to a hockey player from Harvard. So I had written home asking for a copy.

As anyone who has read the book knows, it is mercifully short. It took me a few hours to read, squatting on my steel pot with a backrest of C-ration boxes. The escape was total for those few hours, though it was painful reading about a different world from the one I was living in.

In any other surroundings I might have found the book trite. In Vietnam it made me desperately homesick.

TOWARD THE END OF THAT OPERATION, after we had marched slowly out of the valley toward the banks of the Tra Khuc river, infantry battalion headquarters ordered us to sweep farmland along the riverbanks to the north of Firebase 411. Unhappy to be involved in anything that the higher-ups were plotting, we nevertheless looked forward to it because, at the conclusion, we would be close enough to walk to 411 for our rotation.

The plan called for a coordinated sweep by ground and helicopter gunships through a few seemingly abandoned villages. We were looking for signs of Viet Cong tunnel complexes. For instant firepower should we find them, a number of Cobra gunships would be flying with us, and I was assigned to a Huey above the fray, ready to bring in artillery if needed.

Ed kidded me about being in the safety of the Huey while Charlie Company made the ground sweep. I told him not to worry; I was going to have him join me in the helicopter if I could. To my surprise, Ed, who hated flying, told me he'd rather be in the air if that was possible.

In the early morning before the sweep, a Huey sat down near our encampment. Ed and I boarded the chopper, which was carrying the artillery battalion executive officer. Captain Foley had managed to provide me more cooperation from the artillery battery and from battalion headquarters when we needed support. I trusted him now, although I had known him at Fort Sill to be an unrepentant lifer.

As we took off, Foley described the area we would be working in. I tried to get acquainted with reading a map while flying in circles. From the ground the major difficulty is finding reference points from which to shoot compass azimuths to triangulate your exact position. In the air, the view is very similar to what you see on a map, making target location somewhat easier. But when you're flying in circles, your point of reference continues to change. And as you look back and forth from the map to the ever turning scene below, it's easy to get airsick.

I wasn't too worried about what Charlie Company would find. We had been through the area before and had never come across anything more dangerous than booby traps. So I had peppered the area with artillery before taking off. I fired more rounds from the helicopter before Charlie Company moved in. The operation went along smoothly and quietly. As we had suspected, nothing was found. As the operation ended, we were within two kilometers of Firebase 411, easy walking distance to our next rotation to the hill.

By the end of the day I also felt fairly competent spotting targets from the air, and firing and making adjustments along the gun target line. I had no way of knowing Foley was testing me for a possible assignment for the second half of my tour.

For about a week after our rotation on 411, we worked directly south of the barbed wire on Firebase 411. As always, in a quasi-pacified area, we were set upon by a large number of Vietnamese kids in jungle greens. They sold us Cokes and packaged noodles, and carried our extra packs and tent gear. We never let them carry weapons or ordnance. They were fairly cute, always ready for a handout, and apparently harmless. Nevertheless, we tried to make sure that they learned nothing about our operations, such as where we were going or when we planned to get there.

One of the kids adopted me for the operation. He was probably about 10, quite a smiler, and obviously versed in the ways of getting by in a war zone. I gave him bits of C-rations, and forbade him, unsuccessfully, from smoking cigarettes.

Kwan, as I came to know him, spoke a fine brand of pidgin English, which enabled us to communicate on the most basic terms. "Dinky dow" meant crazy, "number 1" meant good, and "number 10" meant bad. His English version of the language consisted of "want," "you," "me," and "food." So a conversation might go: "You give me food. You number 1. Terry no give me food. Terry number ten." Variations on this conversation went on endlessly. Kwan carried my tent poles and tried as best he could to borrow my steel pot. Once in a while he asked to carry my rifle, but I refused.

During this operation we had another visit from the chaplain. He had left Firebase 411 with us, joining the CP armed with his only weapon: a slingshot. I'll never know whether he checked with battalion command to see whether this was going to be a dangerous mission. I doubt battalion command would have known anyway. But it did seem somewhat suspicious that we had no contact with the enemy on this trip, and that a large number of Vietnamese kids were always on hand, a sign that not much was going to happen.

The chaplain and I did some talking over the few days he spent with us. I found out that he was quite proud of his captain's bars, that he was a Baptist from the South, and that he had become an Army chaplain because it paid well, at least better than he made leading a civilian congregation. He seemed sincere, but it was rather incongruous for him to be in the field where, at any moment, we might be called upon to kill people. When I questioned him on such matters, he responded with a basic "better dead than red" philosophy coupled with a shepherd's flock mentality. The idea of carrying a slingshot was, I am sure, to him quite a joke, by which he hoped to ingratiate himself with the grunts. What it actually did was to separate us from him. Eventually he appeared to be mocking us, soldiers who had to fire real weapons in earnest and might have to use them to protect his life. I'm sure he felt that spending a couple of days in the field with the men helped him to understand their fears and feelings. For us, it made him the object of derision.

I suppose he got his just deserts when he tried to hold a service on Sunday. At the appointed hour, no one showed up. Captain Stancyk had to tell each platoon leader to order one or two men to attend the service. The rest of us were allowed to be absent under the pretext of manning the perimeter and the radios.

If the chaplain knew of this subterfuge, he didn't show it. Acting at all times as if he were the best friend each of us had ever had, he continued to display good cheer and a sense of bad timing, which made even more a mockery of what we were going through. For instance, he had a fish hook, which he tied to a piece of string and fished in one of the bomb craters. I suppose some of us smiled at the sight of him sitting next to the crater with his line in the water waiting for a bite, and we all kidded him about it. At the same time, we had to move him away from one bomb crater when someone noticed under the water a 100-pound bomb that had failed to explode. Fooling around in that crater might have set the thing off. In response, he explained to us that he really did expect to catch something—that these bomb craters had been there for so long that fish were now spawning in them. This "hilarious" fact underscored the futility of the war that had gone on for so many years and that would continue for years to come.

In addition to his pranks, the chaplain approached us individually to sit with him and read a few passages from his dog-eared Bible. Some of the men put up with it rather than face the embarrassment of telling him to get lost. However, as soon other men began to learn of his intentions, they avoided him like the plague.

During the operation we got word from artillery headquarters that Terry, whose tour was soon ending, was to leave the field to get ready to process out and head for the point of departure—Cam Ranh Bay. We all rejoiced that one of us had made it, because it seemed to say to the rest of us that it was possible, maybe a little more than possible, to live through an entire tour. Terry made the rounds of all of the infantrymen, giving many the Black Power handshake, and telling them he would see them back in the "world." I was very happy for him. I also knew he would be unbearable as a returnee—unable to put up with the Army's Mickey Mouse regulations for his few remaining months of commitment, and unceasing in his willingness to bore others with tales of his exploits in battle in 'Nam. But he had certainly earned that right. I just hoped that he would not get into trouble during the last couple of weeks before leaving. Knowing how he felt about the artillery, I thought he had a good chance of ending up in a fight or in the stockade for insubordination.

When Terry boarded the supply helicopter to be taken back to the rear, I saw tears in his eyes as he surveyed his fellow soldiers waving goodbye. He probably knew that no matter what he did in the future, he was leaving some of the closest friends he would ever have.

Having Terry finish his tour in the field made Ed edgy. Usually no one in the field was forced to spend his entire tour there. Terry had done so because he hated the artillery, and the gunners back at the firebase just didn't give a damn about him. Not even the infantry riflemen spent their entire 12-month tour in the field. At some point, they were rotated to work in the supply area or the mess hall. While I had no ability to order Ed out of the field, with Terry leaving, I told Ed I would do everything I could to get him out of the field as soon as I could.

My thoughts about rotating to the rear were constant. When I was sent to the field, they told me that I would probably be there four to six months. It was now four months, and I suspected that new artillery lieutenants had arrived frequently at battalion artillery. The FO next senior to me in the battalion had been rotated to the rear, and I assumed that my number would come next.

It was a strange feeling to be one of the most experienced members of Charlie Company with only four months under my belt. The turnover from my original group was stark. All the officers and NCOs, and 75 percent of the riflemen had arrived since I had. I had more infantry combat experience than virtually anyone else in the field at that moment. Meanwhile, Charlie Company operated at about 60 percent strength.

We had added two new infantry platoon leader lieutenants in the last month, both out of Fort Benning, Georgia's Officer Candidate School, and both without combat experience.

Otherwise, our situation remained fairly quiet. We encountered sniper fire now and then, but we never ran into an enemy force that resulted in a massive firefight. Those few of us who remained from my early days wondered how Captain Stancyk and his new lieutenants would react to a real battle. But we were comforted by the fact that neither Captain Stancyk nor anyone else was interested in playing John Wayne.

I felt sure that if I lived long enough to be rotated out of the field, my chances of surviving my tour would be 10 times better. The rear area was in constant danger of a mortar or rocket attack, but the danger was just as great from some disgruntled enlisted man, half crazed and on drugs, trying to get even with me as an officer or with officers in general. Since my likely job was going to be running a fire direction control center on a firebase, I didn't expect to be ordering soldiers into danger, nor would I have any great responsibility for what soldiers around me were doing. I knew life in an FDC would be extremely boring, but at least it would less dangerous than being in the field with an infantry company.

Photo was taken looking down the barrel of my M-16 after we took sniper fire from the ridge. I dropped some artillery rounds where we felt the sniper was.

As I crossed off each day on my "short" calendar, I grew more and more superstitious and unwilling to take risks. I didn't want to end up like Charlie Company's last casualty—dead just a few days before his DEROS.

We never moved anywhere now without first firing an artillery barrage in front of us to clear out the enemy and any booby traps. I was dropping artillery in our line of march, which made those marches less risky. Arriving at the end of one particularly long, hot march I remember hearing one of the grunts say as he collapsed on the ground: "Today's lesson is about man's inhumanity to man." Even in war, I heard some educated humor.

A FEW DAYS BEFORE THANKSGIVING, CHARLIE Company rotated back to Firebase 411. We remained on the hill an extra day to enjoy the Thanksgiving dinner we'd been promised. We were told that the firebase mess hall was going to attempt a turkey dinner.

The day before Thanksgiving, November 25, I wrote about two celebrities who had come to Vietnam to meet the troops:

"Today I had my first experience with the Christmas visitors and I must say it was great. I heard some ballplayers were at the hill for anyone to meet so I went down to the mess hall and saw [Pittsburgh Pirates play-by-play announcer] Bob Prince and [Baseball Hall of Famer] Willie Stargell. Bob was alone since few people recognized him, but I went up to him and said I was from Pittsburgh and we had a nice chat. It really helps morale here to have these people come so far and yet to such remote places as this. He should be calling you when he gets back ... If he does contact you, please thank him again for coming; it's a great boost to everyone."

In the same letter, I commented on a different side of the morale issue:

"The company has a new first sergeant who has all the bluster and toughness that Hollywood would add. I really have to laugh at the whole situation as he tears up the poor PFC's and NCO's but can't say a word to me. It's exactly what the troops don't need right now, but they are learning to ignore him enough to

live with it. He doesn't go to the field with us, so they know he'll be around only a few days."

On Thanksgiving, the new battalion commander announced that, after our turkey dinner, he wanted to have a basketball game pitting officers against enlisted men. The basketball court on 411 was rather primitive. It consisted of one tall post with an iron rim probably about 11 feet in the air and a half court about 10 yards by 10 yards of packed clay. The enlisted men had an hour or two of tryouts to winnow the many candidates who wanted to play. I was recruited to play for the officers. We had virtually no talented players at all, and certainly no person of color. As the game started, it was clear that the officers would try a teamwork approach with lots of passes, hoping for short, easy layups. Meanwhile, the enlisted men, mostly Black, were ten times better than the officers.

It shouldn't have been surprising that, in the early stages, we officers kept it from a total rout. As our tallest team member, I was playing in the low post. Towering over me was a Black private from the artillery battery who seemed intent on leaning on me and elbowing me every chance he got. Eventually we began to feel the effects of the punishment we were taking. With no referee, only the most blatant intentional fouls were called. Even when play stopped for a flagrant foul, the only advantage was getting possession of the ball.

I resigned myself to losing badly, feeling that we were probably due for this, and to put up with it in good humor. The colonel who had commissioned the game was not there, and neither were any battalion staff. It was left to us players to take as much as we could and then bow out gracefully.

After about half an hour, we reached an uneasy truce by calling the game because of the heat. I gave the opposition the brothers' handshake Ed had taught me and walked away, vowing never to get involved in another basketball game. Ed, who had watched the game, just grinned at me and said, "Good try."

BACK IN THE FIELD AFTER THANKSGIVING I found myself short on MPC when the Vietnamese kids came by with their Cokes. I hadn't been paid in two months because the artillery battery couldn't get its act together to pay us when we were in the field.

But on Nov. 28 I wrote home some exciting news:

"My replacement is in the battalion rear right now (I've been told) and should come out by the end of this week. I won't get my hopes up until he actually steps off the chopper. It will be good for him however to have someone with him the first few days. I came in with no FO in the company and had to pick up a lot on my own. I should be able to help him."

As I had expected, brigade artillery told me that I was to spend at least three days teaching my replacement the ropes. Even though that was three days more training than I had received, I felt I owed it to Charlie Company, and especially to Ed. Unfortunately my rotation did not apply to Ed. He would remain in the field with the new FO.

DECEMBER 1970

THE NEW CHARLIE COMPANY FORWARD OBSERVER finally arrived on December 1. He was dressed, as we all had been when we arrived in the field the first time, in never-before washed jungle fatigues. He also wore a look of stark terror. He was an ROTC graduate in country about a week and a half. He was totally unfamiliar with how to communicate with the artillery guns, and had only done a few practice shoots before being plopped in the field. Battalion artillery told me I should take him through as many shoots as I could during the next three days and nights to get him up to speed.

What worried me most was that he wasn't terribly proficient in map reading. Ed was particularly upset by this, but I told Ed that I was sure that he would be able to keep the new lieutenant straight until he got a better feeling for the job. Ed was now excellent at almost everything, including map reading and triangulation, and he could handle any type of fire mission. With any luck, the new FO would be out in the field a week or two before he ever really had to shoot in anger.

I made as much of a show as I could to the rest of Charlie Company that this new FO was going to be all right. And I was heartened by his willingness to learn. His one request was that I give him my maps, as the battalion XO had suggested.

By now I had quite an attachment to those maps. I had planned to keep them as they were and bring them back to the world as a souvenir. They contained flecks of grease pencil over the entire area of our operations, mementos of some of the battles, firefights, and other horrors we'd been through. The plastic cigarette casings were not a unique cover, but they had made for ease of handling and had repelled most of the sweat, dirt and water that accumulated during day-to-day exposure.

Nevertheless, I knew I had to give them up. If Charlie Company was going to be with an inexperienced FO, they'd at least have the benefit of an experienced FO's maps. And those maps would be a particularly helpful tool for Ed. So, I gave them up.

During my last night in the field, to my surprise, I was able to sleep pretty well. I did, however, contemplate before falling asleep, and during the one or two times I woke during the night, how ironic it would be if a mortar round landed on my tent that last night before I headed back to the rear.

In the morning of December 4, I gave away what little possessions I had that would be useful to anyone in the field, including my buck knife, my remaining Tabasco sauce and my rubber rain pants.

Ed had first pick of everything and he got what I considered the best of it—my mosquito net. The weather was unbearably hot, like most of the days in recent weeks. Nothing was happening other than card playing at the CP and a few patrols by the platoons. As the Huey that would take me to the rear came into view, I grabbed Ed by the shoulders, gave him a big hug, and told him I'd get him out of the field as soon as I could. Then, with a rush of emotion upon realizing that I had survived my time as an FO and was now headed for relative safety, I boarded the chopper.

PART TWO

In The Air

I REPORTED TO CAPTAIN FOLEY AT Brigade Artillery in Chu Lai to receive my next assignment. Foley had a funny look on his face when I arrived. He told me to pack my things and head to Americal Division Headquarters about a mile away. He said: " Congratulations. Your next assignment is to be a brigade aerial observer. You're going to be a Red Baron."

My first reaction was to feel pleased. Red Barons flew missions out of Chu Lai in light planes —like Piper Cubs—spotting artillery either in support of ground operations or, more dangerously, in the mountains to the west where they found or were directed to shoot at intelligence targets. Perhaps to appease me, Foley said the job went to those who had shown they were good at shooting artillery from the ground.

After a few moments of reflection, I realized how stupid I was to be pleased. Instead of getting a fairly safe job at Brigade Artillery Headquarters, or a position on some firebase running the FDC, I was going to be flying daily over hostile ground in an unarmed small plane. Any bullet hole or engine trouble could force it down. Even if the plane did not crash and kill me and the pilot, what chance would we have to defend ourselves in the middle of enemy territory?

Before I left, however, I did have one job to finish. I said to Foley, "Do you need a new RTO here at Brigade Artillery or on any firebase?"

"I can always use a good one," he said, "And we're short one on Firebase 411 at the moment."

"Look," I said, "My RTO, Ed Williams, has been out in the field with me and Charlie Company for four months. Ed was sent out there by the 411 battery commander the first day he arrived on 411. If nobody steps in, he's likely to be stuck out in the field as an RTO for the rest of his tour. You've heard him working with me day after day and night after night over the radio, and you know he's really good. He also knows more than anyone back here about what it's like to be out there in the field, and what those people are up against. He can also read a map better than anyone back here. He will be the best RTO you've ever had at Artillery Battalion HQ or on a firebase. He deserves to get out of the field."

"Okay," said Foley, "I'll look into it."

I flew back to Duc Pho to pick up the rest of my gear. I spent the night in the Charlie Company first sergeant's hut, getting quietly drunk with him and another infantry lieutenant, talking about the bad old days in the field and wondering whether things would remain quiet for Charlie Company. We listened to a lot of Crosby, Stills & Nash and Blood, Sweat & Tears and the Temptations on the sergeant's sound system. The next day, I headed for Chu Lai and my new assignment.

COMPARED WITH CONDITIONS IN THE FIELD, life in Chu Lai as a REMF was cushy. The brigade aerial observers, who flew artillery support for the entire Americal Division, bunked at division headquarters in Chu Lai. This area in the division was the most "stateside." It housed the commanding officer (a three-star general), all of his staff and the other support for the division. The hooch I was assigned to had about six cubicles, and each one had a bunk, a footlocker and enough room for a piece or two of stereo equipment. We had a "hooch maid" who came in daily to clean the cubicle, wash fatigues and shine boots. The latrine located in the middle of the compound had toilets and showers. The only drawback was that rats the size of cats roamed the latrine at night. That made me stay away after dark.

Within 200 meters was the division officers' club—a large thatched-roof building with a stage for U.S.O. shows and movies, and the only athletic facility: the Commanding General's handball court. The nearby officers' mess hall, while not air-conditioned, was nicely furnished with long tables. And compared with C-rations and LRRP's, the food was more than a step up.

A few hundred yards to the east was the South China Sea, with a sandy beach that made Chu Lai look downright comfortable.

An aerial view of Chu Lai from my Red Baron Bird Dog

The brigade aerial observers worked out of Americal Brigade Headquarters. Our area looked like a typical "war room," with large colored-coded maps and miniature displays of battlegrounds in three dimensions. The radio station, called "Salvation," operated out of a rear room. Salvation broadcast warnings to aircraft about artillery being fired. All division aircraft tuned into Salvation to avoid artillery rounds traveling through their air space.

Having a cot and a readily accessible latrine with hot water and showers felt almost like heaven. It didn't hurt that I could get any drink–including a double Chivas on the rocks–for thirty-five cents at the officers' club. The most incongruous part was that we were only about a mile from a beach with lifeguards, who were all blonde California surfers being paid an exorbitant amount to live in a "combat area." They watched over a perfect strip of surfing beach and, during breaks, surfed for the G.I.s to take pictures.

I had to pass a flight physical before I could begin my duty as an aerial observer. When I reported to the division hospital, for the first time in several months I actually spotted an American woman: a nurse walking through the corridors. A wave of homesickness passed through me. As I headed for my physical, I passed wards full of the maimed and dying. These soldiers were spending their last few days in Vietnam before going to the U.S. or some other destination.

My flight physical went without incident until the electrocardiogram. The orderly kept cursing under his breath. Finally he told me that either I had some heart abnormality or the machine wasn't working. He scheduled further testing the next day.

The next day's test involved drinking a solution that looked (and tasted) like liquid chalk, taking an X-ray to see how it traveled through my system. It revealed that I did have an irregularity in my heart, but unfortunately it was not serious enough to prevent me from becoming an aerial observer. Not knowing whether to be happy or sad, I headed off to be issued my flight suits.

Flight suits were, in a word, hot. They were made of green fire-retardant material that did not breathe. In addition, I was issued special leather boots, with the idea that the cloth jungle boots I had been wearing would not protect me if I were locked in a burning fuselage. They also issued me a .45 pistol, the only weapon I could carry in the plane. My final piece of equipment was an aircraft crewman's helmet. It looked like a motorcycle helmet with a microphone mouthpiece and a cord to plug into a radio console. The next day I was sent on an orientation flight to inspect the Americal Division area of operations.

THE RED BARONS FLEW IN WHAT were commonly called Bird Dogs. The official name was Cessna L-19/O-1. They were single-engine, wing-over, two-seat Piper Cubs, painted the obligatory olive drab. Bird Dogs were first built in 1950 and were used as spotters during the Korean War. Ours were from that era. The aerial observer sat right behind the pilot, and the observer had to be thin to squeeze in. The Bird Dog's "skin" was sheets of extremely light metal, enabling it to fly about three hours on a tank of gas.

Photo of a Bird Dog on the flight line before taking off. I would sit in the back.

The cocky first lieutenant who showed me around was clearly full of himself for being a "fixed-wing" Bird Dog pilot instead of a rotary-wing helicopter pilot. He acted as if he owned the airplane company that was headquartered in Chu Lai, and gave me the grand tour with full orchestration. He smirked as he told me I'd have to learn to fly this plane within the next several weeks so, if anything happened to my pilot on a mission, I could land the plane.

We walked to the flight line. As we arrived at the Bird Dog we would be flying that day, he started a ritual I came to know well. He took a small bottle out of his pocket, emptied a little gasoline from a wing fuel tank into it, and then spun the bottle around to see whether any sediment fell to the bottom. If it did, there was a problem. If not, he slowly inspected each wing, inch by inch using his fingers, inspecting the metal. My curiosity got the best of me, so I asked what he was doing.

"Looking for metal fatigue."

Oh, shit! I thought to myself. *I'm going to be flying missions in a plane that's so old, its wings might fall off!*

After we boarded the Bird Dog, I plugged my flight helmet cord into the radio console and listened to Salvation as it broadcast a list of areas to avoid so we were not shot down by our own artillery. I found four channels on my radio console—I could monitor all four at once. By flipping a switch, I could also speak to someone on one of the four stations while monitoring the other three. The first switch was set to the airport control tower, the second to Salvation, and the third and fourth switches were used to call in artillery fire missions. I generally set the fourth switch to the Armed Forces Radio rock and roll station, which transmitted from Da Nang. I soon learned how to listen to four stations and adjust artillery at the same time.

As we taxied in front of the airplane company's main hanger, I got my first glimpse of a large sign painted over the entrance. It read:

"MAINTENANCE PLATOON: IF WE CAN'T FIX IT, IT AIN'T BROKE."

The sign made me laugh a little but it also filled me with dread. I could only hope that it was a joke, and that they were not allowing these creaky, unarmed, antiquated airplanes to fly combat missions if something might be wrong with the engine or the controls.

Once cleared for takeoff, we did a quick pivot at the end of the runway and seemed to take off after only about fifty feet of acceleration.

Aerial view of a fishing village south of Chu Lai

As the Bird Dog ascended, I began to appreciate one benefit of my new assignment: with each few meters of elevation, the temperature in the cockpit cooled. By the time we had reached 1,000 meters, the cockpit felt positively air-conditioned.

"How high do we usually fly?" I asked the pilot through the intercom.

"The rules are we're not supposed to go below 250 meters. But, as you'll see, to get anything done we often have to go lower than that. For purposes of this flight we'll stay up here where it's cool and give you a chance to see the whole area of operations."

Below me spread the vast green lushness–interrupted every few hundred meters or so by a bomb crater–of the northern part of South Vietnam. To the east, the South China Sea, with its light blue color and sandy beaches looked like a tropical paradise. To the west, the rugged mountains, which had been the barrier to our operations on the ground, were a gorgeous green and brown with jungle canopy. In those mountains, the Ho Chi Minh trail wound its way south, often encroaching into Laos. In the middle was the flatland full of rice paddies, where virtually all the people lived and where the fighting was going on. But for the war, it would have been a lovely country to visit.

"We'll start up north and work our way south," my pilot said.

For the next three hours we flew through the plains, valleys and mountains of the American Division. In the cool air at our altitude, it was possible to appreciate Vietnam's spectacular beauty. The only reminders of the war going on below were visible bomb craters and our occasional detour to avoid high-flying artillery shells.

Most imposing were the steep mountainous regions—densely jungled and virtually impassable. I began to realize why the North Vietnamese could travel at will through the mountains, which extended as far as the eye could see to the west. The Ho Chi Min Trail was hidden beneath the jungle canopy. We simply weren't contesting the area in the mountains; every inch of it belonged to the NVA.

The many rivers were the easiest landmarks for locating our position on a map. They wound down from the mountains and flowed east, cutting valleys where the vestiges of agriculture could be seen. Tucked into some of the initial ranges of the mountains were vast areas of terraced rice paddies, carved painstakingly out of the hills over many years. It seemed the farther inland we went, the less disturbed the rice paddies were. Clearly, the farther we got into the mountains, the less U.S. forces had bothered to bomb. Toward the coast, the bomb craters became more and more prevalent. In effect, the areas we had tried to defend and control had been bombed into uselessness.

I asked the pilot what types of artillery missions we would usually shoot.

"Mainly you aerial observers look for something on the ground that looks like enemy activity. Whether it be a hut that might contain some troops, a bunker, or any other structure we might see. We get a call now

153

and then to support a ground action. But mostly it's up to us to find our own targets and shoot at them. You'll learn that once we find a target, unless it's out west in the mountains, we spend most of our time flying around in circles waiting for artillery clearance."

I asked the pilot what other types of missions he flew. "Generally it's for you guys from division artillery. But we also fly some reconnaissance. As a general rule I don't fly more than one mission a day. There are limits on the number of hours per month they'll permit us as pilots to fly."

He seemed quite at ease flying the plane, obviously enjoying it and oblivious to any danger below us.

"It looks like there might be something down there; let's see what we can pick out." My pilot looked out the window over his left shoulder at a spot by a riverbank. He flew a series of circles as we descended closer and closer to the ground.

"What are you looking for?" I asked.

"It looks to me like there's a bunker down there by the side of the river. Let's see if we can pick it out."

I couldn't see a thing. I also wondered why we were voluntarily descending from the air- conditioning into the heat, particularly when it meant going low enough that someone wanting to shoot might be able to hit us. But he was in charge for now, so down we went.

As we hit air pockets and were pressed against the side of the cockpit in our steep dive, I realized that I was lucky that I had never suffered from air sickness. I had the same feeling I used to get on a carnival roller coasters as a kid. But even when we were at our lowest altitude, I never saw anything to shoot at.

"Why don't you mark that on your map? When you go out to shoot, you might come back here and put a couple of rounds down there and see what you get." Dutifully, I marked my map.

I began to see that carrying normal size maps that would cover the whole division was going to be impossible. The Americal Division included a vast amount of territory. The map that I had used on the ground as an FO had approximately a square kilometer per inch. If I tried to carry maps for the entire AO at that scale, there'd be no room in the cockpit for me. My pilot, however, had maps on a much smaller scale—each square kilometer being only about a quarter of the size. The contour lines at times were almost indecipherable from each other. But at least they could fit inside the cockpit. I decided to get a set of them.

When our three-hour mission was up, and we had covered a good portion of the AO, I was reluctant to return to the sweltering heat. Nevertheless, I appreciated that the daily three-hour mission I was going to fly would give me 21 hours per day safely on the ground. If I played my cards right, with a little luck I might live through my tour, particularly because I got to choose where we went on some of the missions.

THAT NIGHT AT THE DIVISION HEADQUARTERS Officers'
Club at Chu Lai I learned from Captain Rocamora, the officer in charge
of the Red Barons, that my official radio call sign would be Red Baron
36. Unlike radio call signs in the field that changed frequently for security
reasons, this was permanent as long as I was a Red Baron.

Rocamora was a short, wiry, handsome Filipino-American who treated
his underlings as kid brothers. He laughed easily, wore tailored flight suits,
and showed us he cared about each of us. He had been a Red Baron before
being promoted to captain, and he knew what we faced day after day.

The other brigade aerial observers were all lieutenants; only two had
previously been FOs, and they were all younger than I was. All but one,
however, had decided to make a career in the Army. They seemed satisfied
with themselves, with the aura of being elite. They were treated as part
of division staff and were entitled to staff privileges. They normally flew
one mission per day, and enjoyed sporting the aerial observer flight suits.
As tactfully as I could, I asked whether there had been any Red Baron
fatalities. There had been, but none that anyone knew personally. None
of the present group had been an aerial observer more than a couple of
months. As we sat drinking, I recall thinking that they were a pretty
cliquey bunch.

The Red Barons introduced me to lower-ranking division staff who came in and out of the bar area as we waited for the nightly movie to begin. Among the staff was a young lieutenant who seemed to have a special air of authority about him. He was introduced as the division censor—his job was to screen all movies that were to be shown to the troops in the division. He told us his instructions were to cut out all nudity below the waist, and all profanity. Soldiers weren't allowed to hear profanity? One had to wonder who gave that order, and whether he was sane. Also, since virtually every sergeant I got to know had a full library of porno movies, the nudity restriction seemed just as silly.

But since this was the Division Headquarters Officers' Club, the censor treated those of us on hand to viewing the cuttings from each movie he had emasculated that day. He passed around film clip with an air of authority, and we held them up to the light for the best view.

Two other groups, both non-military, frequented the Division Headquarters Officers' Club: Donut Dollies and civilian contractors. Borrowing a phrase from the London Blitz, in my mind these two groups were the splendid and the vile. The Donut Dollies, in my book, were the splendid. They were young American women who, as had their predecessors in World War II and the Korean War, volunteered to serve as hostesses for U.S. troops in a combat zone, boosting morale and bringing cheer to soldiers away from home. They were well scrubbed, attractive and exceedingly brave. They took daily flights to fire bases throughout the division to meet with troops, play games with men who hadn't seen a woman from the States for months. Their pale blue uniforms and bright smiles were a reminder of home. A contingent of Donut Dollies was housed near Division Headquarters, and they had privileges to watch movies at the officers' club.

The civilian contractors, on the other hand, were the vile, in my book. These were civilian men who came to the war zone to make money, and they made lots of it. By living six months to a year in Vietnam, they earned many multiples of what soldiers were paid, many earning enough in a year to bankroll a business in the U.S. Their missions varied: support for the base in terms of technology and food service, sales to troops of automobiles and insurance, and less clear assignments that foreshadowed the paramilitary forces who tortured enemy fighters in Iraq. We steered clear of them.

I learned that at least one Red Baron mission was in the air during all daylight hours to bring artillery support wherever it was needed within the division. Red Barons flew a minimum of four daylight missions each day. Division artillery assigned targets to Red Barons each morning based on intelligence reports, requests from different infantry battalions or pleas for help from FOs on the ground. In addition, Red Barons could search for their own targets, observing and firing from the air on anything that looked like an enemy asset: a hooch in the mountains, a group of armed enemy on the ground, or other suspicious enemy activity. At the end of each day, the Red Barons divided the next day's missions among themselves. In addition, the Red Baron who had the 6 a.m. to 9 a.m. mission briefed the Division Command at 4 a.m. on the prior day's missions, on other notable artillery fire missions that were reported and whatever was likely to happen later that day.

WITHIN A WEEK I HAD BECOME accustomed to the routine of flying as a Red Baron. During my next flight, with a pilot whose nickname was Smitty, I called in my first fire mission as Red Baron 36, shooting at the target that my training pilot had pointed out. Smitty was amused to see a green aerial observer at work. He likely knew how to adjust fire from the air much better than I did. But he didn't have any experience on the ground, and when he learned that I had been an FO for four months, he gave me some grudging respect.

Firing onto the suspected bunker, I learned that it was never possible, even at about 250 meters, to see clearly what we were shooting at. However, target location on a map was easy and the adjustments even easier. As I had been told, it took longer to get artillery clearance to fire than it did to adjust onto the target. The best I could tell, as a result of the rounds I fired, something had caved in. Therefore I reported an enemy bunker destroyed. When our three-hour mission was over, we headed home.

For the next month my routine was to fly one three-hour mission a day, seven days a week. I was flying in a Bird Dog somewhere over the division A.O. firing artillery whenever it might help troops on the ground, or trying to hit anything that I saw that seemed worth shooting at.

As a division aerial observer, I particularly enjoyed one perk: shooting all sizes of artillery guns. At Firebase 411 I had had access to a single battery (six guns or fewer) of 105 mm howitzers, the smallest, shortest range and least accurate artillery pieces. But as a Red Baron I could call upon any artillery piece that was within range of a target. That meant I could shoot 155 mm howitzers, 175 mm howitzers and 8 inch guns.

A 175-mm howitzer mounted on tracks so it could easily move from one location to another.

The 8-inch guns were particularly fun to shoot. They had the largest shells and could do the most damage, and they were the most accurate of the artillery guns. The 175 mm guns could shoot the farthest, but they were less accurate than the 8 inch and the 155s. The 155s were usually good for using different types of fuses such as VT (variable time), white phosphorous and armor piercing for tunnel complexes. Compared to the 105 howitzers, these bigger pieces were like driving a Mercedes after being confined to a VW.

I soon learned that the first Red Baron mission of the day—from dawn (about 6:00 a.m.) to 9:00 a.m. was a good one to request. The first mission of the day checked out whether any damage had been done by Division Artillery firing at targets on the previous night. In a sense it was a fool's errand because it was impossible to distinguish the craters created the night before from all the rest of the craters previously created in the vicinity of the target grid. However, since the targets were almost all in the flatland near Chu Lai, we were rarely required to fly into the mountains. That meant there was a lot less danger. I tried to get the early flight as often as I could.

When I did get the early mission, of course, and I only had to fly one mission per day, my "workday" was over by 10 a.m. That allowed me to spend the rest of the day reading or going to the beach. And except for those three hours of flying, I was relatively safe.

When in the air, I quickly became familiar with the various hot spots in the American Division's area of operations. By detouring around artillery firing, I came to know where the most ground action was going on. U.S. troops were actually fighting in only a few places on any given day. Except for the immediate vicinity of Highway 1, the rest of the AO was realistically under the control of the Viet Cong and NVA. The valleys and foothills, which were lined with rice paddies that worked their way into the mountains, were outside the control of any ground troops. Only the Red Barons and the helicopter swat teams ventured out to disturb the North Vietnamese's and Viet Cong's dominion.

DURING MY FIRST MONTH AS A Red Baron I received some gratifying news. One day while flying south, we detoured so that I could fly over Firebase 411 to see if I could pick up any news of how things were going. Looking through my code book I found the call sign and frequency for the artillery XO on Firebase 411. "Charlie Papa 46, this is Red Baron 36, over."

A familiar voice crackled over the radio. "Red Baron 36 this is Charlie Papa 46, over."

I couldn't have mistaken that voice. It was Ed.

Breaking the radio protocol for once, I gleefully called down: "Charlie Papa 46, this is Red Baron 36. Ed this is LT. It's great to hear your voice! How are you doing, over?"

"Red Baron 36, this is Charlie Papa 46. LT is that who you are now? I'm doing fine. They pulled me out of the field about a week after you left. Over."

"Charlie Papa 46, this is Red Baron 36. Good for you! How are things going otherwise? Over."

Ed quickly figured what I was asking. "Red Baron 36, this is Charlie Papa 46. Things have been really quiet. Nothing much to report. I'll let the company know you called and what you're doing when they come back to the hill. And any time you want any artillery, just give me a call. Over."

"Charlie Papa 46, this is Red Baron 36. I'm so glad to hear you are out of the field. You have a good time now, and stay safe. Before we know it, we'll both be 'short.' Red Baron 36, out."

I was so pleased and gratified to know that Ed was out of the field, and to know he was in a job where he could really use his talents. He sounded fine and I assumed he now had a much better chance to survive the remainder of his tour.

ON ONE MISSION, I FLEW OVER the hamlet of My Lai. In March 1968 a platoon of U.S. Army soldiers from the Americal Division under the command of Lt. William Calley murdered between 347 and 504 unarmed South Vietnamese civilians. It became known as the My Lai Massacre. It was a major stain on the U.S. involvement in the war in Vietnam.

My Lai lay surprisingly close to Firebase 411, across the Tra Khuc river, in the flatlands eastward toward the South China Sea. From the air it looked like any other hamlet in the area, surrounded by tree lines and located centrally in a group of rice paddies. The town itself looked totally deserted from the air, and I could see no sign of life anywhere around it. This wasn't surprising because it was difficult to see people from the air unless we got below our so-called minimum altitude. Even then it was chancy whether I could see the top of someone's head. However, I did suspect that the town was abandoned from the lack of any livestock— usually much more visible from the air.

My Lai in early 1971 seen from my Bird Dog

Having suffered through ground combat with an infantry company, I could comprehend in some small way what had happened at My Lai. I couldn't imagine anyone in Charlie Company shooting villagers in cold blood, and during my time in the field we had done nothing to harm anyone who hadn't been shooting at us. But I understood that it would not take much to tip some angry and terrified troops over the line. Having felt the outrage that comes from seeing buddies' torn apart by booby traps, mines and RPGs, and having approached a hostile village that we knew was probably responsible, or at the least had been shielding the enemy, I imagined that, with poor or no leadership, a massacre might result. In addition, the pressure for body count made payback very tempting. If a frightened, immature lieutenant was in charge, I could imagine the worst happening. I suspected that other massacres had occurred; it's just that they hadn't been reported.

UNFORTUNATELY, SOONER OR LATER I HAD to fly missions toward the western region, into the mountains and over hostile territory. No matter how beautiful the landscape or how tranquil it looked from the air, I never could quell the fear of what would happen if our Bird Dog suddenly went down. During each mission into the mountains, I wished I had been allowed to bring an M-16, and I swore at myself for not cleaning and test-firing more often my only weapon: a .45 pistol. I also confronted that, in the rugged, jungle-covered mountains, if we did go down, there was little chance of being able to find a spot where a helicopter could land to rescue us. We had a radio transmitter that would immediately send a distress signal with our location. But would a rescue helicopter to get to us before the enemy did?

I knew that Air Force bomber pilots shot down over North Vietnam were housed in prisons around Hanoi. I had heard rumors that U.S. soldiers captured in South Vietnam were marched north along the Ho Chi Minh Trail to Hanoi. But I could not verify that. I could imagine being held in a jungle prison camp in South Vietnam forever. It didn't seem to make any sense for the enemy to use troops who had marched south from Hanoi to march back to Hanoi just to escort a P.O.W.

I did my best to put such thoughts out of my mind. While in the air, I didn't want to face the reality of who was in the jungle below. During one mission to the west, however, when we were almost over Laos, I spotted an unforgettable sight. My pilot pointed out three parallel paths in the jungle that seemed about a meter wide and at least a half a kilometer long. Then, all three paths stopped. He told me to look at the left end of the three paths and let him know what I saw. As we dipped lower, I could see what he was talking about. Each "path" was foliage already eaten, and at the left end of the paths were three wild elephants. All three elephants' backs were plainly visible as they ate their way through the jungle. I wish I had had my camera that day.

I didn't have any problem once I was back in Chu Lai—the creature comforts of the mess hall, officers' club and showers helped wash away the danger of each day's mission, especially when I had an early flight, and I could anesthetize myself with a second or third Scotch by mid-afternoon.

As it had during much of my days in the field, however, boredom engulfed me. Knowing that I would have to do the exact same thing the next day, and the next, and the day after that, made me begin to take chances again. If the pilot and I decided to make sure what exactly we were firing at, we'd make a low pass. Then, if we thought we had hit something significant, we'd take another pass to see what had been blown up. Even taking small arms fire in the right wing did not stop us from swooping down during the next mission to see where we could drop a few artillery rounds.

We were egged on even more when we observed "positive" results. A direct hit on one of the suspected bunkers in the valley west of the Tra Bong River netted about five secondary explosions. It was like setting off a fireworks display. We whooped and hollered in the cockpit before gleefully reporting back to the guns the havoc their rounds had caused.

Within a few weeks I became more adept at target identification and adjusting rounds onto a target from the air. When we found a target, we circled it, which made identifying accurate grid coordinates dizzying, to say the least. As we circled, I would take a mental snapshot of the target and what was around it, and then drop my gaze to study the map in my lap. Orienting the map to what I had just seen (in terms of compass directions) took some concentration. But the bigger problem was that, once I thought I had the target located on the map, when I looked back at the target on the ground, I was looking at it from a different angle, which made my mental picture irrelevant. We might be as much as 180 degrees from what I had last pictured, and my map was no longer oriented to what I had seen.

Smoke from artillery rounds I fired at a suspected NVA location in the mountains. The strut of the Bird Dog is visible in the upper-right corner.

But target location from the air soon became easier than target location from the ground because I could see landmarks and terrain that I never could have seen from the ground. Let's face it: the view from the air was the same as the view on the map. Once I had a mental image of the target on the ground, and could orient my map, I could establish grid coordinates that were quite accurate. This made for fewer adjustments in any fire mission after the first rounds landed, and added to my willingness to take a chance now and then to see what we had hit. And it didn't dampen my enthusiasm when one day I achieved the aerial observer's equivalent of a golfer's hole-in-one—the first round I called in landed right on the target. Like a hole in one, the chances of it happening were very small, but a good target location gave me a chance. The people back at FDC couldn't believe it that the fire mission was over and we'd hit the target with the first round.

WITH THE END OF THE YEAR drawing near, I knew that my one-week R&R to some exotic (and safe) location couldn't be too far away, and that I needed to get in line. On December 9, I wrote home:

"I thought this would be a good time to give you the full scoop on leave and R&R as it stands now. Each person is allowed one 7 day R&R and one 7 day leave. R&R is a confirmed reservation; leave is standby and hard to get transportation for if the location and time are full. ... So my choice seems to be a leave to [Hong Kong] in March and an R&R to either Sydney or Hawaii either in early February or late April. Hawaii is a possibility because of many friends plus a chance to see the girl I took out in San Francisco just before I left."

The choice of an R&R destination was, to a certain extent, dictated by base and rank. For single white troops, and especially for younger white officers, Australia was the place with the best reputation. Because of Australia's policy against immigration by non-Caucasians, few soldiers of color wanted to go there.

The white soldiers came back with glowing stories about Australian women who opened their hearts and their bodies to the American soldiers. The rumor was that Australia had an over-population of young women, which gave the male population a pretty cavalier approach toward women. A Yank with a seemingly unlimited budget for his one week escape from war, and all the sexual desire in the world, was a perfect foil for any young lady in Sydney who was looking for a good time. Rumor had it that a whole population of R&R female consorts had developed who went week to week with each new shipment of R&R American soldiers.

Bangkok and Hong Kong were the chosen destinations of the non-white soldiers. In the seamier side of those cities, U.S. soldiers could easily find a girl for a week at a relatively inexpensive price.

For the older sergeants, particularly the pot-bellied and crass ones, Bangkok had a special thrill, and I was treated now and then to stories of unnatural acts performed upon these NCOs whenever the subject of R&R came up.

Honolulu was the choice of the married soldiers. The Army encouraged soldiers to have their wives meet them there for their R&R. Stories were rife about the chaplain at Fort DeRussy, the Army base in downtown Waikiki, where the wives met their husbands for R&R, trying to encourage husbands to attend church services on Sunday morning after they arrived Saturday night. For the marrieds, it was a wonderful vacation in paradise in the middle of a year's tour of duty. For the unmarrieds, Hawaii offered much less because it had no network of available women or prostitutes.

Connie, the nurse I met the night before I flew to Vietnam, and I had been writing to each other for the past several months. I had wonderful memories of Honolulu from a visit about seven years earlier, so I asked Connie if she would join me there. Connie said yes, and we started planning for a week's vacation. I learned that an unmarried officer qualified for the Army to make hotel reservations and arrange other amenities in Honolulu. So I applied for an R&R in Honolulu.

FOR MANY U.S. SOLDIERS WHO SERVED in Vietnam, Christmas season brought the opportunity to see Bob Hope and his U.S.O. troupe. For those of us in the Americal Division, however, good ol' Bob knew a bad thing when he saw it. Because of the My Lai massacre, the Americal was tarnished. Therefore, Bob Hope left Chu Lai off the itinerary for his tour.

This left the division with a public relations and morale problem. If the division command accepted the snub, they'd be agreeing that the Americal was not worthy of Bob Hope's patriotic show. Complaining publicly would only make matters worse. Division Headquarters devised a third alternative—if Bob Hope wasn't going to the Americal, the Americal would go to Bob Hope. Since Hope and his troop were scheduled to do a performance before the Marines in Da Nang (a videotape replay would be televised back in the States shortly before Christmas), the Americal Division commander ordered each unit to pick a soldier representative who would travel to from Chu Lai to Da Nang. The lucky troops assembled in Chu Lai early on Christmas Eve morning. A truck convoy would haul the chosen troops approximately 100 kilometers up Highway 1 to the Da Nang amphitheater. The convoy, which would consist of at least 50 trucks, would return to Chu Lai later that day. To avoid any incidents with the local population, the troops were not to carry weapons. Security, however, was a job for the Red Barons. We were to fly artillery cover in small helicopters to and from Da Nang. Luckily, I was assigned to be one of those Red Barons.

As with all such special assignments, an obvious tactical problem was evident to us aerial observers but apparently not to those who drew up the operation. In the event of an attack on the convoy, our job was supposed to be to bring artillery support. But the convoy route was Highway 1, the only area in South Vietnam that was supposedly pacified (and the one that no one was going to admit it was *not* pacified). So if there were an attack, we'd never get clearance to fire supporting artillery. Despite this flaw in tactics, at 5:30 a.m. on Christmas Eve, I boarded a helicopter in Chu Lai and started the first of many trips flying back and forth along the length of the truck convoy heading north to Da Nang to see Bob Hope.

Fortunately, the trip to Da Nang, while slow, was uneventful. Highway 1, which was mostly paved with one lane in each direction and was lined with buildings close to each shoulder, was relatively quiet.

Highway 1 traveling north to Da Nang.

The troops in the trucks were in a party mood, and the convoy was delayed only once, when an intelligence report warned the convoy that

173

Highway 1 had been mined at a certain point. The convoy pulled over for about an hour while mine sweeping equipment checked the road.

During the delay, my pilot landed our helicopter in the middle of the road, and as we stretched our legs, we bought Coca-Colas from an enterprising Vietnamese kid. Assured the road forward was safe, the convoy started again.

When the convoy arrived in Da Nang, we landed in a field, and we made our way to the amphitheater. Under the sweltering sun were thousands of American G.I.'s, all scrubbed to the teeth, sitting on the ground facing a large stage, waiting several hours for Bob Hope and his entourage to appear.

In a letter home dated December 29, I described the show:

"Things went swimmingly on the way up; however we were there only a half hour before the show and the place was already full… We all had to stand up in the rear on the hill overlooking the amphitheater and could attest to all the celebrities' presence only by the loudspeaker system. They looked like ants at that distance. So my chance to see Miss World, the Goldiggers, Lola Folana (who-ha) et al. was somewhat thwarted.

The show included assorted singers and dancers and an orchestra that didn't quite know how to play rock and roll. The show was typical Bob Hope—mildly funny, intellectually somewhat insulting and potentially offensive insofar as it seemed to make light of the war and of the danger for those of us who were fighting it. Of course, he ignored that we were losing. Regardless, the fact that he came so far, brought so many other famous people with him, and endured what I'm sure was a difficult and tiring tour should be considered a tribute to him and everyone involved in the show. I will be forever grateful that he cared enough to entertain those of us whom so many others in the U.S. seemed to have forgotten.

As the show wore on it grew unbearably hot, and I grew tired of straining my eyes to see the distant figures. So I headed back to a small officers' club I'd seen on my way to the amphitheater. I knew the club was air-conditioned and I hoped it had cold beer.

The return convoy back going south on Highway 1 late that afternoon was uneventful until a truck broke down. We realized we were not going to make it back to Chu Lai by dark so everyone spent Christmas Eve at a small firebase called Hawk Hill about a mile west of Highway 1 and two-thirds of the way back to Chu Lai from Da Nang.

When our helicopter set down on the helipad at Hawk Hill, after all of the trucks had pulled into the perimeter and the troops were taken to the mess hall, I walked around the base trying to find somewhere to spend the night. I finally found the artillery battery officers' shelter and begged a bunk from an artillery first sergeant.

It was past dinner hour when I got to the officers' mess hall, but I managed to get a last turkey leg and a little cranberry sauce and mashed potatoes from one of the cooks, who took pity on me as he was cleaning up. I found a seat at a table and had my Christmas Eve dinner alone, eavesdropping on mostly unintelligible conversations among a number of half-drunk officers a couple of tables away. I wondered whether the mail-order Christmas gifts I had sent to my family and a few friends in late November had arrived. I knew I wouldn't be able to open what they'd sent me until late Christmas afternoon. I felt it quite appropriate that my Christmas in South Vietnam would be spent at a firebase where I knew no one, and as I was completing a mission that had nothing to do with winning a war. But I have to admit that since that Christmas Eve 1970, whenever I hear Bing Crosby or Frank Sinatra sing "I'll Be Home for Christmas," I tear up.

We completed the journey to Chu Lai on Christmas morning, and I reported back to Red Baron headquarters. I had been assigned the noon mission so I gathered my maps and my .45 and headed for the airfield. As I wrote on December 29 about that Christmas day mission:

"...we had a truce on and couldn't engage any targets. So we tied green and red smoke grenades on our struts and buzzed the forward firebases to bring some old cheer to those in the boonies."

I CAME TO KNOW THE BIRD Dog pilots pretty well. They hung out after missions in their own barracks, but spending three hours in a small plane several times a week with each of them gave me the chance learn what they were about.

Captain Al Guess was a privileged son of the South if ever there was one. He had gone to prep school and then to Vanderbilt, where he was in ROTC. He had a patrician Southern drawl and carried the hopes and prayers of his family for his generation. We talked a lot about adventures in school, travel to Europe and other vestiges of privilege. He always had washed and starched flight suits and polished boots.

Smitty was much more from the proletariat, quiet and playing his cards close to the vest. But he loved to learn about artillery, so we worked together finding targets and calling in fire missions that included creative use of artillery shell fuses.

My favorite, however, was a first lieutenant named Frank Savino. Frank was chunky and baby faced, but he was smart and had a very dry sense of humor. He loved to tell stories about growing up in the Midwest and about his exploits in high school and college. And Frank was always up for talking about rock 'n roll. He had no problem with my flying the Bird Dog once we had reached cruising altitude, and he taught me a lot about piloting a plane.

One morning as soon as we took off, Frank said: "Norm, would you take over?"

I said, "Sure, Frank." I looked at him seated in front of me. His arms were draped over the controls and his head was hanging. Given this posture, I assumed he was badly hung over.

After a few minutes, I asked, "Frank, are you okay?"

Frank groaned a little and said, "I'm sorry, I'm airsick."

Airsick? My pilot is airsick? I thought. I couldn't believe it!

"Frank," I said, "this makes no sense. You're a pilot. How can you be airsick?"

"Well, it's sort of a long story, but to be candid, I never wanted to be a pilot."

I couldn't resist asking how he got here.

"When I finished college," Frank said, "I wanted to become a Green Beret infantryman and kill Viet Cong. So I enlisted in the Army and volunteered to be an infantry rifleman. But when I finished basic training, the Army assigned me to auto mechanic school."

Leave it to the Army, I thought, *to assign one of the few recruits who truly wanted to fight to a noncombat job.*

"So I decided to see if I could get into combat by applying for infantry OCS," Frank continued. "I passed the test, but instead of being assigned to the infantry school at Fort Benning, as I had requested, they assigned me to combat engineer's OCS at Fort Belvoir, Virginia."

Son of a bitch, I thought. *He actually wanted infantry OCS, but the Army didn't assign him to it.*

"I didn't want to be a combat engineer, so when I graduated from OCS I volunteered for helicopter flight training to be a helicopter pilot. I thought being a helicopter pilot would put me in the thick of the fighting."

Jesus, I thought. *Helicopter pilot was surely the most dangerous position in Vietnam. Only crazy people wanted to fly a helicopter in Vietnam. Everyone else wanted to fly the type of plane we were in: which was called "fixed wing."*

Then Frank said: "I passed the test and the flight physical, but then they assigned me to fixed wing training instead of helicopters."

Stands to reason, given what had happened so far, I thought. *If you wanted to stay alive, you wanted to be piloting fixed-wing aircraft, like Bird Dogs. But Frank wanted the assignment no one wanted, so instead they gave him one that everyone else found impossible to get.*

"The first time I took off in flight school," Frank continued, "I realized I got airsick very easily. I've never been able to shake it. When my tour is over and my three-year requirement is up, I'm getting out of the Army for good."

"Jesus, Frank," I said. "That's some story. Okay, I'll fly as much as you want, but you have to take off and land. I really don't yet know how to do that."

JANUARY 1971

I EXPECTED TO CONTINUE FLYING RED Baron missions in
Bird Dogs for the rest of my tour. I volunteered often to give the 4:30 a.m.
briefing to the division commander and his staff on artillery missions from
the previous day. In return, I often flew the 6 a.m. Red Baron mission.
Getting up so early had an added bonus: it was cooler than it was the rest
of the day. And I got extra information about possible targets for my next
mission.

But my luck ran out. Word came down that the Red Barons were
going to have an added mission. We were to be part of implementing a
new tactic thought up by the division artillery XO—a lieutenant colonel
on the make who seemed to have only one job: think up new ways to get
division artillery into each morning's briefing.

His plan was simple but flawed. He ordered at least one of the Red
Baron aerial observers to fly each day aboard a Huey as a member of what
was called the Air Cavalry: an AH-1 Cobra attack helicopter/combat
assault team. Each Air Cav team consisted of two Cobra gunships, a Huey
with about six special forces infantrymen aboard, and a small observation
helicopter. The observation helicopter was an OH-6 Cayuse, nicknamed a
Loach, an acronym for Light Observation Helicopter. The Loach had two
front seats and a small back seat. It was a small, maneuverable helicopter
designed for observation and attack. Its job with the Air Cav team was to

hover just over the treetops to locate potential enemy troops or Viet Cong hideouts. Meanwhile, the Cobras and the Huey circled above. When the Loach found someone to attack, or more often was fired upon by enemy on the ground, the Cobras would immediately swoop down and fire their 2.75-inch rockets, their 7.62-mm mini-guns and their 40-mm grenade launchers. After the Cobras softened the target, the Huey would land to insert the infantrymen in what amounted to a combat assault to "clean up" what was left. The Huey would take off and circle until the infantrymen called to be picked up.

I described this in a letter home dated January 9:

"The Air Cav is rather a boring place for an A.O. They work with Cobra gunships and infantry in choppers. When they find something they use gun ships on it and then insert the infantry to mop up. I'm supposed to bring in Arty if they need it. Since they use their own firepower and then usually need to refuel, there isn't much work for me. So I spend 12 hours a day riding around looking at the scenery from 2000 ft."

A Cobra gunship, part of the air cavalry team, taking off.

These helicopter assault teams were a new offensive weapon, and I had only recently heard about them. I had seen Cobra gunships shoot up an area during our battle with the NVA battalion while I was with Charlie Company. But the rest of the team operation —the Loach skimming above the trees to find targets, the firepower of the Cobras, and the Huey ready to insert infantry, was new to me.

Below: My view of 2 Cobra gunships. The handle in the bottom left is for the Huey door gunner's M-60 machine gun.

Given the Loach's mission, the pilots had to be more than half crazy and believe they were Maverick from Top Gun. A Loach pilot's life expectancy in Vietnam was short; if he was still alive a month before the end of his tour, he was grounded to insure he went home alive.

Frequently the Cobra team's attack came about when the Loach, gliding at treetop level, was shot down. The Viet Cong and NVA had come to recognize these teams and, when the enemy thought they had the advantage, they would fire on the Loach, then disappear into their tunnels, chalking up the downing of another U.S. helicopter.

The Special Forces infantrymen in the team had volunteered for this assignment to see "action." They were either John Wayne wannabes or high on drugs. They eschewed steel pots, wore camouflaged fatigues, carried knives in their belts, swaggered around with bandoliers of ammunition, and loved to tell stories about the enemy they had killed.

Into this combat assault team, the lieutenant colonel wanted to inject a Red Baron aerial observer. The AO would fly in the Huey gunship with the infantry, in theory to add artillery to the Cobra team's overall firepower.

The Air Cav team, however, wanted nothing to do with an artillery aerial observer. First, the helicopters had limited fuel, certainly not enough to wait around for artillery clearance. Second, the Air Cav team had to attack immediately or the enemy would quickly disperse and disappear. So waiting for artillery was not going to do a bit of good. Third, and most fundamentally, it made no sense for two Cobra gunships with enough firepower to destroy a small town to wait for artillery shells to land and be adjusted. And, if they were to try to use artillery, they would have to clear out of the area surrounding the target to avoid being hit with an artillery round. No self-respecting Air Cav team was going to permit some aerial observer to mess up its action.

As the designated but unwanted aerial observer, I knew there was no role for me in the operation. And I would be a sitting duck in the bay of the Huey whenever the infantry were inserted and retrieved. When the Cobras had finished firing their rockets and mini-guns, as the Huey landed to unload the Special Forces to finish the job, I would be totally exposed to enemy fire. While the Huey was landing, I was sitting in the open cargo door. The infantry would jump out, just as Charlie Company had done in combat assaults, and the Huey would take off to circle until it was time to pick up the infantry. So for me it was like landing in a potentially hot LZ twice. Although the Huey had door gunners providing cover fire as we landed, with no armor or other protection I made a beautiful target. It was as if I were going on a combat assault every day, only I wasn't fighting; I was sitting unprotected and unarmed in the Huey, with no role, but simply hoping not to be shot or have the Huey hit with RPG or small arms-fire.

My view out the bay of the Air Cav Huey during an insertion.
The infantry sergeant is not wearing a steel pot.

The Air Cav helicopter pilots agreed that my involvement made no sense. They told me that they had complained up their chain of command that having an artillery observer would just take up the seat of an infantryman who might bring some actual firepower to the operation. It hadn't done them any good. The program had been approved, and it was going ahead.

So, in addition to my Bird Dog missions, I began to spend a couple of days each week with an Air Cav team, gritting my teeth during any infantry insertion and retrieval when the Huey landed to pick them up.

Flying with the Air Cav. With my helmet on, I could monitor everything
the pilot and co-pilot were saying, as well as hear their conversations
with their command post. I could also talk to the artillery.

Out of frustration, I finally persuaded a Huey pilot to give me a chance to call in a fire mission after we had retrieved the infantrymen from an insertion. Reluctantly, he agreed to stay around as long as his fuel lasted while I hoped to pound the area with a little bit of redleg steel. Predictably, we couldn't get artillery clearance to fire where the Cobra gunships had just bombed a target. Before we had fired a single artillery round, the pilot disgustedly told me we were low on fuel, and we headed back to the helicopter base.

When they flew with the Air Cav, the other Red Barons had the same experience. Each night at the division officers' club, whoever had gone out with the Air Cav that day would report on the futility of the mission, particularly because it took away from what we considered to be a useful job: firing artillery support from the Bird Dogs.

Although I couldn't be any help to the Air Cav mission, at least I got an education in helicopter piloting. Having learned the basics of flying a Bird Dog (except for taking off), it was fascinating to learn how to pilot a helicopter. A Bird Dog had two controls: the stick, which made the plane ascend, descend or "bank," and the pedals, which allowed the plane to turn. A helicopter has a third control. Called the collective, it controls the pitch of the rotor blades; it is crucial for taking off, hovering and landing. As I learned more about the way a helicopter works, I also began to appreciate the complexity of its systems and how really talented the pilots were. I closely observed them taking off, hovering, flying and landing. The physics were fascinating and the amount of dexterity it required was impressive. In a hover, a pilot would anticipate each wind current as he moved the cyclic (in place of the stick) rapidly in all four directions.

I also began to learn what would happen if a helicopter had engine failure. The procedure for getting a helicopter down when the engine fails is called autorotation. In effect, the pilot disconnects the rotor blades from the motor shaft. As the helicopter falls, air is forced through the blades, which keeps them turning. The blades act like a gyroscope, keeping the helicopter under control. The rapid descent forces more air through the blades, which keeps them spinning and allows the pilot to keep the craft in control. Just before the helicopter hits the ground, the pilot pulls up on the collective, reversing the pitch of the rotor blades. The sudden upward force breaks the fall of the helicopter so it can land, in theory, as gently on the ground as in a normal landing.

The helicopter pilots told me they constantly practiced autorotation in helicopter flight school and also during periodic safety checks. I just hoped that whoever was piloting our Huey was good at it, but I also prayed I wouldn't ever have to experience it myself.

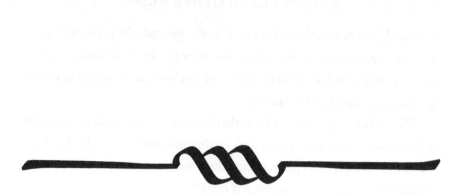

LATE ONE AFTERNOON, AS WE WERE flying back to Chu Lai after an insertion, without warning, the Huey's hydraulic system, which is essential to all helicopter flight systems, failed. While the Huey still had enough engine power to keep the rotors going, for the pilot it was like driving a car without power steering, magnified by hundreds of times. Our pilot was using both arms on the cyclic, trying to prevent the helicopter from turning on its side. He told us through the intercom to hang on. He said that he was going to try to make it to the Chu Lai landing strip. He said he intended to land the chopper like an airplane, only on the helicopter's skids. As we kept losing altitude, we whisked over the treetops. I craned my neck out the door to see how far we were from the landing strip. It was still several kilometers.

The faces of the infantrymen around me betrayed nothing. They were all strangely quiet, but I didn't detect any fear. But they could not hear the pilot's conversation with the tower, as the door gunners and I could through the earphones in our flight helmets as we made our desperate way toward Chu Lai.

I had never experienced landing on a helicopter's skids. I wondered whether or not, as the chopper hit the concrete runway, the skids might send up sparks that could set us on fire. I could see all of the instrument warning lights flashing in the cockpit in front of me.

The other helicopters in our team flew ahead of and behind us to support us if we went down short of the runway. It wouldn't a particularly dangerous area if we went down, since we were close to Chu Lai. But I knew that, at the speed we were going, if we did hit the ground, the Huey could possibly tumble.

Suddenly the runway appeared underneath us. Heading toward us on the runway were several fire trucks and a number of jeeps.

Crash landing with the Air Cav onto the Chu Lai runway.
Our Huey landed safely on its skids.

I waited for the bounce we'd feel as we hit. The first contact with the runway made a loud scraping noise, but the pilot was determined to keep us going straight ahead. I saw him trying desperately to keep the tail from a sideways skid, which I was certain would roll us over. The friction on the runway made a loud screech, but I saw no sparks. As we started slowing down, I watched the fire engines coming up behind us. Finally, the Huey came to a stop. All of us, including the pilot and co-pilot, scrambled off the chopper and dashed away in case it caught fire. The fire engines rushed up, but fortunately were not needed to extinguish any fire. We walked away without injury. I will always have tremendous admiration and respect for the pilot, who appeared exhausted but proud.

VIRTUALLY EVERY TIME WE INSERTED THE infantry, the Loach had been shot at or shot down. Miraculously, we kept safely retrieving the Loach pilots. But the enemy shooters were almost never found. The infantrymen were becoming more and more frustrated.

What seemed incredible to me was that Loach pilots who had been shot down would fly again the next day. They seemed to have no fear or expectation that anything bad would happen to them. This was probably because they were, in the main, 18-year-old warrant officers who felt they were immortal.

We did eventually run into trouble retrieving the infantry. One morning, in the foothills far from Chu Lai, the Loach suddenly went down in a ball of flame. Without hesitation, the Huey landed next to the downed Loach, dispersing the infantry while the door gunners sprayed M-60 machine gun bullets into the foliage. As he left the helicopter, the infantry team leader sergeant was looking for someone to fight.

I gritted my teeth the entire time we were on the ground—probably not more than 15 seconds. Then the Huey took off to circle and await reports from the Loach pilot and infantry.

Air Cav infantrymen leaving a Huey during an earlier insertion.

*My view from the bay of the Huey as the Air Cav infantry returned
to the Huey. Note again: none of them none wore a steel pot.*

But this time the Loach had exploded, and we watched the fire
burning. Over the radio I heard that the infantrymen were taking fire
from somewhere near the Loach.

In less than 10 minutes, the infantry had suffered several casualties.
Our Huey landed to pick them up. The door gunners were also monitoring
the action on the radio through their flight helmets. They knew that
this was likely to be a hot LZ. I could see their frightened faces as we
descended. I looked around desperately for a place to hide in the open bay

of the Huey. I squeezed forward as much as I could into a small indentation between the pilot's and co-pilot's seats.

Over the noise of the Huey, we could hear firing on the ground. Out of a tree line came the sergeant and an infantryman carrying one of the wounded. Two more infantry came dragging another casualty. When they were about 25 yards from the Huey, I realized that, if we were going to get out of there fast, I should help them pull the wounded aboard. Gritting my teeth, I jumped into soft rice paddy mud and lifted one of the wounded onto the Huey.

Once we were all aboard, I saw that one of the wounded soldiers was unconscious and the front of his uniform was soaked in blood. I stood in the open bay of the Huey, waiting for something to hit me in the back. We stuffed another wounded man onto the Huey. I grabbed a soldier with a grotesque leg wound and pulled him aboard as well. The rest of the infantrymen looked dazed as they climbed aboard. I jumped over the bodies and pounded on the back of the pilot's seat to urge him to take off. Quickly, we were airborne.

I surveyed the carnage on the floor of the helicopter. The soldier with the leg wound was sitting up and leaning against the bulkhead. He looked to be in shock. One of the infantrymen was shooting him with a dose of what I assumed was morphine.

I knelt over the one with the gaping stomach wound. I tried not to look at the gaping hole in his uniform. I plugged in my helmet mike and asked the pilot how long it would take us to get to the hospital in Chu Lai. He guessed at least 15 minutes.

With no medic on board, I tried to recall the Army first aid training films we'd been shown. Since the soldier with a stomach wound was breathing, I figured the most important thing was to try to stop his bleeding with what was left of his uniform. I put pressure as best I could around his gut. All I could think to do was gently rock him back and forth. I murmured into his ear: "Hold on, hold on," and "It won't be long, it won't be long."

I had a strange feeling, one that I've never had before or since. I felt that if I kept hugging this soldier, whom I didn't know, and kept repeating that mantra, he would feel me next to him and find the will to live. I also felt that I had never loved anyone so much and that maybe that love could save him. I kept rocking and hugging him and tried to make sure he kept breathing.

Now and then I glanced at the other people in the bay. The eyes of the soldier with the leg wound were now closed—I assumed the morphine had taken hold. The others just stared into open space, glassy-eyed.

Finally, we set down at Chu Lai hospital's helipad. Immediately a group of medical corpsmen leapt into the Huey's bay to assess the casualties. When I showed them the stomach wound on the one I was holding, they grabbed him from me, loaded him onto a stretcher and ran him toward the hospital. Within seconds, the wounded were gone. Our Huey was told to clear off the helipad in case another group of wounded arrived.

We flew to a nearby refueling stop. When we set down, all of us got off and walked over to the safe area during the refueling. The infantry sergeant was there, untouched and swearing under his breath. The other infantrymen still looked dazed but started talking among themselves about what had happened. The emotion I had felt for the soldier I was holding on the flight back began to dissolve as I heard the rest of them talking as if it had been an exciting adventure. But the blood all over my hands, arms and uniform was beginning to dry into a sticky mess.

Unable to light a cigarette because of the refueling fumes, to calm myself I walked away and sat down. I looked off into space. As with virtually all casualties I saw, I never found out what happened to the soldier I had cradled.

WHEN I RELATED THAT EXPERIENCE TO the rest of the Red
Barons, we tried first to get Captain Rocamora to take it up with Division
Artillery. When he told us his complaint had already been dismissed, we
decided to bring to the Division Artillery commander's attention that
we were going out on missions with no reasonable chance of firing any
artillery, and with a great chance of being killed. Shaken by the events of
the day, I agreed to be the spokesman for the group. When I got to Division
Artillery Headquarters the next morning, I was intercepted by a lieutenant
colonel. He was the one who had thought up the scheme to have us fly
with the Air Cav team. He told me I had to first tell him what I wanted
to discuss with the commander.

"Look, all of us Red Barons are fed up going up with the Air Cav.
We've been flying with them now for a month and we haven't shot one
round of artillery. That's because we can never get clearance, and even if we
could, the Cobras don't have enough fuel to stay around to shoot artillery.
Our whole mission is pointless. Meanwhile, we're sitting ducks out there
on the Hueys when they land to insert the infantry, and all we've done is
taken one seat away from another useful member of the team."

His face stiffened.

"They just haven't figured out how to use you," he said. "What you need to do is explain to them where you can shoot artillery. They'd be happy to have you shoot some artillery before they insert the grunts."

"You don't understand," I said. "These people don't want anything from the artillery. The gunships have already softened up the area before they insert the grunts. Most of the time we land it's because a Loach has been shot down. So I can't fire any artillery because we've got to go down to secure the pilot and the Loach."

"You just do what you're told," he said. "The colonel has approved this program, and I want to give it a chance to work."

"I'm telling you it's been going on now for a month, and we haven't shot one round of artillery. There isn't any way for it to work. The Air Cav team doesn't want it to work, and I'm not going to go out and risk my neck as a sitting duck passenger."

"Are you telling me you're not going to fly another mission?"

"Yes."

"Okay, you've refused a direct order. You'll be seeing the colonel later."

Suddenly, I realized I had given the Army grounds to court-martial me. When I got back to the Red Baron HQ, there was a message that I was ordered to report to the colonel that afternoon.

I had a couple of hours to kill. I went up to the officers' club with a book I had been reading. It was Kurt Vonnegut's novel: *Thank Heavens Mr. Rosewater.* I tried to read. It was impossible to think of anything other than what was going to happen to me.

I figured the worst that could happen was a court-martial and perhaps some time at Long Binh Jail, affectionately nicknamed L.B.J. More likely, I'd simply be taken me off aerial observer status and sent back to the field as a forward observer. That was the usual punishment for someone who wasn't playing by the Army's rules. I wondered whether I would be able to survive another six months as an FO. I rehearsed in my mind what I was going to say to the colonel.

Finally, the lieutenant colonel led me into to see Colonel Blackwood. "This is Lieutenant Hile, sir, the one I told you about. He's refused to fly any more missions with the Cobra gunship teams."

"Why don't you leave us alone for a minute," Blackwood said. The lieutenant colonel walked out of the room and closed the door. This was a break for me, and I hoped I could capitalize on it.

I studied Colonel Blackwood. I'd seen him only from a distance before. He was a short man, with a double chin but was fairly young for a full colonel.

"What's this about you refusing to fly with the Air Cav?"

I started from the beginning, explaining to Colonel Blackwood that we had been doing a good job in the Bird Dogs, how we were destroying a lot of targets, and how this new scheme had resulted in a waste of a month's time by the Red Barons. To my surprise, he didn't cut me off, so I continued to describe the futility of the mission. I thought I was doing fine until I told him that we were doing nothing and were just sitting ducks. At that his face hardened.

I realized he did not want to hear this. He thought we were just scared.

So I changed tactics. "Look sir," I said, "it's not that we are afraid. I don't know if you know it, but I was an FO out of Duc Pho for five months. I've got a Purple Heart and went through some of the worst fighting this area has seen in the last year. I'm not John Wayne, but I'm not a coward. If I felt that we could do some good on these missions, I wouldn't complain. The problem is that not only have we not been able to do any good at all, but we actually diluted the gunship teams by taking a seat away from an infantryman. They resent us for doing that, and they certainly aren't going to wait around for us to fire artillery after they've already pounded the area with the gunships. And meanwhile, we're not doing the job we can do in the Bird Dogs."

He didn't say anything for quite a few seconds. He looked out the window, with a look that showed frustration and fatigue. Finally he turned to me and his face softened a little.

"Listen, lieutenant, I can understand your frustration. But I can't have lieutenants refusing direct orders from lieutenant colonels. It's his plan, and I'll review it after another month to see whether or not you've been able to fire any artillery. In the meantime, you are going back out there on that helicopter tomorrow or you're going to jail."

His face softened again. "Just do your job. If this thing isn't going to work, I'll get you back to doing something you do well."

The next day I was back with the Cobra gunship team. I felt a tremendously relieved, however. At least someone with rank had listened. And, most important, I wasn't going to be court-martialed or sent back to the field. I figured I could risk another month with the gunship team with the hope that it would end soon. I told the other Red Barons not to push too hard to fire artillery. In a month I hoped our Cobra gunship team partnership would be over.

UNFORTUNATELY, THAT DIDN'T MEAN THE AIR Cav infantry insertions were over. The next week the enemy shot down two more Loaches. While we were trying to retrieve the second one, things got scary.

When we flew over the crash site, our Huey took fire and we began to lose altitude. As we started to go down, I saw our pilot working his hands and arms hard, but calmly, at the controls. We started to fall fast, but the pilot maintained the chopper on an even keel. While still hanging onto a bulkhead, I looked out to see where we would hit the ground. I hoped that we would not be close to whoever had fired at us. I knew that if the pilot did a competent job, we would feel a sudden jerk as our fall was broken just before we hit the ground.

As the trees rushed toward us, the pilot pulled up on the collective and our descent stopped abruptly. We fell what seemed like a few meters and hit the ground with a small bounce. My heart was in my stomach, but we were alive. I had just survived my first autorotation.

Immediately, we jumped off and formed a makeshift perimeter to secure the Huey and, if necessary, defend ourselves while waiting for another Air Cav team to pick us up. The Loach crew must have seen us falling and, fortunately, we were close enough for them to join our perimeter. Using triangulation, I started determining which direction we should head if no one picked us up soon. But we were in the western territory near the mountains, and it would have been dangerous to try to travel on the ground.

Luckily, we weren't there more than 30 minutes when another Air Cav team picked us up. Right behind them a Jolly Green Giant helicopter arrived to lift up the two wounded choppers and take them back to Chu Lai.

I HAVE TO ASSUME THAT WHAT I said to the colonel had little impact as far as sending AOs with the Air Cav. But fortunately, and typical of the Army, without any warning, the Red Barons were told we would no longer be riding with the Air Cav. In a letter home on January 29, I reported:

"I won't be flying with the Air Cav much more. Two more days and a replacement will take over. I told my boss last night that I would not fly with them any more since I consider it too dangerous. The missions are all volunteer jobs but the AO's were ordered to go. So I was perfectly within my rights. There's no use taking any chances in this stupid war and I think I paid my dues for four months in the field. The whole program is so poorly run that I have said a few unkind things to some higher ranking people. Unfortunately, when a field grade officer makes a decision he feels that it is right even when proven wrong. Hence I'll be moving out of Div Arty and back to my old Brigade at the end of the month. I'll still be an AO, but in my own bird and able to fly as high above the fray as I want"

A few days later, I wrote:

"My flying status is now back to normal, flying fixed-wing three hours a day. I seem to have come out unscathed (although time will only tell). … My tour has reached the midway point now, but if you feel like promoting my morale you could lobby for a ten month tour for officers. That would put me home at the beginning to the summer…"

FEBRUARY 1971

UNFORTUNATELY, I WAS TOO QUICK IN thinking I was done with the Air Cav. I had to fly one additional Air Cav mission in early February. On February 3rd I wrote to my folks:

"On Sunday I flew with the Air Cav for one day to spell the regular observer. The small [Loach] spotted some NVA in a clearing. Higher up wouldn't give clearance to fire [artillery] first so we inserted our infantry and tried to round them up. Needless to say the infantry and the Loach took fire from the NVA. However we still couldn't get clearance to fire back because the ARVN's in the area were "too close" (several thousand meters away). You can imagine what it's like to be shot at and not be able to fire back. So we just took out the infantry and left. You can't win a war that way."

THE RED BARONS HEARD RUMBLINGS FROM division artillery staff about plans to combat an expected enemy offensive sure to happen in early February, at the beginning of the Tet lunar New Year. Ever since the VC attacks during the 1968 Tet holiday revealed to the American public that the U.S. was not "winning" the war in Vietnam, the Allied Command had orders not to be embarrassed again by another Tet offensive.

The Tet holiday fell relatively late in 1971, beginning on February 5. No one expected a repeat of the enemy's massive ground force attack. This late in the war, the VC and NVA knew that the Americans were trying to hand the baton over to the ARVN and were going to leave sooner or later. So the North Vietnamese anticipated that they would be able to take over South Vietnam without great loss of life. During the previous two Tet holidays, the enemy attacks around Chu Lai had been limited to heavier than normal rocket and mortar barrages into the American base from the west, the infamous "rocket pocket."

Although we felt uneasy because the Chu Lai compound had no underground shelters, a rocket barrage did little to disrupt operations. The base was so spread out that individual rockets only resulted in random damage. But, as far as the NVA and VC were concerned, a propaganda benefit could be had. If it was Tet, it was time to shoot rockets into Chu

Lai. Because rockets could be fired from pitch-dark areas in the rocket pocket, the enemy faced almost no danger of effective U.S. retaliation.

That was the problem posed to Division Artillery Headquarters, which was in charge of defending against such an attack. It was a nightly phenomenon for the VC to shoot one or two rockets into Chu Lai. Our standard response, in light of having no way of knowing where the rockets came from, was for the base artillery to fire random rounds into the rocket pocket just to let the enemy know that we were ready to respond. One of the Red Barons' first daily tasks was to fly to the grid coordinates where our counter-rocket rounds had been fired and survey the result. At night no one could see where our rounds landed or whether they had done any damage.

Word began to filter down to the Red Barons that Division Artillery had developed a new plan to deal with the expected Tet rocket attack. As the outlines of the plan became known, we learned that it had been authored, not surprisingly, by the same lieutenant colonel who had put Red Barons into the Air Cav assault teams. This genius's new plan was simple, and as we could immediately see, totally ineffective. The Red Barons, who had been spotting and adjusting artillery from dawn to dusk, were going to be taken off most of those missions for the week of Tet. In the place of most daylight missions, the Red Barons would be in the air from dusk to dawn. We were supposed to be part of the division's line of defense against enemy rocket attacks. If the VC mounted any sort of rocket barrage, the Red Barons were to respond immediately by directing an artillery barrage of our own.

The problems with this plan should have been obvious to the rest of the Americal Division command.

First, was that, in the dark, and given the extensive territory outside the base, chances were slim that an aerial observer would see the flash of a rocket taking off.

Second, even if one of us did see such a flash, in the darkness we would be unable to see any landmarks on the ground with which to establish the grid coordinates of the rocket's launch site.

Third, even if we had the grid coordinates, since we were unable to see anything in the dark, we would be unable to adjust rounds onto the target.

Fourth, and this was one that concerned us Red Barons, if we were to attempt to fly toward any rocket launch site, we would be in grave danger of being hit by our own counter-rocket artillery, fired automatically from Chu Lai randomly into the darkness. This prevented us from flying outside the Chu Lai perimeter toward any target even if we could locate it on a map.

Nevertheless, the plan was adopted and the Red Barons were ordered to fly three hour missions from dusk till dawn, greatly reducing our missions during the day. For a week we flew missions in the dark in circles around the perimeter of Chu Lai. If we saw anything from the rocket pocket, we were supposed to report it. If rounds landed in Chu Lai, we were to do what we could while flying around the base perimeter, as the Chu Lai artillery guns would be randomly firing a counter-rocket barrage outside the perimeter. Boiled down to basics, the plan eliminated virtually all that the Red Barons were able to do during daylight hours and replaced those missions with totally useless Red Baron flights at night.

From the Red Barons' perspective, however, at least for those of us who were not stricken with the John Wayne syndrome, this stupid plan had some advantages. Although we would be awake during a significant portion of the night, we could usually nap during the day. More important, it also took us away from flying many of our daytime missions over enemy territory. Flying in circles around the Chu Lai perimeter was probably the safest position we could possibly be in. While in the air, we were above any enemy rockets that might land in Chu Lai.

On February 3, I wrote home:

"We are flying a 24 hour schedule due to the Tet offensive. This means I was up from 3:00 a.m. to 6:00 a.m. this morning. A schedule like that really messes up your day. And trying to observe anything on the ground when it is pitch black is rather difficult, not to mention the problem of figuring out where it is on a map to fire artillery. But the war becomes more ridiculous every day."

Staring into the night sky while circling the base was extremely boring, and posed one problem: staying awake. To keep warm, given the colder night air, we brought extra poncho liners and a thermos of hot coffee. Books and magazines helped to keep our minds occupied. The pilot and I took half-hour shifts flying in circles and looking out while the other read. Only one time during that week did the enemy shoot a rocket barrage while I was in the air. I was deep into my book when suddenly there was a flash below and an explosion. The pilot said he saw a rocket land near the motor pool. Immediately my radio crackled with a call from division artillery.

"Red Baron 36, this is Tony Ports 45, over."

"Tony Ports 45, this is Red Baron 36, go ahead, over."

"Red Baron 36, this is Tony Ports 45. Did you see anything, over?"

"Tony Ports 45, this is Red Baron 36, I can see that a rocket may have hit the motor pool, over."

"Red Baron 36, this is Tony Ports 45, did you have any idea where it came from, over?"

"Tony Ports 45, this is Red Baron 36, negative, over."

"Red Baron 36, this is Tony Ports 45, we're firing counter-rocket artillery. Continue to circle the base and let us know if you see anything."

"Tony Ports 45, this is Red Baron 36, roger, out."

And so we continued, circling in the dark.

On February 8 I wrote home to my concerned family to debunk a stateside report that Chu Lai had taken an enemy hit during Tet:

"During TET there were no military casualties in Chu Lai, although we did take a few rockets. I think the report was probably sent out of our Public Information Office and therefore was datelined Chu Lai. You should watch out for this in the future. There was some fighting north of here and quite a ways to the south, but we had a relatively quiet time."

In the same letter I discussed the Army incursion into Laos. Once again, apparently I was able to get by any U.S. Army censorship:

"The big move to Laos is of course affecting the units here, but I will most likely never get involved. I imagine there is a big stink in the States going on over the whole thing. It was kept more of a secret here than back there I think. Everyone knew that a lot of troops were being sent somewhere, but no one knew where, even after they started to move. They moved a bunch out of Chu Lai on

[landing crafts] in the middle of the night, and they had to guard a lot of troops on alert to keep them from going AWOL. Especially those who have only a short time left in country. That's about the way this war keeps going. I have no idea whether we have troops on the ground up there, but I know the Air Cav is there and we are firing into Laos. The distinction is somewhat dubious, but the Pentagon can usually get away with it."

One thing I did not write home about: while napping in my hooch during Tet, I was blown off my cot by an explosion in the building next to mine, perhaps 10 meters away. I heard screams but then nothing. I inched out the door away from the blast and heard the shouts of medical corpsmen and others running to the scene. I checked myself and saw no bleeding. My ears were ringing, but I hadn't been wounded. I moved away from the hooch and grabbed my steel pot and .45.

I later learned that it was a "fragging" incident. No one was in the nearby hooch at the time the pin was pulled and the grenade was dropped. I chalked it up to some enlisted man sending a message to an officer who was giving him grief. I didn't go back to my nap that day.

I RECEIVED RESERVATIONS FOR MY R&R trip to Honolulu a little over a month before my scheduled February 12 flight out of Da Nang. I reserved a seat on a C-140 cargo plane from Chu Lai to Da Nang on February 11.

Having concrete evidence of a week's leave from the war had forced me once again to confront the danger I was facing each day. I had been told early on that there was a predictable curve for casualties among Vietnam aviators. When pilots arrived, they were extremely careful. As time went on, however, they began to get lax, which led to accidents and deaths. As pilots approached their R & R, however, their rate of casualties dropped off dramatically. Upon return from R & R, for a week or two pilot casualties were low. Then casualties began to creep back up until about two months before a pilot's DEROS. That's when statistics showed that pilots suffered fewer casualties, likely because they had begun to be more careful again.

Who knows whether this happened because pilots consciously grew more careful as they grew close to leaving. The thought of surviving a full year of combat flying made everyday flights stressful enough. But flying wasn't the only danger. We also faced the possibility of enemy rockets, fragging, and being sent on an even more risky assignment. These added to a developing compulsion that grew stronger every minute to do whatever it took to take one's mind off everything that could go wrong.

That said, making R&R arrangements brought on thoughts of a week of safety, sex and sunshine. Thinking of such revels, however, and trying to make the time pass, led to panic. One thing did seem to help: alcohol. No longer content with steam bath sex, and looking forward to the warmth of a woman's arms rather than her fist, I tried to forget what I had gone through each day, and what I would have to endure the next. I drowned my panic in 35-cent Chivas Regal double scotches at the officers' club.

The Red Barons tried to protect each other. As each of us approached our R & R, we took away his flights for several days to keep the lucky guy safe until his holiday.

I know that soldiers were given leave from combat in other wars. I suspect that leaves happened on a unit basis, which might increase the sense of teamwork, continuity and obligation to return. But in Vietnam, we were individual soldiers. We came and went from whatever unit we were assigned to, and we took our R&R's as individuals, regardless of its effect on our current unit.

The juxtaposition of being on R&R and being in a war zone is impossible to describe. How does one's psyche cope with being taken out of constant danger and suddenly being plopped into paradise for a week? And how does one confront the undeniable fact that, even during that week in paradise, the minutes are ticking before one must return to war?

Once again, the best way I knew to handle it was to numb my brain with alcohol.

FINALLY, I HAD NO MORE FLIGHTS before leaving Chu Lai for R&R but still a couple of days before I could catch my flight to Da Nang. I began to feel that it might have been better if I were flying. The time dragged terribly as I had nothing to do but wait and think about some stray rocket or mortar round ruining my one-week respite from war.

In a letter home, written after my R&R, I described the 24-hour layover in Da Nang:

"I left [Chu Lai] on the 11ᵗʰ and met Ralph Oser in Da Nang where he showed me what it's really like to be in a safe place. The whole area he works in is like the world, considering numerous Officers' Clubs with menus and waitresses, movies that aren't cut up, and a beautiful waterfront city to tour. Then of course there is the regulation forbidding wearing civilian clothes after duty, and no hostile fire has come into Da Nang since Tet of '68. I was accordingly envious. We went to the Navy O Club for dinner (steak) and a movie ("Woodstock"). Then in the morning I went to their beach, which makes most of the ones on Long Island look bad. The surf was great. Then Ralph took me on a shopping trip of the PX's in the area just to window shop and I was on my way.

Finally, after several delays at the airport, I boarded a Boeing 707 for the 14-hour flight to Honolulu.

It's difficult to describe the sensations I had after landing in Honolulu. As I walked out into the beauty and safety of paradise, I breathed in deeply the cool air that smelled so sweet. I listened to the peaceful sound of the ocean waves on the beach and saw the palm tree vistas that were spectacular, particularly compared to where I had been living. The prospect of six days away from war was such a relief. I felt like a prisoner granted a seven-night conjugal visit. Hanging over me, of course, was the realization that, at the end of that week, I would have to fly back to the war for the rest of my tour. Although I wondered if I would be able to get back on that plane, I tried to enjoy every sweet thing I could during those six days and seven nights.

The Army bussed us from the airport to Fort DeRussy, the Army post located on Waikiki Beach. After a mercifully short welcome by an Army chaplain, Connie and I retreated to a comfortable hotel room on a high floor overlooking the beach and ocean to the south and the mountains to the north. Our time together consisted mostly of making love, finding and eating wonderful tropical food in good restaurants, and going to the beach. We ate seafood, poi, pig and other Hawaiian specialties, and tried every tropical drink available. We went to clubs to dance into the night and listened to live Hawaiian music during floor shows.

About two days in, Connie asked if I wanted to talk about what was happening in the war. It was a well-meaning question from someone who understood that talking can often be beneficial. But I immediately felt a physical as well as a mental reaction. My pulse quickened and I had a sickened feeling in my stomach. I also experienced a profound dread. These were reactions I would come to expect often in the years to come.

I told Connie that I would prefer not to talk about it, that it would just bring back the terror, and that all I wanted to do was to forget the war for a few days before I had to go back into the middle of it.

As the fourth day arrived, I was in a downhill slide. I tried as best I could to blot out the war, but it hung over me and worsened with each moment. I tried to remind myself that soldiers went on leave and then returned to the front all the time. But it didn't help. I felt out of place in the United States with hot running water, clean sheets and wonderful food, knowing that I had to go back to Vietnam and all that it meant. It made me bitter to see people around me who were totally ignoring what was happening to those of us who were conscripted to fight. And it seemed so unfair that I was going to have to go back.

I'd heard about soldiers who had gone to Hawaii and never showed up for their flight back. I gave it some thought but never seriously considered that option. Since getting out of the field, as a Red Baron I felt I had a fairly good chance of surviving. I also knew that if I deserted, unless I was willing to live in Canada, I would never get to enjoy the life I expected when I got out of the Army. It was a calculated risk, but I thought I might avoid going back to the field, so I decided to return and took the chance.

I still recall scenes from those wonderful days: teaching Connie to bodysurf at Makapu'u Beach, dancing late at night to a rock band called the Laughing Kahunas (former high school students who kept their band together for years after graduation). But I also recall waking up late at night wondering whether I really could get back on the plane that would take me back to war.

At the end of my six day, seven night R&R, a 707 took me and others back to war. The heat and humidity when we landed was an instant reminder that we were no longer in paradise. In those days and nights in Honolulu, I hadn't forgotten how bad Vietnam was. But now it seemed worse.

MY FIRST RED BARON FLIGHT AFTER returning from R&R was tough. As we combed the wings for signs of metal fatigue, I wondered how I was going to make myself climb into this ancient airplane, and continue to do so for the next several months. I vowed to take every precaution, and to choose only the safest targets, no matter how bored I got, to make sure I survived the remainder of my one-year sentence.

Luckily, it wasn't until a few weeks later, when I was back to a more "normal" state of mind, that we discovered machine gun rounds in the wing of the Bird Dog at the end of a mission. Earlier, my pilot and I had been flying in the north of the American Division A.O. where we had been finding signs of a significant enemy activity. We also had been getting quite a few secondary explosions when we put artillery rounds on our targets. I had seen some flashes of light from below during the flight, but we were flying high enough that we felt fairly safe. When we landed, however, we decided to check the aircraft. Sure enough there were five holes in one wing, each about a half an inch in diameter.

I couldn't figure out how we didn't feel them or hear them, but I chalked it up to my flight helmet and the windy weather that day. I remember feeling that I should be petrified that the pilot and I came that close to being hit. But I was falling back into numbness. I was determined not to let this near miss keep me awake at night. Nevertheless, I decided to look elsewhere for targets for the next couple of weeks.

After my run-in with the lieutenant colonel over using aerial observers with the Air Cav teams, I truly feared doing something that would send me back to the field as a forward observer. In so many ways, I knew I was much better off flying as a Red Baron than living with an infantry unit on the ground. No Red Barons had been shot down during my tenure. I also knew that if I were sent to Fire Direction Control on a firebase, I would not be living in the relative luxury of division headquarters.

A Red Baron was sent back to the field, although fortunately it wasn't me. We found out one morning from Captain Rocamora that one of the infantry companies to the southwest was short a forward observer. One of us would be the replacement.

Captain Rocamora gave the unwanted assignment to Steve Kassel, the most recently arrived Red Baron. We all complained to Rocamora about Steve's reassignment, but inwardly we were quite thankful not to have been in Steve's shoes. We all lived in terror of getting our own call to pack up and head for the field.

Kassel returned slightly over a week later. A newly arrived artillery lieutenant had been sent to relieve him. Steve told us he had been lucky. Because the company had been so badly shot up before he got there, it was content to stay in one place almost the entire time. He managed to come and go in his assignment without being in a firefight.

If we thought it would be unlucky to be in the field, we soon found out it was possible to be unlucky in the air. About a week after Steve returned, late one afternoon Captain Rocamora summoned us all to Red Baron headquarters. Rusty Danielson, the most senior Red Baron, and his pilot, had gone down somewhere far to the southern border of the division A.O.

We received conflicting reports on what had happened. One said that the pilot had managed a crash landing after motor trouble. Another said the Bird Dog had been shot down. There was no word about the condition of Danielson or the pilot.

We used Division Artillery's radio to call as many of the firebases in the southern region as we could for any news about Rusty's plane. We figured that if Rusty had been firing artillery at the time, a firebase might know. However, after about two hours of checking, we still had no word.

We settled in at the Division Artillery headquarters for a long night. A couple of us brought in suppers as we sat by the radios listening for any news.

A few hours after midnight, when most of us were asleep in our chairs, word came through. Danielson was on the radio calling Salvation. He wanted to let us know that he and the pilot were all right. He told us that they had had engine problems and had managed to land at an abandoned airstrip fairly close to a firebase. They hoped to be able to get back to Chu Lai in a few days.

MARCH 1971

WE ALL LEARN IN GRADE SCHOOL civics that our Revolutionary War forebears beat the better- trained and armed British Army by hiding behind trees and acting like guerrilla fighters while following the military genius of General George Washington. When I've mentioned this version of history to some U.K. friends, they all look startled to hear that such a clearly biased tale is taught in our schools.

Whether what we were taught was legend or truth, we must acknowledge that, in Vietnam, we played the role of the British. This became clear to me in carrying out one particular Red Baron assignment: spotting targets for the U.S. Air Force F-4 Phantoms. These fast movers, as we called them, dropped bombs, rockets and other ordnance in support of our operations. And specifically for Red Baron purposes, they dropped bombs on targets in the mountain jungle west of Chu Lai.

One must bear in mind that, just as when Charlie Company faced off against a lightly armed NVA battalion in early September 1970, U.S. forces could bring to bear not just the firepower of an infantry company and supporting artillery, but also armored unit firepower, as well as Cobra helicopter gunship teams. By contrast, the most the NVA had for firepower were RPG's and mortars.

But the truth is that U.S. forces had even more firepower. We had Air Force fighter bombers as well as Navy gunfire from ships just off shore. As a Red Baron, I got to see this firepower up close.

The F-4s, which for American Division purposes flew out of Da Nang, needed the Red Barons for their bombing missions because their forward air controllers (the Air Force's name for aerial spotter) were not permitted to fly below 300 meters. Don't ask me why. The Air Force forward air controllers usually flew in OV-10A Broncos, a fixed wing plane specifically designed for spotting F-4 bombing targets. At the minimum altitude permitted, the OV-10A spotter really couldn't see the target on the ground well enough to precisely place the white phosphorous spotting rounds that established the target location to the F-4, or later to see whether the F-4's bombs had hit the target and evaluate the results. So the Red Barons, who could fly as low as 150 meters (and often lower), gave the Air Force forward air controllers the precise spot to place the white phosphorus marker that the "fast mover" could use when it made its bombing run. Then, after the F-4 unloaded its bombs and other ordnance on the target, the Red Baron would make another pass close to the "deck" and report back to the forward air controller.

I'm certain the forward air controllers felt emasculated by the Red Barons, but our ability to locate a target precisely, and to observe the results, was often essential to a successful bombing run. Our presence meant that the forward air controller was in no danger, however, and I assume the pilots didn't complain.

Once the target round was placed, the F-4s were remarkably accurate with their ordnance. Also remarkable was the earth shattering noise the F-4's made as they dived to bomb the target. Their targets were usually in heavy jungle on the sides of mountains, so I could not tell whether they were actually doing much damage.

Besides spotting for bombing runs for the Air Force F-4s, I had one opportunity to shoot naval gunfire from a ship offshore at Chu Lai. Flying along the South China Sea one day, I had seen some "unfriendlies" go into caves in hills that jutted into the ocean, and I calculated that, with all our artillery batteries inland, their rounds couldn't hit the cave openings that faced the sea and were shielded by the hills. When I reported this find and discussed the problem of bringing our artillery to bear on it, division artillery said they would see if they could schedule naval gunfire that could reach the caves. Sure enough, the Navy wanted to be involved. The next day, on my afternoon mission, I contacted a Navy ship and talked to its version of the artillery's Fire Direction Control.

As I came to learn, one challenge for a ship is that its cannon's firing must be coordinated with the ship's roll. That is a complication we Red Legs did not have, with our guns dug into solid ground. But I was assured that naval gunfire could hit the target.

The grid location for the caves was a snap because they were located on the ocean and the hills that rose from the beach were clearly delineated on my contour map. I was anxious to see how accurate naval gunfire was. The range probable error for our guns was only about 15 meters to either side and about 100 meters along the gun target line.

There was little difference in the "lingo" for a naval fire mission, so the RTO on the ship and I were able to understand each other without any problem. I was excited about this target because I had seen some of the enemy going into the caves, and I assumed they had chosen the location because it was impervious to land-based artillery.

When the ship fired its first round and called "splash," I couldn't see anything that looked like an explosion. It certainly wasn't anywhere near the coordinates I had given. I could only assume it had landed somewhere in the ocean, which made it hard for me to pick it up from the air. We rechecked everything and tried again. This time I saw a round, but it landed far up the beach. Two or three additional rounds did not get much closer.

I still don't know what the problem was, but we shut down the mission because my Bird Dog was running out of fuel. That was my sole experience at directing naval gunfire. I felt a small thrill at being able to boast that I'd spotted ordnance for all three of our military branches: the Army, the Navy and the Air Force.

But after this mission, I was all the more convinced that we were like the British in the Revolutionary War. Pounding away at the enemy with all the ordinance in the world, we were still failing to conquer a poor, relatively undeveloped nation thousands of miles away from our home. The North Vietnamese were staunch revolutionaries, fighting for what they considered their freedom against a much more powerful foreign force. We were like the rich but stodgy British centuries ago who, despite a world-class military, couldn't defeat a weaker enemy because their opponent cared more about winning and learned how to blunt a superior force. To put it simply, we were on the wrong side of this war, and no matter how great our firepower advantage, we could not defeat a more dedicated enemy.

I CONTINUED TO DODGE AND WEAVE to avoid being sent west as part of the Laotian invasion. On March 5, I wrote home:

"I am still in Chu Lai, although more and more units have been sent either north, or home. My old Artillery Battalion went north last week and my old infantry battalion has started going home (or at least taking the colors home — most [soldiers] go to other units). Since I let my opinion on a few subjects dealing with our operation (not the war) be known, I was in to see the Colonel, but the ax has not fallen yet and I have plenty of backing. So all remains in turmoil and I have vowed to keep my mouth closed as much as possible for the next five months unless I get a drop. Of course it also depends on not being sent out on a fool's errand to get shot at. Things are really tense.

In that letter I also mentioned that I had applied for a week's leave to Hong Kong, where I would visit with my dear friends the Soong family, with whom I had spent a glorious summer during college. I would also be able to meet up with Brenda Randolf, a family friend from Pittsburgh I had known for years and who was in school in Japan:

"But less than two weeks to Hong Kong. Unfortunately the move north has pre-empted all the cargo lanes so we get no mail and I can't communicate with Brenda or the Soongs. I certainly hope there's no major SNAFU which requires us getting in touch. I'm also hoping they will have some type of transportation available by that time to Saigon."

Later in that letter I also reported the most exciting news I could imagine since I had arrived in South Vietnam:

"OK, here's a flash gathered since I stopped [writing] for lunch after the last paragraph. The word is that all officers are being given 2 month drops if they are under the two year after commissioning program. I qualify. So under a rather complicated system I should (I say should because I don't have my orders yet) reach the shores of the U.S. around the 20th of June. This is about 50 days earlier than my full year. We must celebrate tonight. It would also mean only 105 days left in this dreary place."

Here's what my letter refers to: when I was commissioned as an officer in August 1969, I was required to complete two years of active duty. For my first year, I had served as an instructor at Fort Sill, Oklahoma. Therefore, at the end of my Vietnam tour in August 1971, I would have completed my required two years and could end active duty in the Army. But under this new program, an early end to my Vietnam tour also meant an early end to my required active duty. This was indeed a double treat. I confirmed this when I wrote home on March 10:

"My scheduled date to return to the U.S. is now 18 June according to the tables printed in the Stars and Stripes. So I am now a "two digit midget" in Army parlance. Less than 100 days to go."

WE HAD JUST TAKEN OFF FROM Chu Lai one afternoon when I got a call from Bob Terry, aka Red Baron 38. Terry had joined us about two months after I came aboard following a tour as an FO on the Quang Ngai River east of Quang Ngai. He was a young, handsome but unassuming lieutenant, probably 22 years old. He was quite bright and had quickly picked up the aerial observer skills.

Terry had a hint of disappointment in his voice as he called me over the radio.

"Red Baron 36, this is Red Baron 38. Over."

"Red Baron 38, this is Red Baron 36. What have you got? Over."

"Red Baron 36, this is Red Baron 38. I've got quite a situation for you up here. We've got an infantry unit and an armored unit pinned down near a village. I've gotten clearance for a number of batteries to fire. But it's taken so long to get clearance that I have to come back before we run out of fuel. Why don't you hurry up here and I'll turn it over to you. Over."

"Red Baron 38, this is Red Baron 36. We'll be there as soon as we can. Out."

The grid location Terry gave was about 50 kilometers northwest of Chu Lai, in a valley that worked its way into the hill ranges just east of the mountains. When I got there, I could see the column of armored vehicles stopped and, I assumed, pinned down on a dirt road. I tuned the radio to the three artillery batteries that Terry had lined up for his fire mission. We had two eight inchers, a battery of six 155s, and another battery of six 105s, all capable of hitting the area. I told them to stand by while I contacted the infantry company below.

"Sterling Dancer 12, this is Red Baron 36. Over."

"Red Baron 36, this is Sterling Dancer 12. Is that you up above? Over."

"Sterling Dancer 12, this is Red Baron 36. That's right. Why don't you put out some smoke bombs to let me know exactly where your forward positions are? Over."

"Red Baron 36, this is Sterling Dancer 12. Roger. You can see the line of armor. We are in a line to the northeast of it in the tree line and to the northwest about to the first building. We've been getting fire from the hut and from the tree line to the rear of the village. How close can you bring it in? Over."

"Sterling Dancer 12, this is Red Baron 36. I can bring it in real close with the eight inch, but I'm going to have to walk it in slowly. Have your people send up their smoke bombs now so I call in the target locations. Over."

When I saw the colored smoke grenades, I called in a different grid location for each of the three artillery batteries. I described the fire mission as "unfriendlies in a tree line." To start with, I asked for regular fuse.

As usual the eight-inch guns were the first to respond. As soon as they told me "shot" I notified the commander on the ground.

My pilot Al Guess posing next to an eight-inch gun. The mountains look west to Laos.

"Sterling Dancer 12, this is Red Baron 36. Shot. Get your people down. Over."

"Red Baron 36, this is Sterling Dancer 12. Roger. Over."

My first conservative target area was about 400 yards from the village. The rounds landed a little bit to the north. I gave a correction to the eight-inch guns so I could slowly walk the rounds closer to our troops. Meanwhile the 155s fired their first shot along the northeast flank. The two rounds were about 300 yards from our closest troops. I moved the next rounds to the left several hundred yards and brought them another 100 yards closer to the line.

The 105 battery was the last to respond. Their rounds were the farthest off. I began walking them in.

I knew this was an artillery aerial observer's dream. I had complete clearance, three different batteries up and firing, and troops on the ground depending on what we could do. Not only would I be keeping them alive, but they could later give an accurate account of the damage I was inflicting.

The thought of having a verifiable body count made it all the more perfect. All I had to do was make sure that our Bird Dog didn't get hit by the rounds I was shooting, and that I didn't hit any of our troops.

Keeping our Bird Dog safe was a little more difficult than normal. With three batteries firing from different locations, we had to stay out of different quadrants in the air as each battery fired.

I had the three batteries on separate switches on my radio and the infantry on the fourth. I monitored all, pushing the appropriate switch when I needed to speak with each.

I had never been on the ground when an eight-inch shell landed. I wondered what the concussion was like.

For the next hour all three batteries fired at targets the infantry gave me in the village and the surrounding areas. I walked artillery up and down the infantry line and moved it in and out of the tree line and hooches. We had several direct hits on the huts and a secondary explosion or two. With three artillery batteries going at once, as soon as I made one adjustment, a round from another battery would arrive. It was a continual barrage of artillery using every different fuse I could think of.

After about an hour of steady firing, the troops on the ground said I had done enough and that they were ready to move in. I told the three batteries "end of mission."

Then I reported to the infantry.

"Sterling Dancer 12, this is Red Baron 36. End of mission on the redleg. I hope we got everything that there was to get. At least you shouldn't have to worry about any booby traps on the rest of your march. Over."

"Red Baron 36, this is Sterling Dancer 12. That was so great. If there was anything there before, it isn't there anymore. We'll let you know if we get any body count. Out."

As the adrenaline subsided, I realized that this had to be the ultimate aerial observer fire mission. I had a fleeting thought, however, of the possibility that there might have been families in the huts. I wiped it away by remembering my own fear of booby traps, ambushes and being on the ground during a fire fight. I was just doing what the Army had trained me to do. In that vein, I felt that I had done as well as I could. Out of the destruction, eager to write our report, my pilot and I flew off, hoping later to hear about any body count.

THE STAIN OF THE MY LAI massacre haunted the Americal Division throughout 1970 and 1971. In Chu Lai, we began to hear rumors that the Army was deciding how to try to upgrade the image of its largest division in I Corps. Some said that the Americal Division would pack up its colors and withdraw those who were "short" to the US. Others said the division would make a cosmetic change, reverting to its historic name: the 23rd Infantry Division. Of course I was rooting they would bring us all home, or at least those who had served a good portion of their tour. In a March 14 letter home I wrote:

"Rumors are once again flying that the Americal is going home. If it does within the next two months maybe I'll come home with it. I could really go for that. Anyway they are collecting info on everyone's DEROS and ETS [estimated termination of service] and how long they have been in the field. Looks like they're wondering where to put us."

Sure enough, in March 1971 the Army took the cosmetic route: the Americal colors were struck and the 23rd Infantry Division colors were raised over Chu Lai. But those of us who had hoped to be pulled out were disappointed. The only thing different was the name of the division. Nothing else changed.

BECAUSE I HAD ACCUMULATED LEAVE TIME from before
I left the U.S., I had a second chance to put the war aside for a week. On
March 17 I flew by transport to Saigon hoping to hop a chartered flight
to Hong Kong. I was entitled to the leave, and I was determined to take it
because, among other things, it counted as days before my DEROS. I was
eager to see my friends in Hong Kong and, fortunately, my OCS buddy
Ralph Oser was going to be there with his wife, Katherine, the same week.

The R&R center in Saigon was much more elaborate than the facilities
in Da Nang, although not as cushy. I got a few glimpses of the city, but
because of places where U.S. servicemen congregated when they were off
post were bomb targets, I elected mostly to hide out in the relative safety
of the R&R center.

On March 18, I got a standby seat to Hong Kong on a chartered flight.
It was a much shorter flight than the one to Honolulu. I met up Brenda
Randolf, and we found a room at a nice hotel in Kowloon.

Brenda and I did lots of shopping and sightseeing with Ralph and
Katherine. And my friends the Soong family, whose son John was my
roommate for two years in high school, and with whom I had spent the
summer of 1964, wined and dined us at some fabulous restaurants. Even
though I was beginning to feel "short" as to my Vietnam tour, and therefore

much more hopeful about surviving, I again avoided discussing what was happening to me and what I'd been through.

After a wonderful six days of delicious food, shopping and scenic sights in a fabulous city with good friends, reluctantly I boarded another standby flight back to Saigon on March 24.

SOON AFTER I RETURNED TO CHU Lai from Hong Kong, the Red Barons were involved in another tragedy, this one infamous in the annals of the Vietnam War. On March 28 Captain Rocamora awakened me shortly after 2:30 a.m. He told me he wanted me in the air as soon as possible heading northwest toward Firebase Mary Ann. As I grabbed my gear, he told me that Viet Cong sappers had overrun Firebase Mary Ann a few minutes earlier. Division artillery wanted a Red Baron in the air as soon as possible.

"I know there's not much you can do until dawn," he said, "but they want a Red Baron out there anyway."

I had flown over Firebase Mary Ann many times. The most western of the firebases in the division, Mary Ann was on a saddle in the middle of rice paddies and jungle in the western foothills. As a Red Baron, I had fired the guns from Mary Ann a couple of times for missions in the mountains. In general, it appeared to be in a very quiet area.

By the time I was in the air I had more details. VC sappers had sneaked within the perimeter and set off satchel charges in the firebase's guard bunkers. Then the sappers had literally overrun the firebase from the south end to the north, killing our soldiers as they went. Artillery "gun bunnies" had engaged the enemy in direct fire with the two 155 mm howitzers. Direct fire comes into play only when an artillery position is overrun. The

232

sappers had swept across the firebase and then exited at the north end after destroying pretty much everything on Mary Ann. The only area left intact was the northeast section of the firebase, where a contingent of ARVN— South Vietnamese Army soldiers—had a small compound. They had left the ARVN untouched.

It was still pitch dark when I arrived over Mary Ann, at about 4:15 a.m. I could see fires burning within the firebase's perimeter. From what I heard over the radio, the fighting on the base had subsided. In the Bird Dog, we could only get within a couple miles of the Mary Ann because of artillery being fired randomly in the dark from the other nearby fire bases. At least one Nighthawk helicopter was engaging targets on the ground to the north of Mary Ann with the use of its searchlights. I couldn't adjust artillery because, no matter how low we flew, in the dark I couldn't see much on the ground.

After about two hours, the sunlight began to reveal the scene below. As I first could discern specific objects on Mary Ann, I saw smoke rising from the burned-out holes of what was left of the bunkers. As the sky grew lighter, I could see that the firebase appeared deserted. Casualty reports were spotty, although most assumed a heavy loss. An armored unit and some infantry were supposedly on their way, but wouldn't arrive until at least midday. Mary Ann looked eerily desolate.

We had less than an hour of fuel left in our Bird Dog. Flying in increasingly larger circles, we looked for any movement on the ground that we might shoot at. There was nothing recognizable as enemy activity. Division Artillery suggested that we fire in the direction that reports said the sappers had been going. I called for rounds aimed at what looked like trails but didn't have any idea whether that was doing any good. Finally, around 6:30 a.m., I was relieved by the next Red Baron and, low on fuel, my pilot and I headed back to Chu Lai.

Back at Division Artillery Headquarters, rumors flew as I filed my report. Mary Ann had been home to over 250 U.S. troops. At that moment the casualties were estimated at least 30 U.S. soldiers killed and as many as 100 wounded. I reported that I had not seen any signs of life on the firebase, and that I could not raise anyone from its artillery battery on the radio.

Division Artillery staff told me that security at Mary Ann had been a concern in recent weeks. Apparently, Mary Ann had not seen any action for at least six months. The U.S. soldiers had become lax. This was exacerbated by reports, generally known by the men on the base, that U.S. forces would soon be pulled from Mary Ann because it had been so quiet.

Based on my experience at Firebase 411, I could imagine what had happened. Mary Ann was so far west that it offered no diversions, like the ones we had on Firebase 411, which was near Quang Ngai. Boredom can envelop a firebase and put everyone off his guard. And if Mary Ann had a drug problem, as did some of the other firebases, inaction might have led to stoned soldiers on guard duty night after night. In such circumstances, the claymore mines and other perimeter defensive tools that deter sappers could become neglected.

I reported that the ARVN section of the hill appeared to be unscathed. This brought a uniform reaction. We surmised that some sort of deal, whether explicit or implicit, had been struck. The ARVN would be left alone if they didn't interfere. I even speculated that the sappers had entered through the ARVN section of the perimeter. However it had been done, the ARVN had not lost any soldiers.

When I was in the field with Charlie Company, Firebase 411 had seemed like a haven to me. It was comparatively safe, and even luxurious when with conditions in the field, where we were exposed to attack at all hours, with foxholes our only shelter. I tried to imagine the Viet Cong storming 411's perimeter. If Charlie Company had been on the hill, at least we would have been able to call on 50 or more combat tested troops. But a single infantry company alone could not have been terribly effective to defend an entire firebase. We would have been spread too thin around the perimeter, and we would not have received much support from those who never left the hill, which included the infantry battalion staff including radio operators, clerks and cooks, who stayed on their firebase throughout their tours. I expected the same would have been true of the artillery gun bunnies and staff.

During the times I had been on Firebase 411, we never had a full-scale training exercise to show anyone how to withstand a full-frontal attack. I assumed there must have been one at some point, but in general the atmosphere on Firebase 411 was one of invincibility despite a few stray rockets or mortar rounds. I remembered how, when we arrived on the base after two or three weeks in the field, it felt like such a relief to be safely there, and that most of our company either got drunk or stoned during portions of the days and nights we were pulling perimeter guard on the hill. I knew, from seeing them, that the ARVN on 411 would no more have fought with us than had those on Mary Ann. At least when we were on 411 we had worked, during the day, to make sure that the wire, mines and booby traps around the perimeter were properly in place and functioning. But if we had been told that we'd soon be pulling out, I'm sure the efforts to guard the hill would have lagged. I wondered how many of those who died on Mary Ann had been "short"—within a few weeks of leaving.

Rumor had it that the 23rd Infantry Division commander, and thus the ultimate person in command of the firebase at the time, would lose his anticipated promotion. A few months later he was relieved of his command. He retired soon thereafter.

APRIL 1971

I mentioned Firebase Mary Ann in a letter home dated April 8:

"We had a bad last two weeks with rocket attacks and several fire bases hit. You probably read about the big fiasco out at Mary Ann. It was the worst beating we've taken in a long time. Heads will roll somewhere in the 23rd Infantry Division."

I also wrote about Mary Ann in a letter dated April 17:

"I suppose you all read about the "Mary Ann Massacre" in Time. There's quite a big investigation going on right now. Four of us flew artillery support for it as soon as it was light enough, but by then it was too late. It's all a problem of people being lax since little happens for months here. The whole bunker line was probably asleep."

IN THE FIRST WEEK OF APRIL, I wrote home that I had learned that orders had been "cut" for me to leave South Vietnam on June 11. I would stop flying on June 4 and leave Chu Lai on June 8. As I wrote on April 8:

"So the time is getting short. Of course it just makes me more anxious and generally uncomfortable since it looks like such a short time"

On an afternoon mission one day to the north of Chu Lai we flew over an area just south of Da Nang. There, for the first time, I recognized hills where the chemical defoliant Agent Orange had been sprayed.

Area defoliated by Agent Orange.

The look was quite distinctive. The herbicide not only defoliated all vegetation where it landed, but also contaminated all the rivers and streams into which it was washed by rain and runoff. The surface looked a little like Mars, except that the red clay revealed by the loss of vegetation also appeared vaguely to resemble the Grand Canyon. None of us knew what effect Agent Orange would have on the local people, as it polluted the watercourses flowing through the villages and cities toward the ocean, or what damage it might cause us and others who were living along the coast.

Smitty and I were searching for a target we'd located in a valley in the foothills a few weeks earlier. We had seen a couple of enemy soldiers with packs. When they spotted our plane, they disappeared into what must have been a tunnel. At that time we had not received clearance to fire. This was a first opportunity to follow up.

We never got there this time either. Instead, Division Artillery ordered us to fly to and adjust fire onto an "intelligence" target. They sent me the encoded grid coordinates, and, after I decoded it using my kak wheel, we headed for the location.

When we got there, we were several kilometers east of the mountains. The grid location was on a plain near a river. Circling the area, as we pinned down the exact coordinates on the ground, we saw it was the center of a small village with about 10 thatched-roof huts. A couple of small boys were leading a water buffalo from the rice paddies into the village. As we took a low pass, we could see a number of women and children in the square but no signs of adult males. I called back on the radio to Division Artillery.

"Tony Ports 24, this is Red Baron 36. We are over the grid location of your intelligence target, over."

"Red Baron 36, this is Tony Ports 24, what do you see, over."

"Tony Ports 24, this is Red Baron 36, we can see a small village with approximately 10 buildings. We took a low pass and can't see anything but a few old women, some children and a few farm animals. Over."

"Red Baron 36, this is Tony Ports 24, we'll get right back to you. Over."

As we waited for the response, I wondered how they'd come up with this as an intelligence target. Chances were that some agent had reported that a Viet Cong or NVA unit was operating out of the town and perhaps there were radios and arms in some of those huts. Nevertheless, it was in a no-fire area, and I couldn't believe that Division Artillery had received clearance to fire there. The way they operated, they wouldn't have known that it was a village until I told them. I figured my report would end the matter, because these intelligence targets didn't often pan out anyway.

"Red Baron 36, this is Tony Ports 24. Over." The voice that came back on was not that of the RTO I'd spoken to previously, but clearly that of a senior officer, which meant a major or lieutenant colonel in charge of these intelligence targets. He sounded a little bit miffed and had clearly been put out by my report.

"We've got an A-4 intelligence report on this spot. We understand that there are going to be bad people there who we want to get. We're firing a first round and you should adjust onto the coordinates. Over."

A-4? That was about as lousy a grade of intelligence as you could find. I'd been checking the results of artillery firing on A-4 targets on the 6 a.m. missions for several months now. None of them ever uncovered a blessed thing. Moreover, by its classification, this was obviously fourth or even fifth-hand information.

I knew what would happen if we suddenly put six rounds of 155-mm howitzer artillery on top of this village. Nothing would be left.

"Tony Ports 24, this is Red Baron 36. We've still got a large number of women and children in the center of this village. I don't see any hostiles at all and no signs of anyone with packs or weapons. Are you sure of your clearances? Over."

"Red Baron 36, this is Tony Ports 24. Listen to me. We've already got clearance to fire on this target. I want you to adjust it onto the grid location. Over."

"Tony Ports 24, this is Red Baron 36. The coordinates you gave me put it right in the center of this town. There are people walking around, most of whom are children. Over."

"Red Baron 36, this is Tony Ports 24." His voice was now crackling with indignation. "We're going to fire a first round in about 30 seconds. You adjust that artillery onto the location. Over."

I tried to anticipate what would happen to me if I refused. If I refused the order to adjust onto the target, I could expect a major investigation or, potentially, a court-martial. By the same token, if we blew up women and children, and I was the one who directed the fire on them, I knew that, the Army would go after me rather than those who couldn't see who and what we were firing on. I decided I just couldn't adjust fire onto women and children.

"Tony Ports 24, this is Red Baron 36. I repeat, there are women and children at the coordinates you have given me. There are no signs of any NVA or Viet Cong. The center of the coordinates is a small village. Over."

"Red Baron 36, this is Tony Ports 24. The first round is going to land in another 30 seconds. Adjust from it onto the coordinates. Over."

"Tony Ports 24, this is Red Baron 36. I can't stop you firing, but I'm not going to adjust it. Over."

"Red Baron 36, this is Tony Ports 24. Shot. Over."

I knew it would take about 15 seconds for the first round to land. I felt helpless. I could only hope that the round would land somewhere off center of the target, as was usually the case.

"Red Baron 36, this is Tony Ports 24. Splash. Over." It was the voice of the RTO. He sounded quite frightened.

I looked for the familiar sight of dust rising from an explosion. The round landed less than 100 meters to the north of the village, in a rice paddy.

It sent the village inhabitants into a state of frenzy as they ran into their houses. They must have had dugout shelters or tunnels inside their hooches to protect them from bombing and artillery. I couldn't tell whether anyone had been hit. I waited.

"Red Baron 36, this is Tony Ports 24." It was the voice of the officer. "What are your adjustments? Over."

"Tony Ports 24, this is Red Baron 36. All I'm going to say is you missed the center of town. Over."

"Red Baron 36, this is Tony Ports 24. Send us your adjustment immediately. Over."

I hesitated for a moment, trying to decide what I should do. After about 15 seconds, I said: "Tony Ports 24, this is Red Baron 36. Negative. I'm not adjusting. Over."

"Red Baron 36, this is Tony Ports 24. I want you to report to me when you get back. Over."

I asked Smitty to fly by the area to see if we could see anything else. He put the plane into a steep dive and we buzzed the area. I got a glimpse of what looked like a wounded water buffalo and boy about 10 years old.

"Red Baron 36, this is Tony Ports 24." It was the RTO again. "Shot. Over."

I guessed that they were firing all six guns in the battery at the same location they had fired the earlier ones because I had given them no adjustment. I watched the ground as word came over the radio: "Splash."

The ground exploded into smoke but we saw no one. Six rounds landed a few meters to the northeast of the town.

But then, to my surprise, I heard a voice say: "Red Baron 36, this is Tony Ports 24." It was the RTO again. "We're ending this fire mission. Over."

"Tony Ports 24, this is Red Baron 36. Roger, out."

"Well," Smitty said to me through his headset, "I wonder what's going to happen now."

"Really, I wonder," I said. I figured I was in deep trouble; at least I would be ordered back to the field as a forward observer within the next couple of days. But if I had agreed to adjust artillery onto the target, I wondered whether I would have been tried for murder like Lieutenant Calley.

As I put my .45 into my locker back at the Red Baron headquarters, Rusty Danielson came running up.

"Did you hear what happened?"

"About what?"

"That intelligence target they asked you to shoot at."

"Yeah, I refused to adjust onto it."

"Well, you're lucky you refused. Apparently that town is the headquarters for some district chief. We don't know how they got clearance to fire there, but apparently the first round killed two kids. It took the district chief about two minutes to get through to Division Artillery to tell them to call off the mission. Now they've started an investigation to determine who's at fault for firing on the village."

"God, lucky for me," I said. "I refused to adjust." Inside, I was both horrified and jubilant. I could never have received clearance to fire there, and I was sure I had seen the kid who died. But I also hoped that they were going to pin this one on that Division Artillery officer who wouldn't listen to what I was reporting from the scene. And I hoped they got him instead of me.

"You'd better talk to Captain Rocamora."

Captain Rocamora had also heard about the incident. I gave him a full account. I told him I'd been ordered to report to the Division Artillery Executive Officer to tell my version. His reaction was sobering.

"Don't go and see him," Captain Rocamora said. "I'll tell them that I told you not to talk to anyone and to wait for the investigation. You better write down your version of what happened right away. It might take a couple of days before they get to you."

"I'm not worried," I said, although I didn't really feel that way. "I've got a witness. Smitty was in the plane with me and he saw and heard the whole thing over the radio."

"Well just in case, you'd better write it all down in your report."

I got in touch with Smitty immediately to let him know he'd be called to back me up.

I found out the next day that I would be interviewed by an investigating officer, a major in the Judge Advocate General Corps, at 4 p.m. the following day. My first instinct was to demand a lawyer. But I knew that doing so would make me even more suspect. I figured that with what legal training I had, and because I wasn't going to say anything that would hang me anyway, I'd take a chance at this point by going it alone. Anyway, I suspected that any legal help the Army would give me wouldn't be much help at all.

My interview was in a conference room at Division Artillery headquarters. The major appeared to be about 35 years old. He had tailored, highly starched jungle fatigues with spit-shined boots. He read me the military version of my rights, then asked if I had made a written account of the events.

I told him I had. He asked for it, and I let him read it. When he finished, he looked up at me. "You know what the Division Artillery Executive Officer says, don't you?"

"No."

"He says you told him that it was clear to fire."

"Son of a bitch," I said. "That's a lie." I tried to keep calm.

"When I got to the grid coordinates they gave me, I saw that it was a village with women and children. That's what I reported. After the first rounds came out, they said they wanted me to adjust onto the target anyway. I refused, and again reported the women and children and no hostiles. At the time, I thought I was going to be court-martialed because

I refused his order to adjust. He's just lucky I did refuse. Otherwise we would have wiped out the whole village."

"Have you got anyone to back up your story?"

"Sure. My pilot. He'll tell you the same thing I told you." I gave him Smitty's name and rank.

"Yeah. Well then, his neck's in a noose too. Of course he'll back you up. By the way, you're grounded until further notice."

During the next couple of days I had a curious sense of detachment, mixed with outrage. I had no confidence that the Army would conduct an impartial investigation. But in going over the events, I knew that a few facts supported my version of events. First, no adjustment would appear on the records of the fire direction control center. So no one could claim that I had adjusted fire onto the target. Second, the rounds that landed hadn't actually hit the village. If they had been adjusted, the village likely would have been obliterated. Third, I had a witness, Smitty, who had heard and seen the whole episode and would back me up. And there was some solace, at least for the moment, that I was no longer flying.

I tried to imagine what type of person, particularly an officer, could lie so blatantly. It didn't really surprise me, however. From Division Artillery headquarters in Chu Lai, firing howitzers was not much different from firing training missions back in Fort Sill, Oklahoma. All the targets were imaginary. This officer likely never saw the damage from any of the artillery rounds fired in this war. He probably never had to look at anyone dying or at anyone's home being destroyed. He probably didn't worry about a massacre he couldn't see. This year in Vietnam would go on his record as "combat" time and "leadership" time. Being in a shooting war would be a great addition to his military resume.

Now, suddenly, his career might be on the line. And all because of a couple of dead Vietnamese kids. The only Vietnamese he'd ever had to look in the eye were his hooch maid and the mess hall boys. Anyway, he'd been given the target by military intelligence. It wasn't his idea to fire on that spot.

I was an obstacle he faced. He could say that the mission included an adjustment since the guns had fired twice and they had resulted in some kills. And six rounds were fired after the ranging rounds. He knew Smitty and I would not back him up. So he might as well go for the throat—my throat.

For me, I didn't have to fly any missions during the investigation. With any luck, it would drag on for weeks. The days went slower, but I didn't miss flying over the jungle or the mountains trusting that a 20 plus-year-old airplane wouldn't fall out of the sky.

If it had been a couple of years earlier, such as during my first year in law school, I would have been horrified that my version of the story was being doubted. But a few weeks after I was forced to leave school behind, I was a buck private in U.S. Army basic training without my constitutional rights. I had been stripped of all decency and dignity in the name of being trained to fight a war that I didn't believe in, and that we had already lost.

Illegal search and seizure? In basic training, they tore open our foot lockers daily to see if we had any contraband candy. Unlawful detention? I had no right to be anywhere or to do anything other than what they told me to do. Cruel and unusual punishment? I had been sentenced to a year of potential death at worst, or maiming perhaps, for the crime of being the oldest undrafted male in my draft board. Equal protection? The majority of those who were serving with me were young men of color. Due process? Tell that to Ed when he was sentenced to the field by a battery commander who based that decision on Ed's race. Trial by jury of your peers? Not in the Army. I assumed that any trial would be before a panel of lifer officers and NCOs whose main concern, like those who prosecuted Lt. Calley, would be to cut their losses at the expense of the lowest ranking soldier.

My detachment then, like everything else, could be attributed to being numb. The relief of being out of the air, at least temporarily, was also a contributing factor. As long as no one sent me to the field while the investigation was pending, I was relatively safe.

But I still felt outrage. When I'd refused to fly in an Air Cav helicopter, I had challenged a judgment call. However ridiculous the decision to put us into those helicopters had been, it could arguably be supported. Here, on the other hand, there was no judgment involved. If I were to lose, the undeniable truth would be ignored. I was being called a liar by a superior who was really the one doing the lying.

For the next several days I did a lot of walking along the Chu Lai beach below Division Headquarters. I even spent a couple of afternoons at the surfer beach trying to work on my tan and clear up a bad case of what I concluded was a form of jungle rot on my back. It had broken out badly with pimples and sores that I was told was a form of fungus. In addition to applying medication, I tried to dry it out in the sun.

On the fourth day, I reported to Captain Rocamora, as he had ordered me to do. To my astonishment, he told me I was clear to fly again.

"What happened?"

"They've dropped the investigation of your actions."

"Do you know why?"

"An RTO at Division Artillery backed up what you and Smitty said. He told the investigators that you told them not to fire, and that you refused to adjust because you saw women and children at the target site and no one with packs and weapons."

I couldn't believe it. Some young enlisted man I didn't even know had saved me. I felt as if a weight had been lifted off my shoulders. But what about the lying SOB who tried to frame me?

"Is anything going to happen to the Major who ordered them to fire anyway and then lied about me refusing to adjust fire?"

"Not that I know of."

Just like the Army. *Asshole!* I thought to myself. I had escaped again, but this time only because of the honesty of an enlisted man I didn't know. I vowed to find out who he was and thank him.

The next afternoon I went to Division Artillery HQ and walked into the command post where all artillery missions were monitored. I asked if anyone knew the RTO who'd been questioned about the intelligence target that had killed some villagers. They pointed me to a Spec. 4 who was on duty in a line of RTOs. I approached him and told him who I was. I said I wanted to thank him for sticking his neck out for me by telling the truth.

He smiled and said: "No problem." Then he grinned again and went back to the fire mission he was working on. I never saw him again.

After all that, I still had to wonder: had I made the right choice in refusing to adjust? Had some dangerous Viet Cong or NVA leader been at that location who might have been killed with a full artillery barrage, but who would now live to plan the killing of more U.S. soldiers? I'll never know. But I've been able to sleep at night because of my decision to protect the women and children I did see, and who likely would have been killed had I adjusted artillery fire.

MOST NIGHTS THE RED BARONS GATHERED at the Division Officers' Club after dinner for the movie. The Division Officers' Club was the nicest club in Chu Lai, but it was also the most stuffy. Because the commanding general was likely to show up once a week or more, the place was kept clean and never became rowdy. It got the movies first and it always had plenty of seating. It was just a short walk from our hooches, and once all of us were safely on the ground each night, the Red Barons congregated there for drinks. Movies provided one of our few escapes. Because the temperature cooled off at dark, we were comfortable, and fairly safe. We saw a different movie each night, and depending on its quality, we greatly enjoyed the diversion.

The other "perk" that came with the Division Officers' Club was a floorshow each Saturday night. The Army hired rock'n'roll bands, mainly from the Philippines, to play for the troops, and this officers' club was on the itinerary. The bands were of varying quality, some decent, more often terrible. But there were a few constants.

One was that each band played its own extended version of Creedence Clearwater Revival's "Proud Mary." Whenever I hear that song now, it takes me back to their Philippine accented pronunciation of that classic as they sang: "Rollen on de Reeeeeber."

Another was that, for some unknown reason, each band's drummer would, at some point, launch into a drum solo. I wasn't a fan of drum solos, and I'm still not, but unaccountably, every band's drummer insisted on playing an extended, and I mean extended, drum solo. It got to the point that, when the evening's drum solo started, we would each guess how many minutes the drum solo would last and then time it. The Red Baron who came closest to guessing the correct number of minutes won a free drink from everyone at the table.

Perhaps most bizarrely, each band closed its show with a dramatic version (in pidgin English) of "Danny Boy." Why each band felt this was the required finale of a show for U.S. troops is anyone's guess. I assume the booking agent loved it and required it, or that it was the favorite song of the commander of U.S. forces. Whatever the reason, "Danny Boy" was always the last song. It never received much applause.

If a band agreed to play requests, the one song immediately requested was the Animals' song: "We Gotta Get Outta This Place." If the band knew it, and most of them did, the whole audience would be on its feet, yelling "Short! Short! Short!" instead of "Yeah! Yeah! Yeah!" before the first line of the chorus. Even in the stodgy Division Officers' Club, the sound was deafening.

IN APRIL, WHILE HANGING AROUND DIVISION Headquarters, we got the drift again that the command might send some Red Barons to participate in the offensive in Laos. The obvious target of this offensive was the Ho Chi Minh Trail and the North Vietnamese troop movements through the jungle just west of the Vietnamese/Laotian border.

I shuddered at the prospect of being a part of such an offensive. To begin with, it would be a face-to-face confrontation with the North Vietnamese Army regulars. I felt sure that there would be larger concentrations of NVA in Laos than Charlie Company had ever come up against off Firebase 411. And I expected the NVA might have weapons capable of shooting down an unarmed Bird Dog.

Additionally, the invasion would be into an area where our forces had no experience. We would have no well-laid-out and protected landing fields, no strategically located firebases with bunkers and no well-developed supply routes. By contrast, it was like home turf for the NVA, who knew the area well. As we sat around the officers' club each night, the Red Barons shared what we had heard of the planned invasion and tried to figure out what it might mean for each of us.

We soon learned that thousands of troops from the 23rd Infantry Division would be involved. Whole battalions of infantry, supported by artillery and with air support, would be pulled from their current positions and sent to take part in the invasion.

At the same time, I heard that the Red Barons were being considered for a different assignment. For some undisclosed reason, while Army units from I Corps were being deployed for the Laotian invasion, Marine units, whose A.O. had been the area from Da Nang north to the DMZ, were pulling out and leaving South Vietnam. This meant that the Army forces of the 23rd Infantry Division would take over the Marines' A.O. and would be even more thinly stretched than before. Captain Rocamora told us that one of the Red Barons would soon be assigned to fly out of Da Nang to support the Army troops in the area. He told us that whoever went would be flying two missions a day, every day.

That wasn't that much more than we had been doing for several weeks anyway. As I wrote home on April 22:

"The hours are once more beginning to increase as we lose people to the end of their tours. For some reason we don't seem to ever get any replacements. I suppose this may be part of the pull out, but they continue to increase the hours we must fly. It's all very much akin to Catch-22. The medical authorities have set limits on flying hours, but when we reach them they just raise the hours."

Ironically, and although I had no knowledge of the testimony at the time, the day after I wrote this letter, former Navy Lieutenant John Kerry testified before Congress as a member of Vietnam Veterans Against the War. In his remarks, Kerry famously said: "We are asking Americans to think about that because how do you ask a man to be the last man to die in Vietnam? How do you ask a man to be the last man to die for a mistake?"

In my own way, without knowing what Kerry had said, or how profound it was, or how influential he would later become, I was handicapping which assignment would keep me from being one of those last men. Should I try to stay in Chu Lai, while hoping not to be one of those sent to the Laotian venture? Or should I volunteer to go to Da Nang, and take my chances flying two missions a day. Although Da Nang was probably less "hot," it would likely almost double my flying time. Then again, I assumed that even those Red Barons who stayed in Chu Lai would have to pull some double-mission days in order to make up for those who went to Laos, and they might also be ordered west with the invasion.

The "choice" was a crapshoot, just another gamble that was a constant element of that war, or any war.

I volunteered to go to Da Nang. I'd be flying two missions a day, but I felt that would probably happen in Chu Lai anyway. Mostly, I wanted to avoid the Laotian invasion. No one had any idea how successful it would be, and I didn't want to take the chance of facing North Vietnamese anti-aircraft, which didn't exist in South Vietnam. The small-arms fire that we periodically encountered, and the helicopter crashes in our A.O. were bad enough. I didn't want to end up in an area where, if my plane went down, I was likely to fall on an enemy position.

MAY 1971

MY DIGS IN DA NANG WERE definitely a step up from Chu Lai. The Army had taken over an area where the Marine flyers had lived, which was next to the smaller of the two Da Nang military airports. It was within walking distance of the beach, and, as I came to learn, had all the amenities that the Marines, with their unbounded energy, could install. The officers' club, PX, movie theater, and steam baths were all handy and much more "stateside" than those in Chu Lai, and they had been built for the longer haul. The people I was bunking with, helicopter pilots in the main, had decorated their hooches with electronics from the PacEx mail-order catalogue. A 10 x 10 room would have stereo speakers with amplifiers capable of serving as the public-address system for a large nightclub. Most refreshing, virtually every hooch had a small air-conditioning unit.

Two things, however, remained the same for me: the Bird Dog I flew in and the pilots who flew it. The Army had simply moved two of our Chu Lai pilots and a Bird Dog to Da Nang. Within the first couple of days, we — the pilots and I — became familiar with the new A.O. Pilots were permitted to fly only one mission a day, so I flew with each of them on my daily two missions.

What I saw from my perch as an aerial observer, however, was frightening. It was hard to tell whether the Marines had done anything to thwart the enemy's movements in the area around Da Nang. The ground was literally honeycombed with tunnels, bunkers and signs of enemy activity. The Marines appeared mainly to have patrolled only the immediate vicinity of Da Nang. Targets were everywhere. In virtually any place I put a round, the ground would cave in, or I'd get a secondary explosion.

Putting aside the military situation, the scenery was spectacular. About 15 kilometers to the west of Da Nang, perched on a large tabletop mountain, were the remains of a lush French colonial plantation. While abandoned and bombed out, we could still see the outline of the gardens, swimming pools, main house and other amenities. The former inhabitants had also enjoyed an amazing view. To the east was the city of Da Nang, and beyond it the sandy beach and South China Sea. To the west were the jungle-clad mountains that stretched to Laos. And because the plantation was situated perhaps 1000 or more meters above the flatland, the climate must have been refreshingly cool compared with Da Nang, with its humidity and mosquitos.

To the north, approaching the DMZ, we saw rugged mountain terrain to the west that continued east to the South China Sea. The tiny valleys and lush vegetation were perfect as an NVA stronghold, and were within a 100 kilometers of the city of Da Nang. We spent hours in the Bird Dog following trails into that wilderness, seeing more and more signs of enemy construction and activity every day. But the tree canopy prevented us from observing what exactly was happening, and protected those below from our bombardment.

Da Nang itself, as Ralph Oser had shown me before I left for R&R, was like a small Saigon. I recognized buildings designed by the French, the more impressive of which were along the Han River, which flowed through the town, much like the Seine through Paris. Vehicle traffic consisted mainly of army vehicles, both U.S. and ARVN. There were a few old, dilapidated European cars, and thousands of motorcycles, scooters and bicycles. I could see that Da Nang had once been a picturesque colonial capital with tree lined streets and beautiful architecture. It was easy to imagine the French riding in rickshaws from their lunch clubs to the stately homes along the river quais or strolling along paths overlooking the South China Sea. Now, however, Da Nang was a dirty, noisy, partly bombed-out city under siege.

Da Nang was bordered on the east by what we called China Beach, a white sandy strip shaded by palm trees that easily could have been a tourist destination. The Marines had taken over most of the buildings along the beach, and it had become a place to kick back, drink tropical concoctions and try to get a tan. If only there had not been a war going on.

What was most overwhelming in Da Nang and its environs was the noise. It seemed that every 30 seconds another aircraft landed or took off from Da Nang Main airport and the smaller surrounding airfields. These aircraft included Boeing 707 Freedom Birds, Army and Marine cargo transport planes and, most ear-shattering, Air Force F-4 Phantoms. Rumor had it, and I half believed it, that Da Nang Main was among the busiest airports in the world.

Flying two missions a day, seven days a week, was more taxing than I had imagined. I began to wonder whether, even though I had avoided the Air Cav missions and would not be part of the Laotian invasion, I had made the wrong choice. After a week, I was physically exhausted. The pilots flying hours were limited. Unfortunately, there were no similar hour limitations for aerial observers. Not only did I have virtually no free time, but I was dead tired at the end of each day. Part of this stemmed from the emotional strain of wondering, each time I climbed into the airplane, whether it would remain airborne for a full three hours. Pilots tried to protect me as best they could, helping me with target location, not asking me to fly the plane much, and cutting the missions as short as they could.

We also made use of a number of diversions. We spent a lot more time above 2,000 meters, cooling off in the natural air-conditioning. We also devised excuses for flying around the Da Nang perimeter.

My favorite excuse came one morning when my pilot, Frank Savino, and I took off around 6 a.m. from one of the smaller Da Nang airfields. Both of us were sleepy eyed and groggy. As soon as we lifted off the ground, Frank said, "I really need some coffee badly. I know where we can get coffee and doughnuts. Want to try?"

Intrigued, I eagerly played along. "If it'll help you fly, Frank, I'm all for it."

"Well, it means we're going to have to land at Da Nang Main." That sounded ludicrous, but I said, "Why not?" Here we were, in an airplane that could fit inside most of the planes that landed at Da Nang Main. It was going to be like landing a Piper Cub at Chicago's O'Hare. We could have landed cross-ways on the runway and had room to spare.

Frank got on the radio to the Da Nang Main control tower and asked for permission to land. The air controller, probably a Spec-4, knew from our call letters that we were a Bird Dog. He seemed amused. Nevertheless, he gave us permission to land, and we got in line for landing with all of the 707s and F-4s.

When our turn came up, Frank took a rather broad turn and we started in from the north. Rather than slowing down, as we usually did before coming into land, Frank had the throttle on full. I suspected that he must have been embarrassed about coming in on such a large runway, over a kilometer long, and that he was trying to build up speed so that our landing would take as much of the runway as possible. The Bird Dog was literally shuddering as we came approached at probably 20 or 30 knots faster than our normal air speed.

We overflew the first half of the runway. Frank didn't want to land right at the start of the runway and then have to taxi its full length to get into the parking area. With the ground rushing below us, I wondered whether or not the tires would hold up at such velocity. We hit the ground and careened along as I desperately held onto the side of the airplane to keep my head from hitting the top of the canopy. Suddenly, in front of us was a cable used for slowing fighter planes as they landed, similar to what you see on an aircraft carrier. It was used in emergencies when F-4's came in too fast.

The cable was probably about three or four inches in diameter and when our Bird Dog hit it we almost flipped.

The air traffic controller turned us over to the traffic director on the ground. Frank and I figured we'd set records for the smallest airplane ever to land at Da Nang Main and for the longest taxiing by a Bird Dog. Sheepishly, we pulled over to the terminal and walked in to find the doughnut shop. Mission accomplished.

After two weeks, Division Artillery sent a captain to see how I was doing. He told me the news that two Red Barons had been sent to the Laotian invasion. The rest were flying double missions every day. So far we'd had no casualties. He looked enviously at the surroundings in the former Marines airmen's hooches. I should have realized that would not be the end.

Sure enough, within 24 hours of his return to Chu Lai, I was ordered to move myself and my gear to the infantry division headquarters west of the city, about three-quarters of an hour's ride by Jeep from the airport. I called to complain.

It didn't do any good. Division Artillery was not about to allow one of its observers to live with the fixed-wing pilots. My bosses wanted total control over me, even if it meant close to an hour's commute to the airstrip for me each way each day. I was told to report to the infantry Division Headquarters village for a new bunk assignment.

Infantry Division Headquarters in Da Nang was very much like Chu Lai. The buildings were temporary cardboard shacks with screens. Located conveniently along almost all the pathways were piss tubes. A piss tube was literally that: a two inch in diameter pipe sticking out of the ground about two and half feet high with a screen secured around the top. Around the base were pebbles. If you wanted to relieve yourself, you just stopped at a piss tube and peed. The smell was terrible.

There was a beat-up mess hall and a command center. I quickly made friends with a captain in the medical corps from Philadelphia. Since there were few infantry people around, I asked him what his job was. He told me that he mainly inspected piss tubes. He also supervised the Vietnamese laborers who burned excrement they removed from the latrines using bunker oil. It was quite a comedown for someone who had only recently finished medical training at one of the best medical schools in the nation.

One positive note about changing my bunk to the Division HQ: I got to attend a Marine Officers' club Saturday night party before all of the Marines pulled out.

The contrast between the Marine Officers' Club and the Division Headquarters Officer's club at Chu Lai was stark. First of all, the Marine's Club was much more plushly decorated. Second, it was packed with loud, boisterous, laughing, hard-drinking Marines. They all seemed to be crazy, and all sported tailored camouflage jungle fatigues. These were much spiffier than the Army's version of the jungle fatigue.

The deafening noise in the club only increased when the floor show started. The Filippino band was typical of the ones I had seen in Chu Lai—inept and impossible to understand. But the audience reacted as though they were the Beatles. And when a female singer arrived on stage and started performing, the Marines raucously passed a hat around. Then they offered her more than $100 to her do a striptease. The place was bedlam for the entire evening. *Semper Fi!*

FOR THE NEXT SEVERAL WEEKS MY days consisted of two three-hour missions — one in the morning, a short lunch break and a second in the afternoon, plus my commute to and from the Army headquarters compound. I grew increasingly fatigued. But my daily routine, however stressful, helped the time pass. During what few hours I had off, time dragged interminably. Boredom seemed almost a worse enemy than the danger of a mission. We found so many targets to shoot at in relative close proximity to Da Nang that I didn't often venture into the mountains or over the jungle. I chose simpler and simpler targets: firing at anything I could rationalize as long as it kept me close to home base. At night, I watched whatever movie was shown, read books, and wrote as many letters as I could. I tried not to think about the fact that I was finally getting to be truly "short."

When a helicopter pilot was within two weeks of completing his tour, he was grounded. For that two-week period, he was feted and toasted in recognition of miraculously surviving his year tour. I saw a number of these pilots in a drunken stupor, stripped of their flight uniforms, looking around wildly, wondering what they were going to do with themselves now that the stress of flying was over. Out of danger, but not yet home, they existed in limbo, each day seeming longer than the next, with nothing to relieve their boredom.

The two flights on my last day as a Red Baron were agonizing. I tried to burn into my memory the little details of the cockpit, the sights below and the effect of the artillery destroying our targets. I also had an eerie, sinking feeling that, at the last minute, something would go wrong. When I finally felt the wheels bump on the runway after my last flight, I thought to myself: *"Holy shit, I may have made it!"*

JUNE 1971

ON JUNE 1, I HEADED BACK to Chu Lai for a week of processing. The Red Barons had been moved out of Division Headquarters and back to Division Artillery. I stayed within a few doors of the same hooch where, during one of my first few days, I'd almost been shot by an apparently berserk U.S. soldier. The newer Red Barons looked wistful as I slept in each day and spent the afternoon, in the heat and dust, going through paper processing at the personnel center. While I was relatively safe, the time dragged terribly.

With about three days to go I was told to report to the medals processing office. When I arrived I was given several forms to fill out in triplicate. The forms acknowledged that I was being awarded the Vietnamese Service Ribbon, a Bronze Star, a Purple Heart, an Aircraft Crewman's Badge and 15 Air Medals.

I had no idea whether 15 was the correct number of Air Medals An Air Medal is awarded for 50 hours of combat flying. I estimated the number of missions I had flown, multiplied that by three, and decided that it wasn't too far off.

After about two hours of waiting, as I was finally about to have my paperwork processed, suddenly the room was called to attention. Four junior and two field-grade officers burst in, and told everyone to make way for a one-star general. He entered in starched, tightly tailored jungle fatigues. He quickly marched to the head of the line. The lower ranking officers told the Spec-4 at the desk to help him fill out the papers. The general was not going to leave until he had received everything the Spec-4 could give him.

About 20 minutes later, the entire entourage left, and I finally presented my own paperwork. As the Spec-4 read through what I gave him, I asked him what had just happened. He told me that a general who had been in Vietnam about four months had just come through. The General had assiduously recorded each minute he had been in a helicopter taking him from one location to the next. Now, by his calculation, he had totaled 50 hours in the air. So he had marched in to secure an Air Medal for combat flying.

I looked at the paperwork for my 15 Air Medals and realized how meaningless it really was. I remembered how Captain Moran had put himself in for, and been awarded, the Silver Star for valor. I remembered how the infantry battalion commander had come out to the field after Charlie Company had taken such heavy casualties, and told us we had saved his career. I remembered how the chaplain had preached to us that those who died were going to heaven for fighting in this war.

I told the Spec-4 I didn't intend to wait around to get the actual medals. If the Army wanted me to have them, they could mail them to me at my address in the U.S.

I got drunk the night before I was to fly to Cam Ranh Bay, where everyone who had completed his tour got in line for a Freedom Bird home. All I could think about was that one last enemy rocket launched into Chu Lai might get me.

IN JUNE 8, I FLEW TO Cam Ranh Bay in a C-140 transport plane. I arrived in the evening and was given a bunk assignment in a large barracks. I was also directed to the Officers' Club.

With nothing else to do, I strolled down to the club to see if I could find anyone I knew. Inside were at least 10 of my OCS classmates. I should have known that a bunch of them would be processing out at the same time, given that many of us had flown to Vietnam on the say day. Ralph Oser was there. So was Bruce Buckalew. Paul Protz, Henry Love and a few others that I didn't know as well were also there.

The first thing we did was compare notes to see if anyone knew of any of our OCS classmates who had been killed. The best information the group had gathered was that Joe Thigpen had died. We suspected there might be more, but we had been so scattered that it was impossible to be certain.

In swapping experiences, I found that only a few of my OCS classmates had actually been in serious combat. Most had gone to units where it was the luck of the draw whether a newbie artillery lieutenant became a forward observer in the field or a fire direction control officer, or had an even safer rear job. Because the war had wound down in most of the south of South Vietnam, most of my classmates had had fairly mundane jobs during the year. Their main enemies had been boredom and malaria.

Bruce had seen some real action, but only for a short time. He had been assigned to an artillery survey company that spent time in the field surveying areas south of the DMZ. Bruce said that they had had to camp out while surveying, and once in a while ran into a firefight. But they had tried everything they could to stay out of the enemy's way.

Bruce also told me about his most harrowing experience. He was on his way to a survey location in a helicopter that went down. Because it was shortly before dusk, he and the pilot, neither of whom was injured, spent the night in the jungle. They decided that if they stayed near the helicopter, the NVA capture them during the night. Therefore, in the dark, they hacked their way several kilometers through the jungle and lay on the ground waiting to be shot or bitten by a snake. Bruce said he lay awake all night until dawn, and then he and the helicopter pilot sneaked back to the helicopter site. When they found no one around, they hid in the bushes hoping that a patrol sent to locate the helicopter would spot them. Around noon it did, and they were dusted off and brought home.

I asked what he thought about during that night. He told me he kept waiting to be caught and marched to Hanoi. He said he thought about shooting himself if he was about to be captured.

The next morning, I checked in to see if I had been able to land a seat on any Freedom Bird. I was told we wouldn't get a reservation for several days, maybe a week.

Several of us decided to go to the beach for a swim. It was beautiful beach, as picturesque as the ones in Chu Lai and Da Nang. Hundreds of G.I.'s were there, all in the same boat: waiting eagerly for a flight home.

We also walked around Cam Ranh Bay base to try to get a feel for how safe we were. It didn't seem to be under any guard, as if the surrounding land was a pacified area. I thought of Firebase Mary Ann and wondered whether the laxness here was just a result of somebody not paying attention.

During the wait in Cam Ranh Bay I tried to sleep as much as I could and went to the beach when I could. At night we sat around a big table at the Officers Club and tried to amuse each other. It wasn't easy. Every day we sat there was an extra day in Vietnam as well as, for most of us, an extra day in the Army.

Finally we were told that in two days we would board a Boeing 707 Freedom Bird for a flight home. We were to report to the airport 24 hours in advance to begin our final processing. As usual, we couldn't understand why processing was going to take 24 hours. But after three years of waiting in lines, I had given up trying to figure such things out.

Bruce and I did our final processing together. We received our final orders and our plane tickets. We got our health records checked and our luggage inspected. That took about 14 hours. Finally we were loaded onto trucks and driven to the airstrip, where we were told to line up in columns of two. Although this was the first time that, as an officer, I'd had to line up since arriving in Vietnam, I didn't think much about it, being overwhelmed by the anticipation of leaving and no longer suffering from the never-ending heat and humidity Soon, however, I found out what it was all about. They brought out a platoon of drug-sniffing German Shephard dogs to smell us and our duffle bags.

When the dogs finished smelling us and our belongings thoroughly, we were led to a barracks and told to deposit a urine sample they would use to check us for drug use. I noticed some fairly antsy enlisted men around me. I had heard that a number of soldiers, for a fee, would give anyone a drug-free urine sample. I wondered how those who were leaving were able to switch samples, after being separated from their base for a good 14 hours.

After the urine test, we waited for another two hours before being led to a remote area of the airstrip. Again, we and our belongings were sniffed by dogs. Then we were led back to the hangar to wait a few more hours.

I passed the time kibitzing with Bruce. I also ran into a medical corps doctor who had been a friend of Ralph Oser's in Da Nang. Now a major, he was on his way back to the United States and, like us, was about to process out of the Army forever.

At long last, we were told that our Freedom Bird had arrived, and we headed for the runway. Carrying our duffle bags and other belongings, we struggled toward the aircraft. On the tarmac we were lined up again with our luggage and given a final sniff by another group of German Shepherds. It was late afternoon when we took the first step up the gangway to the plane. I gleefully made note of my last step on Vietnamese soil.

Inside the plane, the mood of our group changed quickly to anticipation. Spirits suddenly rose as the engines started. I was seated between Bruce and the doctor. Sweltering in the plane before we took off and the air-conditioning system was turned on, we wondered whether we would be served any liquor on the flight back. I remembered that water and coffee were the only liquids available on the trip over.

Finally, the 707 taxied to the end of the runway, turned, accelerated and lifted off the ground. A raucous cheer arose from all of us in the plane. I kept saying to myself over and over again: *"I made it! Fuckin' A! I made it!"*

About two hours into the flight a soldier approached the doctor for what was the first of a steady stream of visits. A rather desperate looking E-4 came down the aisle, looked furtively in each direction, and leaned over to him.

"Hey, doc, I need something bad." I could see the sweat on his forehead and the pale, pasty look of his skin. His eyes were sunken.

"I don't have anything. You saw them sniff me too," the major said. I wasn't really sure what the soldier could have thought an Army doctor would have to give him on an airplane anyway. Where could he get a fix? The soldier returned to his seat, shuddering.

Within the hour he was back, as were several others. The doctor had to tell them again that he had nothing. He confided to me they wouldn't let him bring any medications with him because he was not on the plane to treat anyone. I began to wonder how many of the soldiers on the flight were addicted to drugs. I wondered how much they all would suffer during the 20 hour flight.

Our Freedom Bird had a layover in Guam for refueling. It was about 2 a.m. Guam time. Nevertheless, the duty-free shop was open for business when we arrived. The place became packed with soldiers spending their last few dollars on cameras, stereo equipment and watches. I wondered how much the shopkeeper had paid to get the airport franchise.

Guam looked like a tiny slab of rock in the middle of the Pacific. Its sole purpose seemed to be a site for a military base. I had heard lots of stories about the Marines who spent time on the island, and I wondered what they did for diversion. I assumed it was the same that the Marines did in Da Nang—got loud, drank a lot and visited prostitutes.

We re-boarded the plane about two hours after landing. The euphoria had worn off a little after hours sitting in cramped seats and as boredom overtook us. We were told we were destined for an Air Force base in Washington State, many hours away.

As usual, no one had told us what processing out would entail: how long it would take, what we would have to do, where we would stay. Accustomed to being left in the dark, and simply happy to be on my way to freedom, I drifted off to sleep. I wondered whether any of the addicts had been able to get a fix while we were on the ground. I assumed that such a need was universal on all freedom flights and that an industry must have cropped up to fill it.

TWELVE HOURS LATER WE LANDED AT McChord Field, an Air Force base near Seattle. As we piled off the Freedom Bird, we walked past a gamut of posters warning us that we had to go through customs, and that if anyone had contraband, including guns, drugs or pornography, he would be arrested. So much for welcome home! Under Army rules, we had not been allowed to tell our families exactly when we were leaving, or when we would arrive in the States, or where that would be, so no one was there to meet us. For the foreseeable future, we were also forbidden from calling our families.

I wondered why we needed to go through customs and a search of our belongings. Having had everything rifled through multiple times before we got on the plane, and having only been in an Army-controlled duty-free zone in Guam, there appeared no reason to search us again. Having nothing to hide, I stoically got in line. I noticed, however, that Bruce was a little bit fidgety. Each time we passed a sign warning us about contraband or pornography, he grew more edgy. Finally he turned around to me in the line and said, "Do you think they'll go through my bag?" I asked him why he asked. He told me he had a collection of pictures that he thought could land him in jail. I told him to get out of line, take the pictures out and dump them. He said he was sure they weren't going to check his bag.

We finally got to the head of the line. Bruce was in front of me. The customs agent grabbed Bruce's duffle bag, opened the top, reached in as if he knew exactly where to go, and pulled out a dozen pornographic 8x10s. He studied each one. Then he put them back into the duffle bag, stamped okay on the bag, and let Bruce through. I escorted my ashen-faced friend onto the bus.

We had landed at dawn. By the time the planeload cleared customs, it was about 8:30 a.m. A caravan of buses drove us to Fort Lewis, Washington. It was Saturday morning. I couldn't get over seeing a highway that was full of nonmilitary vehicles, of watching civilian after civilian, and seeing the peace and serenity of the Washington State countryside. About halfway through our bus trip the road took us by a golf course. There in the early morning dew was a foursome of middle-aged men using golf carts and preparing to tee off.

This sight overwhelmed me with bitterness. These men had been playing golf, I supposed, a couple times a week for the entire year, while my fellow soldiers and I had been at war. To me, these golfers appeared totally oblivious to what we had gone through, what was going on in Vietnam, and how their government was lying to them while sending us to fight and perhaps die in a losing war. To me, they were simply ignoring what their country was doing to us, and what we had been put through. How could they be playing golf, denying what was happening every day and every night while we were fighting for our lives?

When we arrived at Fort Lewis, a single E-4 greeted the caravan of buses. He took the enlisted men to a mess hall. He pointed out to the officers a PX area and some base restaurants. He told the officers to come back in an hour, telling us he would find us a place to sleep. He announced that all processing was halted for the weekend, and we could not begin to be checked out until Tuesday. He had no idea how long our processing would take.

Although we had finally arrived in the U.S., we had no U.S. currency, no civilian clothes, and no authorization to leave the post. We had not been permitted to have family or friends greet us, and now the Army told us that we were going to have to sit idly by for at least another 48 hours before we even knew how long it would take before we were set free. I thought back to the golfers I saw on the bus ride. They obviously weren't interested in us; I could only conclude that neither was anyone else.

We headed for lunch and a long, boring weekend. Fortunately, that afternoon we found a bank of pay phones near the PX, and we used them to call our families and alert them that we were safely back in the States. My family was thrilled, but of course they wanted to know when I'd be home. I had to tell them I had no idea.

Ironically, as we waited over the weekend at Fort Lewis, on Sunday, June 13 the *New York Times* published its first story revealing what was in the so-called "Pentagon Papers." The *Times'* revelations about the Vietnam War were not, of course, publicized to any of us in Fort Lewis. We were not alerted that the Pentagon Papers revealed that four Presidents had lied about the U.S.'s role in Vietnam from the late 1940's though the mid 1960's. Nor did the only newspaper we had access to, the *Army Times*, describe that in 1963 President Kennedy approved the assassination of South Vietnam's President Diem. We were not informed that, as early as 1965, the Pentagon had concluded that we were losing the war in Vietnam and couldn't win it. We did not hear on the nightly national TV news that, years before we were sent to fight, and perhaps to die, Secretary of Defense Robert McNamara had become convinced, but could not bring himself to tell the public, that the U.S. role in the war in Vietnam was a lost cause.

On Monday, June 14, we were informed that the officers would start their out-processing on Tuesday afternoon. All of the enlisted men would be processed first, which would take at least 24 hours.

By Wednesday morning we had completed most of our paperwork. We had two more hurdles: a physical exam and getting our paycheck.

On Thursday morning we were told to report to a medical clinic. We filled out numerous forms and received information on how long to continue taking our malaria pills. We were also given a cursory physical examination.

Finally, we were ushered into a room. A man in a white lab coat came in and handed each of us a form.

He explained that the form was a release of all Army liability for any injuries or illnesses that we had now or might develop as a result of being in Vietnam. He said that if we signed the release, we could leave Fort Lewis that day. If we did not sign the release, we would have to stay at the base for several more days for medical examinations to determine whether the government would be responsible for any long-term ailment, illness or disability. I signed the form without hesitation so I could get out of there. As I left, I received two months supply of pills they said I needed to take to prevent a delayed case of malaria.

Shortly after lunch, we went to the finance office for final pay. After another hour long wait, my last in the Army, I received a paycheck and was able to cash enough money to buy an airline ticket home. Then four of us took a cab to the airport. It was Thursday, June 17, 1971. My sentence was up. I was back in the U.S., and I was no longer on active duty in the Army. I was alive and free.

Epilogue

Needless to say, upon my return to the United States in June 1971, the war and the carnage on both sides in South Vietnam did not end. More than 2,000 additional U.S. soldiers died from June 1971 until the end of the war, and untold Vietnamese citizens, including Viet Cong, NVA and Vietnamese civilians, died as well. In December 1973, President Nixon ordered the Christmas bombing of North Vietnam in hopes of pushing the North Vietnamese government to peace talks. That failed. The Army continued to have troops in Vietnam until the fall of Saigon in 1975.

Soon after my return to the U.S. and release from the Army, I joined Vietnam Veterans Against the War. I marched with thousands of fellow Vietnam War veterans down Broadway in New York City in November 1971 to protest the war. Who knows whether it had any effect on Nixon and the Pentagon. But the solidarity I experienced with my fellow veterans was a real rush.

In early spring 1972, after I was back in New York at Columbia Law school, I was walking through a lounge in the Journalism Building when I ran into Carl Potz, a fellow soldier and friend of Ralph Oser's from Da Nang. We had a couple of meals together with Ralph during the middle of my tour, and I had also seen him in Cam Ranh Bay for a day or two before we left.

When I saw Potz I involuntarily shuddered, my pulse quickened and I felt sick to my stomach. I had been totally immersing myself in school, trying to catch up with my classmates for the past few months, and had tried to push what had happened to me and the rest of my fellow soldiers to the back of my mind. Seeing Potz, however, brought it all back.

We greeted each other and both had the same question: What happened to you when you first got home to your family?

He answered first. "I was able to stand it for about three or four days and then I walked out and went off by myself on a trip to the mountains for a couple of months."

"The same for me," I said. "I was home with my family about 48 hours when I couldn't stand it anymore. I called Bruce Buckalew, who was in the same boat, and we immediately walked out on our families and headed for California."

I learned it was a fairly common reaction. Many of us felt so alienated from our families and close friends that we couldn't relate to them. We assumed that they couldn't comprehend what we had experienced and didn't want to hear about it. They seemed more comfortable if we didn't talk about the war. Although they might have felt a twinge of concern, or guilt, about having a close relative or friend in danger, they couldn't change the war and what was happening to those who were dragged into it. The horror that we had gone through was something they assumed we wanted to put behind us. But in my mind, and I assume in the minds of many fellow veterans, the war was still going on, even though I was now home.

I remember that, during the first hours with my family, my mother told me several times how tough it had been on her and my father for me to be in Vietnam. She told me about all their friends being so thoughtful by asking them to dinner to take their minds off my being away in a war. I suppose her expression of the war's effect on her was understandable, but it only made me feel bitter and alone.

For two days after I arrived home I had tried to begin to describe what had happened to me and others. When I did, I had that same unpleasant physical reaction I had had in Honolulu when Connie asked me about the war: a quickened pulse, a sick stomach and an overwhelming feeling of dread. But I didn't have to go on because each time the reaction from my family was the same: let's not talk about it now. Let's talk about something else.

I spent two months that summer with Bruce Buckalew in California trying to recover from my fragile mental state and hoping to be in a better frame of mind when I went back to law school. Bruce and I talked very little about Vietnam. We drank a lot and, having moved in with Connie and her roommate, lived moment to moment. We didn't try to make friends or explore what we'd do in the future. We just existed in our own world, letting ourselves bask in freedom from the war, even though it was still hammering inside us. Bruce decided to head for Europe indefinitely in the fall. I was determined to head back to law school. Neither of us felt the need to make any long term plans.

I will be forever grateful for two gestures that impacted me shortly after my return, however. First, when I asked Columbia Law School if I could re-enter in September 1971 as a second year student, they told me that they had filled all the places in the second-year class. However, Columbia said it would make room for me, as they would do for other veterans who had been enrolled but then drafted, and they welcomed me back that fall. About 50 Vietnam veterans returned to Columbia Law that year. You could always tell us because, to keep warm in winter, we wore the green fatigue jackets the Army had allowed us to keep when we mustered out. So my graduating class in the spring of 1973 had around 350 students instead of the normal 300.

Second, when I applied for a summer "clerkship" with law firms in the fall of 1971, I was shunned by all but one: Curtis, Mallet-Prevost, Colt & Mosle. That law firm hired me at the demand of a partner who was a WWII veteran. He insisted that as a Vietnam vet, I be given a summer job over others with better first year law school grades.

I also remember driving from Pittsburgh to New York City for law school that fall. My mother, who was in the passenger seat, later told me that this was the happiest day of her life because I was back from the war and able to return to school. She wouldn't have understood the agony I was still going through. As we entered New York City on the interstate, a truck in front of us backfired. I almost drove us off the road as I looked around for incoming fire. I was overwhelmed by the bitterness of having almost lost my life so many times and having wasted three years to fight a war that was a lost cause. While I had been away, for many Americans, everything had gone on just as if I and my fellow soldiers didn't exist. To me it seemed the war that we had been sent to fight was an unpleasant fact that many Americans were able to sweep under the rug.

During those next several years, I suffered from what I assume was a form of post-traumatic stress disorder. The "whop-whop-whop" sound of a helicopter immediately brought back memories of Vietnam. When the subject of the Vietnam War came up in conversation, I could feel my blood pressure rising and I felt that sickened feeling in my stomach. I avoided movies and books about the Vietnam War, and I remember having to leave the theater during Oliver Stone's movie "Platoon." I didn't talk to other people about being in Vietnam unless they had been there themselves. I felt that being a veteran of that war labeled me as either a psychopathic killer or a dummy who couldn't avoid the draft. It wasn't fashionable to be a Vietnam veteran. It took many years, as I assessed it, for the country to begin to accept us as worthy veterans who had done their duty honorably.

In the '70s and early '80s the image of the Vietnam veteran portrayed on television and in the press was of a drug-addicted or crazy person who might suddenly flash back to 'Nam and begin shooting everyone in sight.

Our government's treatment of Black and brown soldiers in Vietnam altered my opinion on the death penalty. I was never strongly opposed to it before my tour. But after seeing how the Army discriminated against minority draftees, I became convinced that no branch of the U.S. government could be trusted to make a fair and unbiased decision about who should live or die.

I also felt bitter that those in power, and particularly those in Congress, had shielded their sons from serving in harm's way. Only one son of a member of the House of Representatives or the U.S. Senate served in the Vietnam war. That son was Al Gore. Every other senator or congressman in office during the Vietnam war managed to keep their sons safely away from serving in Vietnam.

Two events suggest how long it took for me to recover from the war. The first was 10 years later, in January 1981, when I watched the news of Iran's release of the 52 American hostages. The media and politicians portrayed it as a great victory and homecoming. Yellow ribbons adorned the trees and buildings on the route the hostages took to the White House as well as to their homes elsewhere in the country. Cheering throngs met them every step of the way.

I watched in anguish. Certainly the hostages had been through an ordeal. Their lives had been in grave danger for more than a year. But it had been a quirk of fate; no one had knowingly sent them into captivity. Hadn't we, who had been drafted and dispatched by our country to fight, and possibly to die, in a war that our country had lost, deserved at least as much of a celebration when we returned? Why were there no ribbons on trees and bands playing and crowds cheering for us? I flashed back to the men I saw playing golf as we rode from McChord AFB to Fort Lewis when our Freedom Bird arrived back in the U.S. Those men symbolized, in my mind, what my country thought of our homecoming.

The second event happened in November 1982. That night a TV newscaster reported the dedication of the Vietnam Veterans Memorial in Washington, D.C. The report showed the wall with all the names of my fellow soldiers who had died. The reporter described the ceremony and commented on all the Vietnam veterans who had attended and paid homage to their buddies. I broke down and wept.

End

Appendix: Letters Home

3:00 PM 7 AUG 70

Dear Family,

I'm sitting in Ben Hoa Airport about to be shipped to Chu Lai where I'm assigned to the I Corps with the Americal Division. It will probably be several days before I get to my unit because of orientations.

The Pearsons, my date & I partied non-stop for three days around S.F. managing about 5 hours of sleep total. My date was a nurse who works near Palo Alto and went to Ohio State. Nevertheless, we had a good time. Chuck drove me to Travis AFB on Tuesday morning where I met six others from class 16 including Ralph Cox, one of my favorite people. We took off at noon for the 20 hour flight — all in daylight since we were flying west. Stops in Anchorage and Japan were enough to tire us out. Airlift International is not a company to buy stock in: all they had for beverages was coffee and water. We got to Ben Hoa at 1:30 AM yesterday and went immediately to Long Binh to be billeted at the 90th Replacement Bn.

Ralph and I got our jungle fatigues etc during the day and I located Peter Bacon. We spent all afternoon in the officers club trying to drown our sorrow at being sent north instead of staying around Saigon. Peter is safe and relatively comfortable in his own trailer and expects to go to Law School fall of '71. We hashed over all events since the Harvard game of '68 and retired at 9:30.

At 1:00 AM we were awakened to ship out on a 6:15 flight. Leave it to the Army to make sure you're on time. So far the heat & humidity have been bearable but somewhat oppressive in mid-afternoon. Conditions are horribly primitive, especially for the enlisted men. Everyone acts somewhat jumpy but tries to make light of the whole

285

situation. Ralph and I have asked each other about a hundred times what we're doing here and to no great effect. At least we're officers and the treatment is good. My jungle fatigues fit like a tent but they're cool.

The vacation was so great it may take me awhile to adjust. Everything went so well that it's a real letdown to stop it. At least I have plenty of buddies with me. I'll be back on August 30th, and the Pearsons have promised a good time again in S.F.

I'll write again when time allows, hopefully with an address.

Love,
M.C.

---

26 August

Dear Family,

After four days in the field we have returned to Hill 411 to protect the artillery for a few days. This is the major rest that the infantry gets on a rotating basis, and it means showers, clean clothes, hot meals, and cold beer. After 2 weeks, it all seems pretty luxurious. As one who never was the camper type, I really appreciate any creature comforts we get. After four days I had problems sleeping with myself, even outside.

The Artillery in our area has a bad reputation because of problems caused by the My Lai incident. We can't fire anywhere near villages or huts, and must get political clearance from the Vietnamese before any firing. Most of the time we can't fire at all, or if we can, not where we need it. As a forward observer with the infantry, this can be both

286

frustrating and hair raising since I'm only trying to support myself and the people around me. Also our company had before me was a sergeant & was prone to fire on his own people as much as the enemy. So my biggest job has been to convince the infantry I'm safe & can do them some good and then try to talk the arty into firing.

I just got back from a trip to Quangtri for ice for our beer. Population is 60,000, but it looks like another San Felix. All the roads are dirt, and the outskirts are all huts and cardboard shacks. The ARVN's have a big headquarters there so I didn't feel too unsafe. We still had to carry M16 locked and loaded with steel pots. The really discouraging part is that our areas are so primitive.

Our company commander is very good and has a prior tour here.

I have much more confidence in him than I usually would in the infantry, and we're beginning to work together to get some tactics on call. The infantry really treats me well, and I hope I can return the same soon. I'm taking the platoon leaders and squad leaders out tomorrow to teach them to adjust mortars and artillery. Since I stay in the command post with the CO while the platoons maneuver, they will have to adjust what I can't see.

I'll close this now and try to get some extra sleep for our next two weeks in the field. No mail has reached me yet, most likely because of the address mixup. Happy Labor Day, and hope the golf & tennis are both in good shape.

Love,

MC

287

2 Sept

Dear Family,

I've had some more mail from you including mother's letter about the Scrapmit. I'll try to keep you posted on events here, but writing from the field is somewhat different depending on how much we're moving.

Right now we are having air strikes put in the valley and are waiting for a few hours. You may read about this fight in the papers, so I'll tell you what it's like. We came down here with the tanks and in four days un-covered an NVA regiment in the draws of the Nui Dawn valley. Yesterday they brought in two more companies of infantry plus bombs, air strikes, gun ships and napalm. C Co is the blocking force now — that means we're in the rear to meet anyone going through the sweeps — because of our somewhat weary state after the first four days. I spent most of the morning with our CO and the Battalion Cmdr monitoring radios as the progress of the sweeps. They've pulled back now for more air bombardment.

It's about time, I guess, for a comment on this stupid war. We had two platoons of Popular Force Vietnamese go with the infantry today and as soon as the shooting started they hid and refused to fight. Here are the South Vietnamese with two companies of infantry, a troop of tanks, all the air support in the world, and they won't fight the NVA who have been bombed for two days and have only small arms and a few anti-tank rockets. But the NVA put up with all we have and hold their ground. You almost have to conclude they deserve this place, not the South Vietnamese. The Americans fight well, but Nixon's stupid Vietnamization is a hoax, at least up here. From where I'm looking, I'm just hoping we don't

288

lose any more men in this ridiculous place. We fight well and hard, but for no good reason. I only hope I'll be out of this area soon.

I got two cards from Brenda on her way to Japan and a letter from Brant. I'll try to get some R&R around March to see Brenda, and also try to take a week's leave late in my tour. Right now I'd like a shower and a scotch and water more than anything, but it will come in a few days when we return to the hill.

Keep writing: the mail is the best part of my day. Hope those Eli have a good season and Broadway Joe returns to the Jets. Are the Reynolds coming for the World Series?

more later

Love

ML

5 Aug [ ]

Dear Family,

The fighting has stopped now and I'm combatting a heat rash now. This morning we got food and water for the first time in three days — a banquet was had by all. We had been drinking stream water with purifying tablets which makes it taste like iodine. I even managed to shave and wash a little. Mail came for the first time in four days and I got a letter from Mother and a Sports Illustrated from Brad. It has been well passed around by now.

We routed the 60th NVA Battalion and got credit for 40 kills. However, they were bigger than Vietnamese, and they are investigating the possibility of Chinese help. I sure hope not. If things go as planned we'll go in for a rest in four days. We can really use it, especially some cold beer + soda and maybe a few hot meals. I have learned to cook C Rations to an edible mess, but the last two days it has seemed regular monsoon type deluges, and we've spent the morning drying out and trying to make some fires. We also [sent] to LRP's out here — long range reconnaissance patrol meals which are instant type — which enables us to add water to achieve beef stew, chicken & rice etc. They are somewhat like a lump in your stomach but make a good change from C rations. So far (knock on wood) my stomach hasn't rebelled too badly. Only my skin from the dirt. I'm also drying my socks & boots for the first time in a while. Such breaks should come more often.

We have with the company 3 Kit Carson Scouts: former VC who have come over to our side and work as scouts for strategy and uncovering booby traps. They are funny to talk to in their pidgin English, but prove invaluable in their jobs. I have been using

One of our KCS is sitting here with me—the only one who can write. His name is THIN

them to do harassing fires at night where they suspect enemy escape routes and base camps.

It's somewhat disconcerting to hear artillery shells go over your head all the time. Last night they fired all night on a valley about 500 meters to the west of us, and the shells whistled all night. I stayed awake to make sure none landed short on top of us. And you hear the whistle, you know it's above you & won't hit you. Two days ago I brought it in to 300 meters from us — I had the whole company down in trenches as each round hit. Then we'd look up & see where the smoke was & adjust it. They'd love it in OCS.

Well, I've been rambling. See you all soon in a letter. Hope the lull keeps up here.

Love,
M.

6 Sep

Dear Family,

Yesterday was a good, quiet day and I even got a chance to wash, shave, trim my moustache and wash my hair. For dinner I had a hot LRRP spaghetti + meat sauce and wrote many letters. Then at night I had a hairy experience. Each night when we reach our defensive position I plot defensive targets for artillery my likely enemy attack positions. Then later at night they fire them in to make sure they are where we want them. We shoot white phosphorous up in the air first to make sure they're safe and then fire the same location "on the deck" for pin point. Since there are other companies around us now, it's hard to make sure they aren't close to a DT. I only know where our company is.

Anyway when they fired our second target last night up in the air, it came close to where I thought another company was

situated. I told the guns it was safe for us but not, I thought for another friendly element. They argued with me that it was either safe or not safe, but I refused to let them fire on the deck. Five minutes later the other company got through to the guns to say the WP round was right over their heads, and please don't put it on the ground. They had failed to tell the guns they had moved an element out during the night. Sweet vindication and much relief from this FO and plenty of static to both the guns and the other company's F.O. It may give me a small amount of satisfaction to know that in one instance it was worthwhile for one to be an officer who can save some lives and limbs.

Another comment on this war prompted by a column by Stewart Alsop (whom I don't usually listen to) in Newsweek. He called of the

fighting situation here being messed
up because only drafters are fighting.
All enlisted men who signed up
were given the chance to choose
their job and of course choose
non-combat specialties. The NCO's
who re-ups do the same thing.
This is very true, and the result
is a non-professional combat force
of 18 or 19 year olds who get the
worst job + have no experience. 95%
of our company is PFC, Spec 4
personnel, all drafted with no
higher NCO leadership. Each platoon
should have an E7 platoon sergeant,
3 E6 squad leaders (staff sergeant)
and E5 team leaders. Now our
highest squad leader is E5 (he made
his rank over here). We have three
E6 platoon sergeants and 2 E6
platoon leaders (a lieutenants job).
So, you have a civilian, drafted
fighting force with no experienced
leadership, and a professional
rear in the soft jobs.
    Of course this is bound to happen

when the army tries to keep people
by job incentives. But it shows
how horrible the draft system
is: if you're drafted, you'll
be the one being shot at; and you
better learn by yourself how to
protect yourself because there's no
experienced people with you.
Since a high percentage of drafters
are black, you create a bitter
bunch of trained killers. This war
will have continuing repercussions
for many years to come. And the
drafters are the ones losing their
lives. It's no wonder the career
people love this war and re-enter
to come back.
    Enough of this. I got a letter from
Howie today about the concert and
a letter from Brad about the ballgame
and the races. Hope the Steelers can
muster some sort of competition this
year. The football schedule was well
read by everyone, with much argument
+ sentiment for various favorites.
        I'll write again soon
                 MC

11 26

Dear Family,

Just a quick note to let you know everything remains quiet, and we'll be going in to the hill in three days. We are back with the tracked vehicles for a few days, and I'm hoping we can ride them in instead of walking. I never was much of an infantry sort, and five miles with my pack won't be a picnic. But anything for a cold beer.

We all took a bath in a nearby river today with the villagers and their cows. We figured it was safe if they were willing to risk their animals. Besides the NVA have apparently left for the time being, and the VC haven't reappeared.

I got a letter from Brenda from Japan, and she seems reasonably comfortable, although I have the feeling her family is less than affluent by Ryan standards. But one of my latest lessons is you can adapt to anything if you have to. Just don't ever ask me to go camping again.

More later — maybe I can get this out on this chopper.

love,

MC

293

12 Sep

Dear Family,

I had decided there is one thing I could really use out here that maybe you can send me - a cheap instama tic. It's about the only size camera that I can carry out here + use effectively for pictures of what will be more interesting than when I get back at the firebase. I tried to buy one over here, but the PX's here have absolutely nothing. Ordering through the PX will take several months. If you can send a small instamatic with about three rolls of 20 exposure slide film I should be able to get pictures of what the war is like in the field instead of taking a Minolta 3,000,000 with all the lenses out one day when I'm off. I never was much for photography field trips.

We had our second encounter ambush with claymore mines go off on our perimeter last night - and bagged our second rabbit. But you should have seen the people scurry when the explosion went off. At least it keeps the troops alert.

The artillery continues to be ineffective and dangerous from our firebase, and I plan to make a big stink when we get back in. They fire opposite of what the FO's call for + usually land too close to our troops after a delay long enough to allow the enemy to escape. I've had several close calls with our forward platoons both by inaccurate guns and wrong fuzes. I'm about to call off all Arty until they can investigate what's wrong. Last night another FO called for one round up in the air to check proximity of fire to his company & the city sent a battery of rounds on the ground which just about blew away the whole company.

Of course it goes both ways. Last night I fired a defensive target and one of our ambushes called up to say it was right over them — they were 1000 meters away from where they thought they were. I'll have some gray hair when I get back.

I'll close for the time being to search out some shade and trim my moustache. It's red and blond, and coming in very thick now. I'll send you a picture and you can decide if I look more like Clark Gable than before.

Love,
RB

295

5 Sep

Dear Family,

I got letters from both of you here at the hill today saying you received some mail from me. This two week delay does cause some problems, but I do get your mail both on the hill and in the field almost daily, and I've been writing either daily or every other day for about two weeks now, so you should be hearing from me. Most of the back mail has come through, and I have written to Brule through his parents (with a note to them) since I haven't yet gotten his letter.

Most of the questions Dad asked have been answered concerning food & mail. Our "permanent" rooms — I've been living out of a ruck sack since reaching the infantry, but I do have some stuff in storage back at base camp. My wallet is in a safe.

News here is sparse; about once a week we get a "Stars & Stripes" Army newspaper which is slanted and rather Vietnam oriented; and I find a Time or Newsweek now and then.

When we got to the hill I had two packages waiting: a beautiful Buck survival knife from Home, and a food package from Brenda. We killed the food in about an hour during a card game with beer. Of course I can't take any with me to the field, but the CP did enjoy a change from our usual C ration fare.

I've been hearing from Brenda on and off and also the girls I met in S.F. I try to write a letter or two a day to keep the mail flowing in, but it becomes hard after awhile to find things to talk about. It can be rather dull when we're not in contact. Long range lessons are not new to me, but they do have their limitations.

I wrote to Uncle Harry & Aunt Lea and Gary, but replies take so long you tend to forget what you covered in the last letter.

I really had it out with the Battery Cmdr when we got back, and I may have made a few enemies here. It is rare that I have really told someone off, but the artillery support was

so bad, I felt something had to be done. He was belligerent and defensive since he'd been getting it from all sides anyway; it may have been the wrong thing to do, but I'm very concerned for the safety of our company, and my disposition suffers when I get such a response from someone not getting shot at & merely protecting himself. It also helps that I'm not worried about my Army career. He has tried to pin some of it on me, but I've been backed up by my FO party, our CO, and the other FOs in the field. I hope things improve.

I wrote to Jamie concerning the knife & plan a thank you to Brenda tonight. Back to the field in two days. Love MC

13 Sep

Dear Family,

We're sitting on top of a mountain the choppers took us up yesterday afternoon. Last night was cool and clear, with few mosquitos. But today we have to climb another mountain and I'm not looking forward to such a hike. My pack is heavy enough on flat ground.

We'll spend some days up here and then have our first six day rest starting the 26th. Actually I don't know how much good the rest will do me since I picked up a bug in our three days on the Well. I may start fixing my own food all the time if the real stuff on a fire line makes me sick.

Yesterday they pulled one of the other FO's back for a rear job. If things then go as planned after two more months the same should happen to me. Let's hope.

Neither Bruce nor Ralph Oser got field jobs and I'm beginning to feel discriminated against. But I have a million war stories they don't.

Time to move out. More later.

Love

MC

20 Sep

Dear Family,

Another day, another few
dollars. We're sitting on top
of a hill about 3500 ft
high, having walked up with
our packs, no mean task in the
sun with that much weight.
But here the nights are very
cool and there's a breeze all
day. The view is spectacular,
the kind that Dad would
require. Now if only the
rain would stop and the
NVA would go away.

I became a fair haired boy
for a day today. Early this
morning Cpt Morgan and
I were making a binoculars
reconnaisance of the valley
to our rear. I spotted a
small water fall and pool
and I spotted about 4 NVA
taking a bath in it. They
were about 3 miles away
so I called back for some
artillery and we hit the

waterfall after one adjustment
killing two of the enemy. When
I called back to Battalion
that we had gotten two the
place went mad. The Colonel
came out to look over the
area (from our location) and
wanted my full story for
posterity and suggested all
sorts of arty tactics for tonite
in case they come back. Anyone who comes back for a bath
after 2 batteries of arty hit
the area is crazy. But the
arty has been so bad of late
this is the biggest thing
they've had and everyone
wants to get all the facts for
their real war story about
how they got two deaths.

Of course maybe I should
feel some sort of emotion
about killing people but
this war has pretty much
drained me of moral qualms.
It's such a stupid, base in
a life time thing to have

an easy, safe shot at the enemy that all I can do is laugh at the rifle it sets off back at the firebase.

I was much happier later in the day to fire support for one of our platoons in trouble – they got hit on a hill and I got enough heavy stuff on the enemy for our people to pull back to their trenches. No one made much noise of it.

So the war goes on. In 9 days we get a big break back at Deck Phe, with free beer and three days of movies, floor shows etc. I also will be awarded my Army Commendation medal which arrived last week. Now if they'd only give me my promoted papers – I still don't have anything that says I'm a first lieutenant. Oh well, you can't expect everything.

Not much more to report. I want to get some mail off to Howie also since he's been burning the mail routes lately in astounding fashion. After all these years it's really amazing.

Love,
M C

22 Sep

Dear Family,

Nothing much has happened for the past few days. We've been trying to get two platoons up a hill (with the assistance from some scattered NVA. The terrain more than anything is against us since the mountains are so steep and the woods so thick. I'm somewhat frustrated with arty because I'm on another hill about 1000 meters away with our CP and two platoons and can't observe most of the stuff we call in.

I have my FO/O with the two platoons, and he's getting a lot of practice firing + adjusting, but it just shows the old story - they have someone just out of AIT with no training doing an E-7's

job because it's in the field + the NCO's stay in the rear. Since one day our platoon leaders was wounded and one platoon had no NCO's we had an E-5 with two years experience leading two platoons. The men were scared and didn't want to move up the hill. We had to send a Lt from another platoon and an E-6 over to them to go up the hill. What a war!

Our Company has had a drastic change of personnel in the last month and most of the people are scared and inexperienced. Unless we get some leadership in the platoons we might as well just sit in one place. Otherwise people will get hurt. They sent us a new Lt platoon leader in country one week with

no combat experience. I
don't think he'll help very
much. Cpt Morgan is
realistic in figuring we'll
just have to move slowly &
do little until people get
some time to get oriented.
Otherwise the company will
fall apart.

Of course we also have
the problem that no one
wants to be a target in a
war that means nothing.
We have no use for taking
land, just finding the
enemy & that means getting
shot at. So morale in
the maneuver platoons
is rather low.

The last paper I saw
was for Sep 4 - and the
Pirates were still in
worst place. I don't
think they'll go any-
place against Cincinatti,

but I remember the Mets
and Jets, so no predictions.
Hope the big weekend
is a success and someone
beats PC at Jetto.

See you next time

Love,
NC.

24 Sep

Dear Family,

First of all, happy birthday to the division - maker. Since I haven't been near a PX or store in over a month a card was rather hard to come by. I hope the weekend in Philly + New Jersey was a success.

Second - the letter you sent first class got here in the same time as regular airmail. I guess it doesn't make too much difference.

Third - you wanted some Pidgin Vietnamese - English ok. I eat beaucoup chop-chop in ti-ti time. Di-di mao before I ca ca-dac you, Madame R. The above translates as I ate a lot of food in a short time. Get out of here before I kill you, fallen

woman! Very colorful as you can see. I've about exhausted the printable vocabulary of my Vietnamese.

I killed three VC yesterday on a mountain top with artillery. Whoopee. Of course everyone was once again exhilarated, but I found the bloodthirsty hoopla somewhat incongruous. As a confirmed killer now I'm not sure any woman will like the look in my eye and the wild appearance I take on when spotting a potential victim. I also wonder if this will always haunt me à la Tom Smith (?) in The Man in the Grey Flannel Suit. I doubt it.

However it does afford one a certain amount of status among the people here. All the grunts want me to fire at anything that moves and they give me time

as many rounds as I ask
for back at the firebase.
All this is fine as long as
they don't decide to keep me
in the field longer to have
a higher body count. The
only senior NCO to me in
the battalion will be getting
his rear job in a week
rumor has it, and maybe
I'll get out sooner than I
expected.

It's looking a little dark
for my R&R in Japan since
they are cutting out Japan as
an R&R spot next month.
Unless I buy my own ticket
I don't think I'll be able
to go. Another thought
would be for Brenda to
meet me in Hong Kong.

I got a nice letter from
the Buckalews yesterday
Mr Buckalew is having
a hard time selling
Bruce's Triumph GT6+

Oh, the pleasures of a
foreign sports car.

Well, I'm adjusting
a road runner arty
mission now for one of
our elements needing a
recon by fire. Must
get back to work. We
go in the 26th. That
shower will feel good.
Moustache really thick!

Love

NC

29 Sep

Dear Family,

I suppose I've been in the Army long enough to know that there is no justice and if you can get screwed, you will, but this last brusher takes the cake.

Every 90 days each company gets a 3 day "stand-down" in the rear where the troops can relax, don't pull guard, can party, and get some USO entertainment. This is looked forward to as much as R + R because for the field troops, it's the only chance to let off steam + get out of danger.

Today we are supposed to be on stand-down but the higher-ups canceled it + sent us back to the field because a company found 5 NVA. Last week our company found a platoon, had 10 people wounded and got no help.

Now another company saw some people and we have to go help them. The morale is now non-existent in the company but the higher-ups won't listen anything to help their careers. The really stupid thing is that one of the other companies that just completed stand-down was not sent out here. They are returning for a second tour of guarding the hill. Talk about SNAFUS. It's all so stupid and meaningless, with the draftees paying the price once again.

I had planned to make a mars call to you all on stand-down, but that is out the window for the moment.

The Pirates still seem to be clinging. I'm somewhat surprised to see the merger of Goodbody

not knowing if this is out
of pure financial want or
a desire by most of the
brothers to retire. I may
have to use my savings from
this year as capital for
Hile - but if Gary is hurting
maybe we can get a loan
from Papa's Laundry.

Well as senior FO in
the Battalion, and having
killed more people last
week than the rest of the
infantry combined, I'm
in the midst of experiencing
the charisma of John
Wayne. Just get me out of
the field. Waiting for
the Camera. Thanks for
sending it.
          Love,
            MC

7 Oct

Dear Family,
      Sorry for the delay in
writing. We got caught in
a storm in the mountains
for five days - everything
wet & cold, no re-supply of
food & water or no re-support and
we just tried to stay warm
& dry for the duration. There
was major flooding in
the lowlands, bridges out
& towns under water, and
we had to wait until it was
over to get out. They then
brought us back to the rear
for our pseudo R & R, and
I tried to call you from the
MARS station the last two
nights. No luck.
      The enclosed picture was
taken unexpectingly by
our First Sergeant the last
time we were boarding the
hill. You can't see my
moustache very well; I assume

you it is quite red & brushy.
The sandbags are the bunker
where the CP stays. You can
see my ruck sack and M16
and the roof and an ammo box
wall in the foreground. The
mountains in the rear are
similar to what we're navi-
gating further south. The
artillery battery is off to the
left on the hill.

I received the Instamatic
when we got back here - it
works fine and should give
you a better idea of the area
& what the infantry is like.
Since it's light & inexpensive
I can carry it with me.
When I get the pictures
developed I'll send them
home with a commentary
on each. I'll try to get as
many rainbow-powerline
shots as possible.

To answer a few questions,
I haven't received Sports Illus.
trated yet. We have cheese

and crackers in all C-Ration
packs. There really isn't any
type of food I can use right
now, except some un sweetened
instant iced tea.

On news coverage, it's getting
worse. I learned of both the
Pirates winning their division
and Nasser's death through
your letters. I don't think it
will get better until I'm in
the rear & can begin to search
out TIME and other magazines
and maybe a Stars & Stripes
under a week old & into it.

On fellow officers here, the
majority of Lt's are armor
twisted, although not soaped
in Eastern Liberalism as I am
a lot having gone through ROTC
The career people are somewhat
harder to put up with especially
the Cpt & well grade West
Pointers. Few OCS people
are cluster.

Well I hope the golf

tournament is going well and
you decide on a cottage. Time
continues to tick, somehow
slowly. Bruce wrote saying
he had heard from you and
that he has a soft job near
Saigon. The Buckalew luck
again.
                    Love,
                        M C

11 Oct
Dear Family,
        I can't remember whether
I wrote to you since we got
back from stand-down. At
any rate we spent two extra
days guarding the hill because
of bad flying weather, and
then were lifted back into
the mountains. We had
seven days of rest, so I suppose
we should be ready for this
15 day operation. It wasn't
very easy to come back out,
but at least we're set here
for a few days before we
start walking. I got some
pictures of our "combat
assault" with the camera,
and should be able to show

you what it's really like. I'll take a roll of 20 here + then have my liaison officer send out another roll. This way the unused film doesn't get wet.

I got a letter from Brenda today, who seems to be getting more used to Japan + even picking up the language. She has now turned 20 and seems very happy to be off on her own. She is thinking of coming home over the Trans Siberia RR, but I think she will miss seeing Omar Sharif. I'd follow her if Julie Christie were along the way.

Sorry to hear about the debacle of the Seniors golf tournament. I guess we can say that outside business interests are keeping Dad from concentrating on his game. Maybe a few weeks in Latrobe will help.

I haven't heard anything about the Pirates. I imagine the World Series has started by now. I am counting on Yale having beaten Brown last weekend + suppose the silence on this matter from Philadelphia to indicate the same. Otherwise Howie has kept me closely informed on the talent in his area. I'm curious whether

Lilian has gained a place
on Mother's list. With
Gary getting married
next month, Wacky can't
be far behind, and that
would put her list completely
out. My uncle would have
to dine upstairs. Fortunately
he is accustomed to that.

Well, as you can see
there isn't too much more
to report. If I see any of
the filthy commies, I'll
be sure to pour lead on
them, or steel, as they
say in the Arty.

291 and a wake up.
Love,
NC

---

19 Oct

Dear Family,
We are still out on the
mountaintop covering our
two platoons below. I've
been firing a lot of Arty
as covering fire, and doing
very well until today. We
spotted one VC down in our
last night's position and
I fired about 40 rounds on
him but one round had
bad powder & landed only
about 50 meters from
us. Luckily no one was
hurt.
So I'll have to start all
over again convincing
the infantry that Arty is
safe and effective. We

and been doing so well up to now.

I got a letter from Uncle Harry saying all is well in Garden City and that on top of a new VW he is bargaining for a newer Mercedes. I'm sorry to see the Corvair go - if only for the fear it put in everyone else on the highway.

We go back to the hill in three days, and I hope to have a full roll of film taken to have developed. The Commission report on campus unrest underlined my old point - Spiro, you're doing more harm than good.

Little else.

Love
me

Dear Family,   16 October
This may take awhile to get to you since we're on top of a mountain in a typhoon. It's really rather unpleasant. Poncho hootches are not made for 90 mph winds and driving rain. And of course we're out of food. Rain water is plentiful however and we're making the most of what shelter we have. I suppose I can tell my grandchildren about it. Whoops, that's a dirty word.

However, we continue to march. We just laid the tincom for our ark, and have 33 more days to find a mountain. Were they pigeons or doves?

17 Oct Would you believe—

311

I had to stop writing this to move out. But the storm we went, looking for Charlie. We finally made it to our present location at dark last night, somewhat wet + tired. But the storm ended at midnight + we got resupplied this morning.

I got some R of the L from Wayne with a few unexpected Chaplains attached to lighten my day. The Bde is down to 5 candidates, in Glee Club + very little going on.

I'll try to answer some of your questions in the last few letters. First of all the VC/NVA are much fewer than a year ago, and they are mainly in the mountains. The movement

of communities into the lowlands with all mountains free fire areas has cut off most of the enemy's food supply, and the Rice denial program in the low-lands has them very hungry for this monsoon season. However in the mountains the terrain gives the enemy the advantage and very good cover. So searching the mountains is still dangerous + rather unproductive. Since there's so little food in the mountains there isn't too much reason to go get there except to keep them from stockpiling for after we leave. The VC are very low on manpower + have NVA helping them now. This is the line we get but it seems to be true from what I've seen.

The lowlands here are quiet & appear pacified with ARVN's in control. Of course the US is doing all the mountain fighting.

On pay — I have $500 a month going directly into the Soldier's Savings plan drawing 10% interest. $50 a month comes to me in cash, and in the field I have a hard time spending it. The remainder, around $50, goes into an American Express checking account for my R+R. So I should have some money over here. In June my pay will also go up for over 3 mos duty.

I became eligible for R+R in January but probably will shoot for March with leave in May or June.

In-country mail is just that, stays here & goes direct.

I got some pictures of arty today, hitting a hill as a prep pretty close to us - about 100 meters. I'd like to get some closer shots, but have to wait for the proper situation.

So the time goes - in three days I'll have two months in the field. As the senior FO I get a lot of preference from the battery as far as fast & accurate fire, and I've been pinpointing it lately. Has had there won't be a civilian job that uses these talents.

I've been making some delicacies with my France, Vietnamese noodles & c

313

4 November

Dear Jimmy,

Well today is my anniversary - 3 months in country, and it was rather discouraging. The job I was going to get fell through because my boss job fell through, and to top it off I learned that they are going to rotate one of the other FO's before me because he came in country before I did. I have twice as much time in the field as he does - no better?

That's the way things seem to go. We have a new company commander. Capt Morgan has a rear job at Brigade & tomorrow he'll go in. Our new CO came out today. At least he's been here before and seems to know what's going on. Capt Morgan and I never got along very well so I hope things won't be too much different.

Tomorrow we go back to the hell for four days. Unfortunately we have to walk back, a rather long trip. I hope it remains overcast so that it won't get hot. We'll stay down in...

rations. However, if you ever see the "C Ration Cookbook" in any stores, we could use it out here.

If you think anyone, especially Maurie would like a small cassette tape recorder, I may be able to get one in the PX & get it to you before Christmas. I'm still waiting for my rear job before I send a list, but a small portable electric fan will definitely be on it. Also a copy of Erich Segal's Love Story to cure my curiosity.

More later. See you in the mail.

Love,
N.C.

...materials as much as possible for lightweight moving.

Enclosed is the invitation to Gary's wedding. I thought you would appreciate the very colored sentiments. I wish I could have seen the newspaper announcement about the troth being told since he & I always joked about writing each other's. "Mr. Goodbody, who attended the Hotchkiss school and Yale University, where he was a member of the Whiffenpoops and Saint Anthony Hall, as in his final year at the Harvard School of Business after a two year tour as a Peace Corps Volunteer in Brazil." I bet even the wording is the same.

Things are quiet. I just put the final trim on my mustache and should have some pictures of the bushy appendage any day now.

I think Yale lost last Wednesday month. Oh well, maybe next year.

Love

M—

---

6 November

Dear Family,

Enclosed is my first roll of slides from the instamatic. I am amazed and ecstatic at their quality considering the camera & the treatment it's put up with. I'll try to give you a picture by picture description which will help unravel what it's like here. To preface the whole thing, this is one trip out from start to finish, a sweep from the mountains into the Wo Sohn Valley which took twelve days.

#3 This is in the Pickup Zone for our combat assault from the firebase. There are two of the eight Slicks (Slicks?) that took our company of 100. As you can see we sit on the floor, feet out & the rudder on, seven men to a chopper.

#4 A closeup of one about to lift off. The blond is my Recon Sergeant, SSgt Terry Williamson. He's back in the bush for 9 months & is one of the best combat soldiers I've seen, he's crazy.

#5 A view of the mountains & the Wo Sohn valley below taken from the chopper on the way in.

#6. Our left was first to the landing zone and I took this of the second lift to come in. Everyone piles out running & sets up a hasty perimeter. This was so cold & wet, that means we weren't fired at when we got down. However there is still a problem of booby traps - one CO from another company was wounded last week on an LZ by a mine. The Arty "preps" on LZ before the landing to try to clear out the enemy.

#7. Well there he is, mustache & all. Sgt Rock all good to my left at the LZ. We had secured the area. This is next morning as we are about to start walking down into the valley. Notice the M16 gingerly held, my rucksack, the mortar round, and the sticks for hootch poles - they're hard to come by & we try to keep them. My map is in my big pocket. The white stuff on the ground is shaving cream.

#8. We got partway down the mountain and then got word to stay high because a typhoon was going to hit. We set up here for the duration of the storm. Cpt Morgan is on the right with his CO, woolen

#9. nightshirt. His RTO, "Kirp", is on the left, getting the last bit of sun as we build our hootches. A deflated air mattress is in the foreground.

#9. There are the CP hootches for the typhoon. My RTO, Ed Williams (1stC) is settled in front. At the right foreground is our medic, Gustavo Haro from Ecuador, who got extra mtg by joining the Army, & is enjoying it now. He would fall to the US Inf & I speak Spanish when I can remember enough. Kirp & Cpt. Morgan & the other RTO from Boston - are in the rear. Notice the radio aerials inside the hootches & sticking up. The tarps were blown down & the poncho hootches in the winds.

#10. Well, you can see the typhoon winds are starting. This is Sam Gresher (1LT & 2nd Platoon Leader - from Seattle) in the nightshirt I have on my wet weather parka. In the rear is the hootch in the dirt from our foxhole & in the distance, the valley.

#11. This is a break here of a few day after the typhoon we walked down into

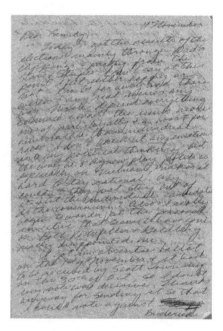

the ridge on this side of the hill. We fired along the top again all night to keep him from coming back.

#49 This is the next day - we were picked up to go back to the firebase. This is a chopper flying with part of the company landing out the door as usual. The door gunner with an M60 machine gun is in the rear.

#50 Same shot trying to get our own door gunner in it. At this time we're contemplating our first beer in two weeks + something besides C rations for dinner.

There it is in all its resplendent glory. I think this will give you a better idea of what it's like here and why I'm looking forward to a rear job. More pictures when I finish this next role.

As a boon to beg - would you get some prints of no 7 + 10 - about three of each to send the Pearsons, Brenda, etc. I'm very proud of my work to the

I'll close for now - write later.
Love, Mike

and foremost of the Democrats
by they John Doe Peeves, I think
they'd probably have to register
that way.

I got packages from Fran
began full of filler, I will
water a few of them with older
use them in the usual here
got sunken hill yesterday
will only sending the company
into Paradigm... joy I still
low... there how to take it
but we lost two wounded to
a only try the day before, so
it'll help morale even though
not...

let me know if there's
anything I can send you
Elizabeth - I think I'll keep
you some clothes - no... anything
I hope you can read this
we too busted on this side
aren't bad enough, ing by the
will be sent to me by those
person who owns judgment.

I think I'll try either Sydney
or Hawaii for my leave, either
before or after R & R.

As one of the "old-timers" in
the company I have more war
stories than anyone to tell
but I'm beginning to wonder
what happened to my rear job
they have already started rotating platoon leaders back to
the rear who came to the field
after I did. But they aren't
getting any new arty Lt's and
the ones transferred from
other units have already been
to the field & may be getting
the jobs that open. It also
works that when they have
someone who does a good
job & has experience they prefer
to have him there. That's why
Cpt Morgan was in the field
so long. But I have lost my
Recon specialist CR & R and
he won't be back out because
he's only got a few weeks
left. Also there's no replacement for him, and my I

so in there won't be anyone else out here to call in Arty.

Despite all this my morale is still OK, and as long as we don't run into too much it's all "good time", as they say. I've gotten used to the existence at any rate and so far my health hasn't been affected either by disease or jungle rot. I did get bitten by a centipede the other day, a painful experience for about twelve hours, but no ill effects.

We're about to go on a VR (visual reconnaisance) in a chopper to see what we have wrought for the past few days. More film should be coming soon — I hope you got the slides I sent. More later,

love
M____

Dear Family,

I'm hoping that you have received my letter about buying a wedding gift. I think I've been writing about twice a week, and if some mail has gone astray, I'd like to know about it. We get it in sporadic bursts here — going several days to a week without it and then getting it all in a bunch. This makes it rather difficult to keep up a steady flow going out, but you should be hearing from me once or twice a week.

Our Battalion Commander was relieved this week; the circumstances are rather vague & we really don't know what he did wrong. There have been several mining incidents on the road leading to the firebase from Quang Ngai. There doesn't seem to be anything that can be done since the mine sweep team that goes out every day doesn't

320

pick up the charges, and the road isn't paved so there's easy access to digging a hole. Really all they can do is pave the road, but even after about ten incidents with about 12 killed there's no help from the rear to pave the road. That's the way it goes here – the troops that have left are support personnel, so we're fighting the war with about half the support we should.

Now they are giving troops for Christmas to anyone going home before Feb 15. This will leave everyone very short. I just hope the 'ceasefires' are effective. The leave program to the states is for anyone over four months, but the requirement of having to have a ticket back in case the MAC planes are full is rather discouraging. Quite a lot of career people who are married will take a stab at it. I don't have that much leave before my ETS.

25 November

Dear Family,

Tomorrow is Thanksgiving, and they are giving us an extra day on the hill so that we can enjoy the dinner. I've been enlisted to play on the Officers vs Enlisted Men basketball game as part of the festivities. Since it never was one of my better sports I expect to take much abuse.

I sent in the second role of slides to be developed. I think I could use about two more roles; its Kodachrome X for instamatic, which is special since it comes in a cartridge.

Yesterday I received

two books, the one on Nixon which I've wanted to read, and the Alfred Hitchcock anthology. It should be good reading in the field next time.

Last night we sneaked a bottle of Chivas Regal onto the hill and had a very pleasant party although my fingers got rather worn on the guitar after no practice in the field. The company has a new First Sergeant who has all the bluster & toughness that Hollywood would add. I really have to laugh at the whole situation as he tears up the poor PFC's & NCO's but can't say a

word to me. It's exactly what the troops don't need right now, but they are learning to ignore him enough to live with it. He doesn't go to the field with us, so they know he'll be around only a few days.

Today I had my first experience with the Christmas visitors & I must say it was great. I heard some ballplayers were at the hill for anyone to meet so I went down to the mess hall & saw Bob Prince and Willy Stargell. Bob was alone some few people recognized him, but I went up to him & said I was from Pittsburgh and we had a nice chat. It really helps morale here to have these people come so far & get to such remote places as this. He should be calling you when he gets back & I think he has a picture of Willie, he & I. If he does contact you, please thank him again for coming, it's a great boost to everyone.

Time for a company meeting. I'll write more when we go out. Happy Thanksgiving.

Love,
MC

28 November

Dear Family,

We are in the midst of coke kids galore right now. Of course their price (50¢ a can) remains steep, especially for one who has not been paid for two months. As soon as I get a rear job I'm going to have to go to the finance office in Chu Lai & get the thing straightened out. This is another typical Army deal. My FO party is assigned to the battery at the firebase so we don't get paid by the infantry who come to the field. The BC won't come to the field to pay us, and he can't keep our money more than two days because they need their reports in. So unless the company is on the hill on payday the F.O's party doesn't get paid. I've gotten $30 since coming to Vietnam — all the rest is somewhere on the books in Chu Lai. I'll get it sooner or later, but they should be able to do a better job than this. I have to go get it myself & I can't do it while I'm the F.O for a maneuver company.

I received your food package while we were on the hill. The onion flakes are really good in just about all our cooking &

the 1st Sergeant took the pizza back to the rear to make when we're on stand-down in a few weeks. We devoured the ham & cheese package at one of the company meetings before leaving the hill. everyone is very appreciative of any change from C's. We all thank you.

My replacement is in the Battalion rear right now (I've been told) and should come out by the end of this week. I won't get my hopes up until he actually steps off the chopper.

It will be good for him
however to have someone
with him the first few
days. I came in with
no F-O in the company
and had to pick up alot
on my own. I should
be able to help him.

Dad's letter on the
oligopoly problems of the
cement industry was much
appreciated. Old Alan
Smith doesn't crapply much
anymore.

Chopper is coming
so I'll put this on
Love,
[signature]

---

9 December
Dear Family,
I'm waiting for my project physical
to be completed, and thought this would
be a good time to give you the full
scoop on leave & R & R as it stands now.
Each person is allowed one 7 day R&R
and one 7 day leave. Both is a confirmed
reservation: leave is standby & hard to
get transportation for if the location
& time are full. The Army's new deal,
a two week leave to the US is in lieu
of leave - you still get R&R. But
you have to have a confirmed seat
back, paid for. This is a good deal
for people who are married, but
not really worthwhile for someone
who is single. Several organizations
have chartered planes to put the
cost down somewhat, but it
still runs somewhere around 500
and up for the east coast. And
the demand far exceeds the supply.
That leaves me with an R & R
+ a one week leave. Brenda wants
to see Hong Kong, and I have tenta-
tively planned for March.
I should like to see Sidney, but
every single male in Vietnam wants
to go there and standby seats are
almost impossible.

325

To my choice seems to be a
leave to HK in March and an
R+R to either Sydney or Hawaii
either in early February or
late April. Bangkok is a possibility
because of many friends plus a
chance to see the girl I took out
in San Francisco just before I left.
Right now I'm leaning towards
Hawaii in February, but the
application has to be in by the
end of this month so I'd better
make up my mind.
Well, you can see it's quite
complicated but it's something to
look forward to. More when I
get into the job a little.
Love,
MC

29 December 70

Dear Family,

I've been trying to call you for the past four days from
the Mars station with no luck due to crowds, flight times
etc. I hope to get through tomorrow morning, but in the
meantime I'll send news of the Christmas season in Nam
and hope you'll get it on arrival back in sunny Pittsburgh.

At about 11:00 PM on the 23rd we got the word that 3 aerial
observers would be needed for duty on the 24th to act as
security for the convoy and taking troops to the Bob Hope
show in Danang. I was one, giving me a free ticket to the
"show of shows" and a chance to see some of Danang. Things
went swimmingly on the way up; however we were there only
a half hour before the show and the place was already full.
We all had to stand up in the rear on the hill overlooking
the amphitheater and could attest to all the celebrities'
presence only by the loudspeaker system. They looked like
ants at that distance . So my chance to see Miss World,
the Golddiggers, Lola Falana (who-la) et al was somewhat
thwarted. On the way back on of the trucks broke down and
we got only as far as a firebase north of here at dark.
So I spent Christmas eve on Hawk Hill, with no running
water etc bunking in with an old Arty 1st Sergeant that I
cajoled into providing shelter. It wasn't exactly like
setting up the manger set, but then again I wasn't expecting
eggnog at Betty and Scoops the following morning. I
begged a ride back to Chu Lai on Christmas day in time to
take up my 12 noon flight and fire some good old Artillery
if the whole Chinese Army was massing. Otherwise we had
a truce on and couldn't engage any targets. So we tied
green and red smoke grenades to our struts and bummed the
forward firebases to bring some old cheer to those in the
boonies.

Christmas evening I opened my packages, which were numerous.
I had two from the nurse in SF including a 25 lb food cache ,
some cookies from Kathy Buhl, goodies from Mrs Ryan, and
Nuts from the Marottes and Aunt Blanche. Thank you notes
are on their way, but I need the Marottes' address if you
would be so kind. Of course I tried on the bells and shirt,
which are just perfect for R&R. I'm launching into the
James Bond book and will give John Hersey a whirl soon.
Also the Peanuts book on francais is a classic and it certainly has reminded me of a million idioms I'd forgotten.

The day after Christmas I took a class of FO's out for
their first shoot on arriving in country. We were at
an OP (observation post) in the middle of nowhere when
the major at N-5 decided that we should stay all night
so they could see how to fire illumination. So another
night in the sticks for LT Hile. I just can't seem to
get away from the war and all the wonderful sounds of
night firing around a perimeter. Oh well, such is life.

Enclosed is the bank card with signature and the ballot
about Great Men in American Business. You can see my
reaction. Maybe a nasty letter to Yale will fill this
void in instruction.

I expect that your vacation in Florida is another classic
of repose and golf and the new car is running fine. The
color alone will redeem it in my sight. But for the
money I am not sure why you didn't go for a Thunderbird
(the trunk doesn't sound any bigger). I'm trying to
decide what to do for my own transportation when I get
back. What does Howie think of the Vega, or is that a
dirty word along with the other Detroit Iron.

I'm hoping for R&R on February 12 and leave on March with
the two twos. I'll let you know what Uncle Sam has in
store. With the payraise as of 1 Jan and my flight pay
I should be able to enjoy myself to the fullest.

Happy New Year.

Love,

NC

---

9 January

Dear Family,

I'm flying with the air car today
and we are sitting around on call. I
hope I have enough to finish this letter.

The air car is rather a boring place
for an AO. They work with Cobra gun
ships and infantry in choppers. When
they find something they use gun ships
on it and then insert the infantry to
mop up. I'm supposed to bring in
arty if they need it. Since they use their
own firepower & then usually need to
refuel, there isn't much work for me.
So I spend 12 hours a day riding around
looking at the scenery from 2000 ft. And
with the monsoons its rather cold
up there. Luckily any day now the
permanent air car AO will come
over here and I will be back to my
usual flights. I can't say I will
be disappointed to leave.

My R&R has come through for the
12th of February. That's something to
look forward to. The ten months tour
has not yet materialized, and I'm beginning to think it never will.

But at any rate the new pay raise plus flight pay made it pretty profitable to stick with it. I've already got $2000 in the savings account drawing 10% interest plus $900 in my checking account for R&R + leave. I'm sure I'll spend that. I'm about to buy a combination AM-FM portable cassette tape player for $50 to let me make war to music.

Well, the rain keeps up, and it doesn't look like we'll fly again today. Famous last words.

Love,
MC

3 February

Dear Family,

It's raining and so we are not flying. I'm listening to my new cassette recorder - AM/FM radio that arrived from Hong Kong. Quite a piece of equipment: it's about 14" X 10", weighs about 10 lbs and runs either on batteries or regular house current. I can record on it, and it has a collapsible aerial for the FM. The tapes sound much better than the radio, but I must admit we're not exactly close to any stations. The nearest one is Da Nang, quite a ways up the coast for FM.

I also picked up my new sport-coat yesterday after getting my shots for Hawaii. It's a blue muted silk, light-weight, six-button double-breasted Edwardian. That sounds more like a bird than a sport.

cool, but it really goes well with the clothes you sent and will come in very handy both in Hawaii and Hong Kong.

We are flying a 20 hour schedule due to the TET offensive. This means I was up from 3:00AM to 6:00AM this morning. A schedule like that really messes up your day. And trying to observe anything on the ground when it is pitch black is rather difficult, not to mention the problem of figuring out where it is on the map to fire artillery. But the war becomes more ridiculous every day. On Sunday I flew with the Air Cav for one day to spell the regular observer. The small LOH (light observation helicopter) spotted some NVA in a clearing. Higher wouldn't give clearance to fire first so we inserted our 12

infantry and tried to round them up. Needless to say the infantry and the LOH took fire from the NVA. However we still couldn't get clearance to fire back because the ARVN's in the area were "too close" (several thousand meters away). You can imagine what it's like to be shot at and not be able to fire back. So we just took out the infantry and left. You can't win a war that way.

Glad to hear that you received some of the stuff from the Coop, altho I ordered 12 college seal glasses (JE, Pierson etc) for Mother. At any rate I expect the bill here. If it comes to you, just send it here. We could make all sorts of monopoly - socialist institution comparisons, but Mother is sticking up for her store, so I will desist. She always did like to go in there.

Dad's theory of inflation about over servicing the public is pretty well taken. However it shows the old Keynsean problem, actually in a way he never thought off. Remember you can have either inflation or unemployment. Well, if we cure this kind of inflation by laying off the extra clerks and ticket buyers we have unemployment plus a dip in buying power etc and the typical result you have in the States right now. If you really want to get theoretical, remember that none of these service features has anything to do with variable or marginal cost of the product. They're all fixed costs and thus can't be priced. Just like the railroads.

I'd try to find something unkind to say about oligopolis, but if Ralph Nader is willing to accept them as a fait accompli, how can I protest?

Glad to know who Chris and Bob Hooper are, for hopefully they will be candidates for the C. Sammis award one of these years if we can dig out any skeletons.

One week to R&R. Then I'll have a month to leave. Brenda is going to leave Tokyo on the 27th of February and take a boat to Yokahama, Taipei and other exotic ports. I'll meet her in HK on the 18th. I wrote to John and hope we'll get to see all his family.

Donnie says he met a girl who

likes Tom Rush. If ever a match were made in heaven .... I guess there is a sizeable element of fans to keep him going all these years. Actually now I'm being hoist in my own petard since he now has Joe Cocker as an example of my depraved taste. I'll have to be a little more diplomatic.

I'll talk to you all on the phone soon. How about meeting me in Hawaii for John's wedding?

Love,

MC

---

8 February

Dear Family,

I got a letter from Mother yesterday dated 3 February, which is pretty fast service, even with the day lost by the dateline. She mentioned the attack on Chu Lai. During TET there were no military casualties in Chu Lai, altho we did take a few rockets. I think the report was probably sent out of our Public Information Office and therefore was datelined Chu Lai. You should watch out for this in the future. There was some fighting north of here and quite a ways to the south, but we had a relatively quiet time.

The big move to Laos is of course affecting the units here, but I will most likely never get involved. I imagine there is a big stink in the States going on over the whole thing. It was kept more of a secret here than back there I think. Everyone knew that a lot of troops were being sent somewhere, but no one knew where, even after they started to move. They moved a bunch out of Chu Lai on LST's in the middle of the night, and they had to guard a lot of the troops on alert to keep them from going AWOL. Especially those who have only a short time left in country. That's about the way this war keeps going. I have kno idea whether we have troops on the ground up there, but I know the Air Cav is there and we are firing into Laos. The distinction is somewhat dubious, but the Pentagon can usually get away with it.

I'm enclosing the latest instamatic effort, still high quality. I'll also put my usual documentary along so that you will have a program with which to tell the players apart.

I got a package of cookies from the Cyphers two days ago and will send a nice note. They are really good, and shouldn't add any weight to my slim, trim form with all the exercise I get from handball. I can't quite figure out why Mother thinks I'll gain weight when I get back. I'm still the same lean and mean, body that women love and men fear, and expect to remain that way for years to come. Also got a letter from Uncle Harry about his trip out to the Golden Triangle area.

When you get this I should be in Hawaii. Will call.

Love,

MC

5 March

Dear Family,

I am still in Chu Lai, although more & more units have
been sent either north, or home.
My old artillery battalion went
north last week & my old infantry
Bn has started going home
(or at least taking the colors
home — most go to other units).
Since I let my opinion on a few
subjects dealing with the operation
(not the war) I was in to see
the Colonel, but the ax has not
fallen yet & I have plenty of
backing. So all remains in turmoil
& I have vowed to keep my
mouth closed as much as possible
for the next five months unless
I get a drop. Of course it
also depends on not being

sent out on a fool's errand to
get shot at. Things are
really tense.

But less than two weeks
to Hong Kong. Unfortunately
the above writer has pre-empted
all the cargo planes so we get
no mail & I can't communicate
with Brenda or the Soongs.
I certainly hope there's no
major SNAFU which requires
us getting in touch. I'm
also hoping they will have
some type of transportation
available by that time to
Saigon. There I'll have to
try to get on an R&R flight.
If I don't I'll buy a ticket
on a commercial flight.

The enclosed article was
from Newsweek, sent to me
by Chuck Pearson. I wasn't

sure you would see it since Irene is more in evidence (a little dig there, I suppose); but it sounds pretty gruesome.

There is word that officer tours will be shortened this week — here's hoping. I'm really looking at the Vega right now as a good possibility altho NYC is not a great place to try to keep a car. Do you have any ideas on what I should do for transportation? I'll also need something for the summer to run around.

OK — here's a flash gathered since I stopped for lunch after the last paragraph. The word is that all officers are being given 2 month drops if they are under the two year after commissioning program. I qualify. So under a rather complicated system I should (I say should because I don't have my orders yet) reach the shores of the U.S. around the 20th of June. This is about 56 days earlier than my full year. We must celebrate tonight. It would also mean only 105 days left in this dreary place.

Well, I'll let you know when I get definite word.

Love,
MC

10 Mar

Dear Family,

The mail delivery is really erratic at this point — I got a letter from Dad sent 4 March today but the book by Lindsey got here two days ago. I suppose that is the one he sent second class — but it took only 4 days to get here. And apparently my mail is taking awhile to get to you. I also got a letter from Mother saying she hadn't heard from me + that it one arrived today, was mailed the 2nd.

Anyway, my scheduled date to return to the US is now 18 June according to the tables printed in the Stars & Stripes. So I am now a "two digit midget"

in army parlance. Less than 100 days to go.

I must say Mother kind of "spilled the beans" as Marge did (I think it was Marge who spilled the beans on Uncle Hollister) by telling Mrs Ryan I was in Hawaii. My circumspect discretion in affairs of the heart was severely jeopardized (However, Brenda didn't believe it (as far as I can tell) and so all is go for March 18th in Hong Kong. She is launched on a trip to Singapore, Malaysia, Bangkok + Taipei right now + we will meet on the 18th for a week. Should be a good time if all the arrangements go as planned. However my problem is to get to Saigon someway with in-country flights no longer flying due to our Laotian blunder. I'll make it somehow.

Hope you got the slides I mailed this morning with all the great travelogue bit. My birthday fast approaches, but what I really need is some clothes for when I get back, so why don't we postpone it until then?

Howie sent me a Janis Joplin tape which is a first exposure in Chu Lai & has won me innumerable friends who are copying it. My collection of tapes is soaring & should be great by the time I reach the States.

Here's to HK and 100 days.

Love,
M.

---

14 March

Dear Family,

Congratulations to the new supervisor and best wishes for continued success and an easier workload! Of course I wondered if the barges on the Monongahela had a special salute.

In three days I will be attempting to wend my way to HK. It can't come too soon since things are getting rather unpleasant and hectic. Luckily today is Sunday & the weather is very bad, so I have a day off. Last night we had a floor show from Australia at the O Club which, while not stateside quality, was a good diversion. The most poignant moment was a real Aussie accent trying to sing Johnny Cash's "Folsom Prison Blues." Just didn't sound right. Boy, do I dislike Johnny Cash anyway.

I have read & digested Dad's Yale letter on being a national asset. I agree wholeheartedly, of course, feeling that old Eli is the greatest place in the world - a place that is so much different than anywhere else, even and especially Andover &

Columbia. Long live that venerable institution.

Rumors are once again flying that the Americal is going home. If it does within the next two months maybe I'll come home with it. I could really go for that. Anyway they are collecting info on everyone's DEROS & ETS & how long they have been in the field. Looks like they're wondering where to put us.

I should start thinking about ordering some of the PX buys here to bring home, and if you can think of anything & anyone

336

who needs or wants, let me know. I can order anything & have it sent home. I have a footlocker also that I will ship home with goodies. Special deals on jewelry, watches, cameras & electronic components

A game of handball in the spring. Maybe I'll break my leg. Sounds like a good idea.

Love,
MC

8 april

Dear Family,
I hope you had a glorious time with Mother's relations in the other California. I imagine it will be some time before I can beat Dad with all the practice he is getting on the golf course. I thought of buying some new clubs in Hong Kong, but Dad spent so much on other things I held off.

Thank you for the Easter basket, which arrived on Wednesday. We all had a piece and argued about whether it was ad Wednesday or not. I think the various church councils would have been appalled at the lack of expertise shown by so many college graduates. Take that, Billy Graham.

337

I also enjoyed Jim Bouton's _Ball Four_. As an old Yankee fan I found it somewhat heretical, but certainly amusing. I had hoped he wouldn't choose the old Jim Brosnan day by day formula, which has become trite; but all in all it was great to see so many sacred cows deflated.

I called Appur's Records two days ago to find out when I would get my orders. They have already been printed & the date is now the 11th of June. I will have Chu Lai on the 8th & hopefully stop flying the 4th. So the time is getting short. Of course it just makes me more

anxious and generally uncomfortable since it looks like such a short time. I've been thinking of going to Bangkok on leave for a week just to cut down on the hours I have to fly.

We had a bad last two weeks with rocket attacks and several fire bases hit. You probably read about the big fracas out at Mary-ann. It was the worst beating we've taken in a long time. Heads will roll somewhere in the 23rd Inf Division.

I wrote to Jamie at the Biles and hope he will find a few minutes to send me a word on his new job. I want to

now also if they have a
Brazilian enterprise we
can use in Hillsbod.
     Brenda is now back
safely after betting
Taiwan. The Bubble will
be in Seattle when I get
there in June.
     Count the days.
          Love,
            NC

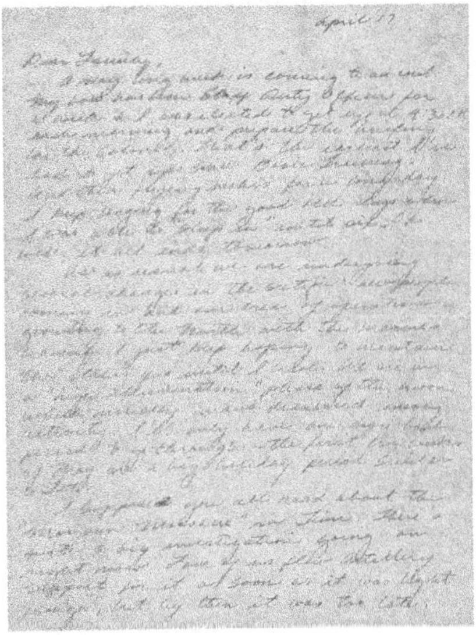

April 11

Dear Tammy,
A very long week is coming to an end. My last has been thirty thirty officer for I will as I anticipated to get off at 4 with underwear and prepared the reading for the command. That's the second that two of I eff on four then Saturday.

[remainder illegible]

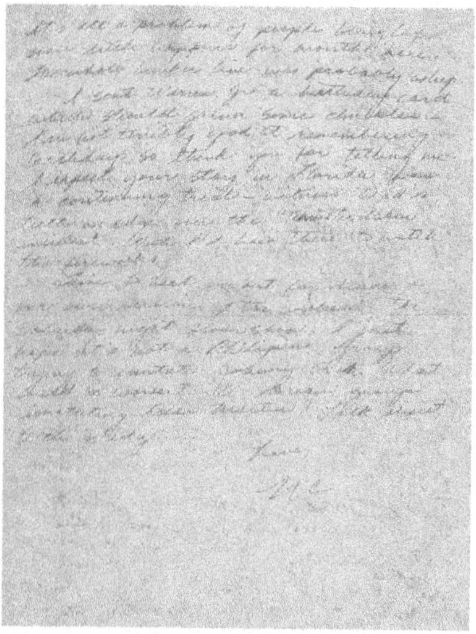

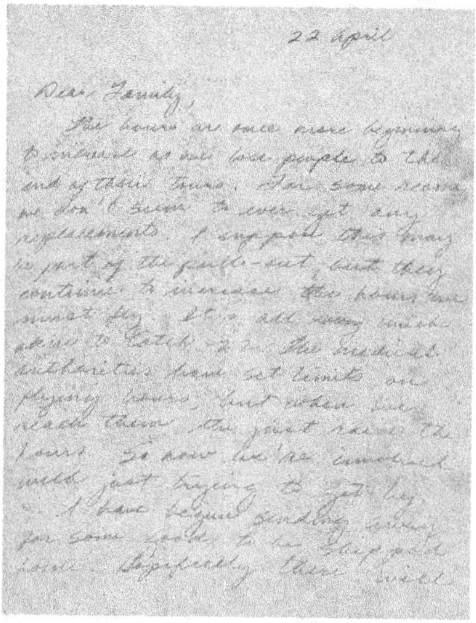

22 April

Dear Family,

The hours are once more beginning to increase as we lose people to the end of their tours. For some reason we don't seem to ever get any replacements. I suppose this may be part of the pull-out, but they continue to increase the hours we must fly. It's all very much akin to Catch-22. The medical authorities have set limits on flying hours, but when we reach them, they just raise the hours. So now we're involved with just trying to get by.

I have begun sending money for some goods to be shipped home. Supposedly these will

not be any duty since I have
orders sending me to the U.S.
I'd get a cassette deck and
a new watch along with my
clothes. I'm ordering Mother's
silk screen this week + waiting
for word from Sonic on the
car FM cassette.

Glad to hear you all got
along with Mother's relatives
in Florida. From the scope
of the score cards I may just
be able to take Dad after some
practice. But never on the
Nicam system. He never loses those.

Under 50 days now + the
time is dragging. Should have
a good reunion on the West Coast
with the Bulls & Pearsons. Not
to mention ...

                    Love,
                    NC

Glossary of Military Terms, Acronyms and Slang

Aerial Observer or AO— Artilleryman who spots targets and adjusts artillery onto them from aircraft instead of from the ground.

Air Cavalry or Air Cav— A combat team consisting of Cobra helicopter gunships, a Loach and a Huey carrying a team of infantry.

Americal Division — The 23rd Infantry Division. In the Vietnam War, the division was headquartered in Chu Lai in I Corps, which was the U.S. Army's designation for the northern sector of South Vietnam.

AWOL —"Absent Without Official Leave." Army acronym used to describe a soldier who was not at his post or where he was supposed to be.

Battalion — An infantry battalion usually has four companies: commonly the companies are named Alpha Company, Bravo Company, Charlie Company and Delta Company. An infantry battalion is led by a battalion commander, usually with the rank of lieutenant colonel.

Brigade — The next larger infantry group, consisting of several battalions.

Bungee stake or pit— A type of booby trap consisting of a sharp stake hidden in a camouflaged pit. If a soldier's foot went into the pit, the stake could go through a jungle boot into the foot. The stake usually was covered in feces to cause infection in the wound.

Chinook — Army twin-engined helicopter (officially a "Boeing CH-47 Chinook") used to carry heavy loads of troops and material, including artillery pieces.

Company — Infantry unit of approximately 125 soldiers led by a captain and commonly broken down into four platoons and a command post (CP). Each platoon is normally led by a lieutenant. Platoons are broken into squads, each normally led by an NCO.

Da Nang Main — The main military airport in Da Nang, South Vietnam for the largest aircraft, including C-130 cargo planes, Air Force F-4 Phantom jets, and Boeing 707s for R&R flights.

Danger close mission — An artillery fire mission in which the enemy target is very close to your own position.

DEROS — Army acronym for "Date Expected Return from Overseas." The end of a one year tour.

Division Artillery — Artillery command that coordinated artillery support to a Division's infantry and armored operations.

DMZ — Demilitarized zone, in Vietnam a land area that divided North and South Vietnam as established by the Geneva Convention in 1952 and supposedly not used for military purposes.

Drop — Army slang for shortening a 365 day tour in Vietnam.

Dust off — Army jargon for airlifting a soldier out of the field by helicopter.

E-1 through E-9 — Letter and number designation used to denote an enlisted soldier's rank. For instance, a buck private was an E-1, a Private

First Class was as E-3, a corporal was an E-4, an E-5 was a sergeant and an E-6 was a staff sergeant. A first sergeant was an E-8 and a sergeant major was an E9.

Eight Inch Gun —An artillery piece with the largest caliber rounds used in Vietnam. It was the most accurate artillery piece, and had the longest range: over 12 miles.

Fire Direction Control or FDC — The command center of an artillery battery. The FDC received fire missions from the field, usually over the radio. FDC then plotted the grid coordinates of the target, calculated (using a sort of slide rule or early computer) the settings for the guns to hit the target, and gave other commands to the guns. FDC also told the gunnery personnel what type of artillery fuse to use for a particular fire mission. In Vietnam, FDC was usually located on a firebase in a bunker next to the artillery pieces.

Firebase or Fire Support Base— An encampment to provide artillery fire support to infantry operating in a particular area of operations. Typically, a firebase had at its center a battery of six artillery guns that could shoot in a 365 degree arc.

Fire mission — Shooting artillery rounds for any purpose at the request of a forward observer.

Forward observer or FO — The FO is the artillery's eyes and ears in the field, spotting targets and then adjusting artillery rounds to hit them. In the Vietnam war, forward observers generally were imbedded with infantry companies to provide artillery support.

Freedom Bird — Army slang for an aircraft providing a flight home from South Vietnam.

Gun target line — The imaginary line from the artillery guns to the target. When shooting artillery, the FO and his company did not want to be on this line because of the risk of being hit by round due to range probable error of any artillery round.

Huey — Bell UH1 Iroquois helicopter (also nicknamed "Slick") used for resupply, medevac missions and troop insertion in combat assaults.

Howitzer — name for a category of artillery pieces capable of shooting explosive artillery projectiles accurately onto targets many miles away. In the Vietnam War, the Army used different size howitzers. The smallest caliber, 105 mm, was capable of shooting as far as seven miles. The middle caliber, 155 mm howitzer, could shoot as far as eight miles. The largest, 175 mm howitzer, had a range of twenty-five miles.

Hump — Army slang for carrying a pack, weapon and other ammunition and ordnance.

In country —In South Vietnam.

Intelligence target — A target whose location was based on intelligence reports gathered from various sources by military intelligence.

Jolly Green Giant — Sikorsky HH-3E helicopter used for troop insertion and combat search and rescue missions.

Kak wheel — a coding device used to encode messages, particularly grid locations, to be sent over the radio.

Kit Carson Scout — former Viet Cong soldiers who "turned" and fought with and supported U.S. Army units in the field.

Loach — Hughes OH-6 Light Observation Helicopter. These were small and very maneuverable helicopters used by, among others, the Air Cavalry to find enemy targets.

LRRPs—Long Range Reconnaisance Patrol freeze dried meals which could be eaten by adding boiling water. Consisting of meals like beef stroganoff and spaghetti and meatballs, they were a welcome break from C-rations.

Million-dollar wound —A wound that takes a soldier off the battlefield but does not permanently disable him.

MPC—Military Payment Currency, a type of scrip in dollar denominations used by U.S. forces in South Vietnam.

NCO — Non-commissioned officer. NCO's were all considered (and called) "sergeants" Their classifications were from E5 to E9.

O-1 — designation for an officer with the number showing his/her rank. Thus O-1 was a second lieutenant, O-2 was a first lieutenant, O-3 was a captain, etc.

OCS — Officer Candidate School, the six month course that an enlisted soldier takes to become a commissioned officer.

PF — Popular Force military units of Vietnamese who supported the ARVN and U.S. forces.

PX—Post Exchange, the store on an Army post where troops can buy food and other supplies.

Phonetic alphabet —military convention that makes letters more intelligible when spoken, especially over the radio or other communication device. For instance, under this convention A is Alpha, B is Bravo, C is Charlie, D is

Delta, E is Echo, etc. ending in Z is Zulu. Numbers do not have a phonetic equivalent except "nine," which is pronounced "niner."

Range probable error — the potential variable in distance an artillery round may travel on the gun target line because of temperature of the air and explosive, wind and other factors.

Redleg — an artilleryman, so-called because the U.S. artillery branch's color is red, whereas the infantry branch's color is blue.

REMF — used by those in the field for anyone classified as a Rear Area Motherfucker.

RF — Regional Force military units of Vietnamese who supported the ARVN and U.S. forces.

R&R — Rest and Relaxation. In the Vietnam War, each soldier was entitled to one week of R&R at a location outside Vietnam during his tour.

RTO — Radio Telephone Operator. RTOs carried the radios that allowed infantry or artillery to be in contact with the rear at all times to receive messages, report locations and events and, in the case of an artillery RTO, call in fire missions.

Salvation — Radio frequency that broadcast on-going artillery fire missions to aviation flying in the American Division so that the aircraft could avoid being shot down by friendly artillery.

Sapper — An enemy commando trained to penetrate an enemy perimeter to plant and ignite explosives.

Shake and bake — An enlisted soldier who received additional training after Advanced Individual Training, and was immediately promoted to the rank of E-4. These soldiers were generally sent to Vietnam in a combat role and given responsibility normally given to NCO's because of the lack of NCO's in the field.

Short — Having only a few days or weeks before the end of one's tour in Vietnam.

Shot — Radio jargon used by Fire Direction Control to announce to a forward observer that an artillery round has just been fired, thus enabling the observer to know that a round will soon land.

Sniper —A soldier trained to go on missions alone or with a small group to search out and kill the enemy using a specially designed M-14 rifle capable of firing longer than normal distances.

Splash — Radio jargon used by artillery Fire Direction Control to announce to a forward observer that an artillery round is now landing.

Spec-4 — An enlisted man rank equal to a corporal (E-4) with specialized training in a particular area.

Tunnel Rat — A soldier, usually short and wiry, with special training to enter enemy tunnels to search for Viet Cong or NVA.

"Walk in" artillery rounds — Adjusting artillery during a danger close artillery mission. The concept is to shoot the first rounds far enough away from your position to not risk hitting yourself and your own men, and then slowly move it closer to you and onto the enemy.

Acknowledgments

Holly Richardson, my talented legal secretary during the 1980's, was the first person to hear these stories. Holly volunteered to transcribe audio tapes of my experiences in Vietnam if I dictated them. So, while driving to and from work and on longer trips to court appearances in Northern California I recorded my first account of these events. Her excellent transcription later enabled this memoir to become a reality.

Mike Kail, my wonderful friend since our days together at Yale, was the first to read the early drafts of this memoir. His excellent edits and encouragement were instrumental in the completion of this memoir. Just as important, Mike's guidance in so many different ways in getting this memoir published was also invaluable.

Belinda Beckett, the love of my life and my wife of the past 40 years, read an early draft of this book and gave me encouragement, suggestions and edits which improved this book immensely .

Brenda Beckett, my sister-in law and a talented editor, read two early drafts of this memoir and provided excellent suggestions and edits. Her encouragement was instrumental in the completion of this work.

My parents, Norman E. Hile and Mary B. Hile, who both passed away more than 20 years ago, contributed significantly to this memoir by saving the letters I wrote to them from Vietnam in 1970-71. I discovered these letters in our attic recently as I was working on this project. These letters helped not only to provide day by day quotes but also allowed me to place in time and context so much of what I experienced many years ago during my tour in Vietnam.

Jim Makol, a wonderful friend for many years, worked on improving the quality of the photos, and Jim's talents made them usable for this book.

Patty La Duca edited the manuscript when it was in a later draft, and her editing talent improved it significantly.

Ryan Greenleaf, a talented photographer, took the author's photo.

About The Author

Norman Hile is a retired attorney. Drafted into the U.S. Army in 1968, he served from 1968 to 1971, including a combat tour in South Vietnam from August 1970 to June 1971. He was awarded the Bronze Star, the Purple Heart, 15 Air Medals and two Army Commendation Medals.

Mr. Hile received his B.A. from Yale University in 1967. He received his J.D. degree from Columbia Law School in 1973. He became a partner in the law firm of Orrick Herrington & Sutcliffe LLP in 1980, and led the firm's Sacramento office for over 20 years. In addition to his civil litigation practice, Mr. Hile has represented condemned prisoners on California's death row on a pro bono basis for over 30 years. The Sacramento County Bar Association named Mr. Hile its Pro Bono Lawyer of the Year in 2018, and the Ninth Circuit Court of Appeals awarded Mr. Hile its John P. Frank Award in 2019 as a lawyer who "demonstrated outstanding character and integrity; dedication to the rule of law... and a lifetime of service to the federal courts."

Mr. Hile resides in Sacramento, California with his wife, Belinda Beckett. The couple has two daughters and four young grandchildren.